DRUGS AND THE WORLD

Axel Klein

DRUGS AND THE WORLD

Axel Klein

REAKTION BOOKS

Published by Reaktion Books Ltd
33 Great Sutton Street
London EC1V 0DX
www.reaktionbooks.co.uk

Printed and bound in Great Britain
by Cromwell Press Ltd, Trowbridge, Wiltshire

British Library Cataloguing in Publication Data

Klein, Axel, 1961-
    Drugs and the World
    1. Drug abuse – Social aspects
    I. Title
    362.2'9

ISBN-13: 9 781 86189 381 9

Contents

Introduction

Over the past two decades there has been such an increase in publications, research and policy initiatives that it is becoming increasingly possible to make sense of a 'drugs field', at least in the UK, parts of Europe and North America. In other parts of the world, too, academics, policy-makers and the wider public are displaying a growing interest in finding out more about what mind-altering substances can do to individuals, families and entire societies. Always a complex issue, research has been advancing so rapidly that the field is fragmenting into subdisciplines and ever narrower specializations. This is apparent from the range of academic journals concerned with the treatment of addiction, education and prevention, or international policy issues, to name but a few examples. Drugs also play an important supporting role in disciplines such as criminology and sociology, and are, of course, of concern to pharmacology, chemistry, law and various branches of medicine and public health.

Scholars and public alike have been exposed to relentless media coverage ever since the 1950s. Whether it is concern over new drugs such as ecstasy, crack cocaine or methamphetamine, the repackaging of old drugs such as cannabis in its new guise of 'skunk', the titillating indulgences of celebrities, the sinister underworld of organized crime, or the environmental devastation caused by crop eradication, drugs are rarely out of the news. In a medium defined by the present, emphasis is always placed on the immediacy of the problem or the novelty of the threat, but the drug story in all its lurid detail of degradation and debasement has been around for over a century. In keeping with another convention of the genre, it is the exceptions – dysfunction, crises and spectacular excess – that are reported, not the vast majority of unproblematic experiences and encounters. This is regrettable as large sections of the public have no direct experience of these 'drugs' and rely on the media not just for entertainment but also for information.

What allows newspapers to over-report, say, the deaths of young people taking MDMA and under-report aspirin overdoses, is the legal framework and government policy that has declared a range of substances, including MDMA, illegal. Governments have been concerned with the regulation of 'drugs', and the penalization of transgressions, for nearly a century. Reluctant at first, the authorities in the UK as elsewhere have now taken on the fight against the drug peril as one of the core functions of government. It is in the US, however, where these efforts have been called 'a war on drugs', and have initiated an expansion of the powers and the punitive apparatus of the state that is without parallel in the history of modern democracies. In countries like China, Saudi Arabia, Singapore and Malaysia, where 'traffickers' are executed with a chilling regularity, the 'drug war' allows for governments to signal their vision of what constitutes a proper society, to underscore what constitutes the authority and the function of the state, and how dissent is dealt with.

It is the government then, which in the UK, as in most other countries, drives drug policy with so-called 'information packs', public 'education' messages aimed particularly at the young, and by funding the police force and prison services, that sets the framework for what is permissible and what is not. While the media remains free to sensationalize personal tragedies and paint vastly distorted pictures of risk and dangers, it is far more constrained in reporting positive aspects of 'drugs' or the relative safety, say of cannabis, in terms of overdose risk. In a policy climate of 'zero tolerance' of drug use, politicians are quick to come down on any hint of irresponsible reporting. The media, in turn, scrutinize individual politicians for their personal conduct and governments for their calibre lest they become 'soft on drugs'.

It is against this background of disinformation, alarm and disaffection that much of the recent work on drugs has to be situated. Drug use is a stubbornly persistent social phenomenon in spite of massive campaigning by media and drastic policy by government. In no other area of social policy are the positions of policy-makers so out of step with a significant section of the population. Nor has there been such a steady, if not exponential increase, in any form of behaviour that policy-makers have tried systematically, and often brutally, to eliminate, as there has been in drug-taking.

In most European countries governments like to emphasize the public health approaches of national drug policies, in contradistinction to the more aggressive methods and terminology used in the US. Even within the European Union considerable differences remain in attitudes towards drugs. In Sweden, for example, successive governments have shown little tolerance of drug use, with overwhelming popular support, while the Netherlands has depenalized drug possession, and have partially regulated the consumption of cannabis via the famous coffee shop system. Such deference to the principle of subsidiarity needs to be placed in context, however, as room for manoeuvre is actually limited by a series of international conventions quite independent from the EU. It is in fact the United Nations that has intruded upon this particular aspect of sovereignty via a series of conventions that are jealously guarded by an appointed group of treaty custodians, the International Narcotics Control Board (INCB). These treaties, drafted under UN auspices, perversely allow governments to arrest, incarcerate, kill and maim their own citizens, but not to provide clean drugs to sick addicts or to keep young drug users out of prison by decriminalizing petty offences. Treaty defaulters, including the Governments of Canada, Switzerland, Germany and even the UK, when downgrading cannabis from class B to C in 2003, face the wrath of the treaty guardians. Any Member State or group of Member States wishing to depart radically from the prevailing consensus would have to repudiate the treaties, an as yet unprecedented step that would challenge the entire edifice of inter-governmental decision-making.

The pressure that the different factions of the regime, politicians and national governments, international drug control bureaucracies and the media are exerting on each other is therefore pushing inexorably towards ever more comprehensive measures of control. The expectation held in some quarters during the 1970s, that a generational shift would lead to an overhaul of the system, has foundered on grand disclaimers – former US President Bill Clinton confessing to having puffed a cannabis cigarette, but without inhaling, for example – or professions of regret. While drugs have entered the panoply of consumption choices readily available to most young people in Europe and North America, and countries as diverse as South Africa, Jamaica, New Zealand and Iran, and have been normalized even for non-consumers, the official discourse has not led to a loosening of restriction but, on the contrary, to an extension of controls. Not only is the list of controlled substances being continuously expanded to take in what are known in the European Union as 'new synthetic drugs', but bans are also being imposed on traditional plant-based drugs, such as khat, which are becoming available outside traditional areas of consumption, one of the many by-products of globalization. Moreover, the use of traditional and culturally integrated psychoactive substances including tobacco and alcohol is being constrained further. The mechanisms of control, then, are becoming ever more effective and sweeping, in a spiral of widening governmental powers and mirrored by the narrowing sphere of individual liberty.

How deeply entrenched the discourse has become is illustrated by the simple sleight of classificatory hand that has allowed a small number of advocates to shift the referent for the signifier 'drug' from medicine to poison. Most English language speakers today will understand by that term a given number of illicit substances, not necessarily restricted to, but in most likelihood inclusive of heroin, cocaine and cannabis. The equation of 'drug' with the illegal is in fact one of the great feats of the control experts. It has created a popular understanding of an aggregate where problematic substances are producing problematic behaviour that needs to be controlled. Labelling a given number of substances as 'drugs' has allowed, first, for these to be distinguished from non-drugs and, secondly, for everything not listed there, from alcohol to Prozac, to acquire a clean bill of health simply by dissociation. The final benefit derives from the slippery descent of the drug user. Branded and stigmatized, he or she becomes the object of a legion of tough and soft cops, law enforcers and therapists, who make it their business to prevent the drug users from succumbing to the error of their ways.

The vested interests of these different professional groups are the foundations of the regulatory system, which is systematically piling on ever tighter controls. In few areas is professional self-interest so bound up with the acquisition of power and, as I will argue throughout, divorced from a clear base of evidence to demonstrate its efficacy. What may be lacking in terms of science is often compensated for by moral righteousness. Drugs have indeed become a symbol with many different meanings. For some they evoke social disintegration and cultural decline, for others the defence of drug use is the defence of civil liberties and of citizens against the new totalitarianism. It is this symbolic quality of 'the drug issue' that divests any objectivity from bipartisan debate on the subject. Instead, drugs have become a battlefield in what in the US has become known as the 'culture wars' and can trigger an electric moral charge. It is a topic on which people hold passionate views, often a melange of personal experience, conviction and righteous anger. Replete with ambivalence in our value system, drugs are second only to sex in their ability to wreck the careers of public servants, though figures from the entertainment industry, by contrast, seem to thrive on both.

Meanwhile politicians in opposition or otherwise out of power frequently appeal for an honest debate on drugs. This is a coded admission of the folly of the current controls and the hypocrisy of government ministers and law enforcers, many of whom have experience of drug use themselves and are now at the apex of the control system. Yet any review, however slight, threatens to unwind a vast system of powers and entitlements and is therefore immediately resisted. This makes the very agencies we tend to look towards for guidance in many areas of life – professional associations, government ministries or UN agencies – the least helpful. We therefore depend on independent assessments and studies of the different aspects of drug control. Fortunately there is by now a rich seam of literature on the drugs nexus and the control apparatus. While our knowledge of such subjects as drug production, pharmacology, the chemical structures of substances old and new, the interplay of neurotransmitters and different parts of the brain, and the trajectory of addiction is growing exponentially, it is equally clear that argument and study are having no impact on policy.

Trying to answer why this particular area of public policy-making remains so isolated from scientific advance, and what lies beyond the symbolic dimension that drugs have assumed, is what has prompted me to write this book. The findings are by no means conclusive, but there is a model taking shape to explain the virulence of the repressive apparatus that has been build up over recent years, and which needs to be understood before reform can be achieved. My own position on drugs is quite clear: all drugs are dangerous substances, because they open new dimensions of seeing, thinking, feeling and being. They are encountered in all cultures, inevitably seated right at the heart of social life and at the core of rite, ritual and religion, all those areas that give meaning to life beyond the drudgery of everyday existence. Historically, people have been protected from the power of substances by a web of customary rules of use and avoidance, depending on age, sex, family membership, the calendar and so on. This close relationship between a culture and 'their drug' has been severed by two processes. One is the swamping of choice and diversity that is often associated with globalization. Advances in transport and the growth in trade have made it easy to ship plant-based substances well beyond their original cultural zones. Cultures of recreational drug use have also triggered the design and development of new substances, which are continuously coming onto the market with no customs of restraint attached. Herein also lies the crux of the second process, with far more devastating consequences: commodification. Drugs are now traded as one product among many. Some drugs are legal, some are not, but most are brought to market with the sole intent of providing retailers with the highest possible return.

In contrast to food items, the satisfaction threshold for most drugs is much higher. In the UK, for example, many people carry on drinking alcohol well after the meal is finished. Drug users, from chocoholics to heroin fiends, are insatiable. Once this demand is connected to a supplier, the entire system of checks and balances carefully built up over time is thrown into disequilibrium. It is the accumulation of capital and the industrialization of production on the one hand, and the unfettered demand of a mass market of individualized and atomized consumers on the other, that lies at the bottom of our current set of interconnected drug problems.

A cultural analysis, however persuasive, does not provide ready solutions as culture is something that lies well beyond the quick fix. Yet it allows us to devise interventions that encourage and support protective factors and mitigate the risks. It helps us distinguish between cause and symptoms, by locating drug use within a wider culture of consumption, and by treating many of the associated problems as questions of public health and social exclusion. Finally, it helps us turn our gaze towards the regime of controls we have constructed over the past 30 years, and recognize its most blatant absurdities – from aerial fumigation of the rainforest to systemic corruption of police forces – not as occasional lapses of intent, as might occur in any public scheme of such magnitude, but as chronic features of a project that has spun out of control.

As so often when the error is fundamental and the scale gigantic, the greatest difficulty lies in detecting the incongruence of intention and achievement. Surely all the 183 countries that have signed up to the Single Convention of Narcotic Drugs cannot be in error? Worse still, even if we concede that mistakes have been made, these are surely outweighed by the benefits. The current casualties of the global war on drugs, from environmental devastation, to mass incarceration, to the erosion of liberties, are a price worth paying to protect us from the onslaught of an unfettered drugs boom. I am arguing this defeatism is no longer credible. We have the know-how and the ingenuity to devise systems that afford far greater levels of control over drugs that are currently in the hands of underground suppliers. We owe it to our children and to the next generation of young people to find a way of safeguarding their physical health from risky adulterants and unknown dosages. Most of all, we need to find a way beyond the pyrrhic stratagems employed across the world today, whereby young drug users are arrested, incarcerated and branded for life with the stigma of criminalization in order to save them from the danger of self-inflicted drug use.

Many 'experts' close their eyes to the colossal collateral damage effected by 30 years of drug wars. Lives ruined by imprisonment, lives lost to the hangmen, and families devastated by the incarceration of a breadwinner are never factored into the tally. Yet we need to focus not only on the impact of drug production and use, but also on the role of policy and practice. All costs need to be listed for a global analysis. Unfortunately many of the key professionals have a stake in maintaining a system that can only disguise its failings by continuously expanding its activities. This book, then, seeks to unmask some of these failings, count the total costs, and expose the systemic corruption on which an unworkable system has been built. Moving from a failing drugs war, which exacerbates social deprivation and penalizes the weakest members of society, towards a functioning regulatory system could be done in a series of small steps over several years. It is neither rocket science nor revolutionary, but it will not come from within the bastions of the control apparatus. Reform, for this is what it is, has to come from outside, pushed by activists and supported by an informed public tired of the waste and suffering caused by decades of failed policy.

1 Taking Leave of Our Senses: Drug Use and Drug-taking in the 21st Century

Drug control in a historical perspective

The faculty of reason is a fundamental principle behind our definition of what it is to be human. One of the great legacies of the Enlightenment has been the liberation of humanity from the shackles of ignorance and autocracy, to ring in an era of autonomy and self-determination based on a rational understanding of the world around us. Meanwhile the growing confidence of science helped to elevate the status of man versus his creator, by dislocating God from the centre of social and natural affairs, and to loosen the chains of superstition and custom. In this process the control that had been exerted over individual behaviour by church, the feudal lord and tradition subsided. Their place was taken by the individual will, seated in the faculty of reason, nurtured by education and training, and facilitated by transparent and accountable institutions of government. In the post-Enlightenment ideal, social stability and communal welfare have depended not on fear and brute force, but on individual self-control.

Notwithstanding occasional setbacks, such as the inexplicable emotive power unleashed by nineteenth-century nationalism, and the rearguard actions fought by religious fundamentalists, particularly of Christian and Islamic persuasion, the scheme has evolved into a principle of national and, importantly, global governance. From the opening, however, it was beset by an inexplicable difficulty in the form of 'peculiar substances'. During the early modern period proponents of the Enlightenment lamented the corrosive effects of the 'demon drink'. The increasingly articulate puritan critiques of alcohol-induced inebriation were delivered at a time when science as the study of nature was intertwined with the first phase of globalization, and busily engaged in the taxonomic ordering of the world. Scientific curiosity complemented and reinforced mercantile self-interest that procured for the European centres of commerce and study both the specimen for analysis and the cargo for commerce and consumption.

Patterns of consumption, which for most of Europe's agrarian history had remained constant, began to change quite dramatically. New products such as coffee, tobacco, tea, sugar and cocoa arrived as luxurious curiosities that quickly caught on. The dual process of global trade and scientific experimentation delivered to the modern European consumer a whole range of substances with the potential to significantly alter mood and mind. Some of these were taken into the pharmacopoeia of medical practitioners, while others became first luxury goods, then staples. Yet these products contained dangers unrecognized in the first flurry of excitement. Plants discovered around the world by intrepid explorers continued to fire the imagination and ingenuity of European scientists intent on uncovering their secrets by isolating psychoactive alkaloids right up to the nineteenth century. The two scourges of contemporary drug control, morphine and cocaine, were first discovered by isolating and extracting the psychoactive alkaloids from poppy juice and coca leaves. The refined products were promoted as panaceas and marketed as 'over the counter' medicines, at the same time as the assault on alcohol was reaching a climax. Indeed, heroin synthesized from morphine was marketed by the pharmaceutical company Bayer as a morphine substitute in a cough syrup sold from 1898 to 1910 in a combination pack with aspirin and the diuretic Lycetol (Dimethyl-piperazidine tartrate). The cough syrup was finally withdrawn from the German market only in 1958.

In Britain, the US and much of northern Europe, the temperance movement had matured into a powerful political force by the late nineteenth century. Though often associated with other causes, such as female suffrage, it was in essence a single-issue campaign against the production, distribution and use of alcohol. Alcohol, in its many guises, was seen as the scourge of the urban poor in the rapidly industrializing towns, responsible for social deprivation and much of the ensuing misery. Campaigners such as William Booth, the founder of the Salvation Army, sought to realize social benefits by focusing on a single cause. This entirely reformist approach was, and is, much despised among revolutionaries, as it drew attention away from the structural conditions of exploitation, to home in on the patterns of consumption among the exploited. Moral crusaders, then as now, lay the blame for abject conditions at the door of the victim. Temperance reformers were not trying to redress exploitative relationships by raising wages or redistributing wealth or improving working conditions, but agitated instead to deprive the workers of one of the only sources of pleasure at their disposal.

It is not surprising, perhaps, that the temperance position was shared by paternalist industrialists, motivated either by genuine disgust over the appalling social conditions suffered by the urban poor and by a genuine philanthropic concern, or by shrewd calculation that simply ameliorating the worst deprivation would forestall more violent upheavals. Beneath this class-focused discussion of sectional interest and the distribution of wealth and power lies a cultural theme that took shape in the early modern period and remains with us today. It explains why the revulsion for habitual drunkenness that inspired so many political agitators in the nineteenth century was so easily adapted and transposed onto the growing number of addicts to opiates, cocaine and other substances in the twentieth century.

Alcohol addiction in the nineteenth century and problematic heroin or crack cocaine use today have both been seen as subverting the foundation of the social order that is vested in the rational autonomy of the self-determining individual. The actual intoxication itself is an offence to what in post-Enlightenment terms is the pinnacle of human achievement – the seat of reason – now occluded by a synthetically produced mimicking of pleasure. It may be said that switching off the endogenous apparatus for rational thought is a choice every individual should be free to make. But temperance campaigners in the past, and proponents of drug prohibition today, have argued on the other hand that drugs, through their psychotropic action and addictive properties, erode the very capacity of the will to make a free choice. Alcohol and drug users then forfeit their right to autonomy and self-determination, and thereby invite the intervention of the authorities as custodians of the rationality and enfeebled will of the individuals afflicted, guarding society from the intrusion of alcohol and drugs.

There are considerable variations in interpreting the respective rights and roles of individuals and the collective. In countries with welfarist traditions, such as Sweden, the assertion that the individual can be saved from him/herself by the intervention of a benign state is very persuasive. It is firmly rooted in the notion, stemming from Aristotle, of the 'good society' with responsibility for creating the conditions in which individuals can prosper. When it comes to dangerous substances, the state is called upon to intervene so as to curtail their availability, especially to younger and more vulnerable members of the community.

Whether individuals should be allowed to erase the very intellectual faculties that render them human in the first place echoes the discussion over the ethics of suicide. The sanctions against suicide were for centuries based on religious principles of the sanctity of life. With the elevation of reason itself, however, God was displaced as the reference point for moral reckoning. Direction for moral conduct has since then been provided by the declaration of 'universal principles', as well as the interests of society itself. With regard to general social interests, drugs are odious in that they foster selfish, egotistical behaviour and neglect of responsibility. Moreover, their effect on individual behaviour is to lower the threshold of inhibition. It is indeed this very facility that is appreciated in cohesive and integrated societies, where drugs are used to facilitate relaxation and social interaction. But in parts of the world, now or in the past, such as the industrial cities of Victorian England, or much of contemporary urban Africa, where the state's presence is shadowy, where the bonds of tradition are weak, and customs are still in the making, the removal of internal control poses a threat to an already fragile community. Substances that lower the inhibitory thresholds and which may even spark off antisocial behaviour are potentially dangerous for the individuals and communities affected.

Individual autonomy and the function of social control are further undermined by one of the most obnoxious effects of drugs on the human psyche – addiction. The phenomenon is of relatively recent origin, dating back to the temperance campaigns in the US of the late eighteenth century and the early nineteenth, and its formulation owes much to the work of Benjamin Rush, the New England medical doctor who became one of the founders of the Temperance League. The propensity of individuals to over-indulge in alcohol has of course been reported since antiquity, and drunkards, such as Falstaff or the Rabelaisian revellers, were stock characters in medieval and later literature. Periods of intense alcoholic binges on high days and holidays, at harvest festivals or during carnival, were woven into the calendar. Beer and wine were so integrated into the dietary patterns of most European countries prior to industrialization that we may well assume that many adults spent most waking hours under the influence. What changes in the modern period, however, is the assessment of the condition of chronic drunkenness, which is regarded alternately as a moral weakness in the individual or as a disease. In either case, the diagnosis opens the way for dramatic intervention, without challenging the underlying definition of humans as rational, self-determining individuals.

Indeed, this intervention by the state is based on the under-standing that the addict has suffered such neurological damage as to be against his own will. The impetus to engage in the drug-using behaviour is so strong as to overcome all restraints and inhibitions and compel the addict to direct his/her behaviour towards the drug. Drug control, as first advocated by the anti-saloon league, is simply a means of aiding the weak of will to resist temptation and retain their faculties. Over the past century, the proposition has been secularized and transformed into a political principle (albeit a paradoxical one): that the weak internal controls of individuals have to be supported at social level by the authority of the state to protect the freedom of the citizen from him or herself.

Ironically, the substance against which the crusade was waged in the first place, the demon drink, remains widely available in ever changing packages on supermarket shelves in most western countries. But the anxieties over individual degradation and social dislocation that prompted the first agitation remain with us, now transposed onto a new set of substances, most prominently cannabis, opiates, cocaine and a growing list of synthetics such as amphetamines and LSD. In clear contrast to the mid-nineteenth century, however, we do now have in place a complex regime of controls, invested with considerable powers over the liberty and property of individuals afflicted by 'addiction' or implicated in any other way with these now forbidden substances.

When setting out to rid the world of alcohol, the temperance movement had modelled itself on the campaign against the slave trade, a spectacularly successful moral crusade that had achieved the rescinding of commercial licences at home and the projection of naval power abroad. It was difficult at that time to anticipate how the extension of a formal control apparatus on as deeply entrenched a cultural practice would play out, at a time when both police forces and public health services were in their infancy. Most activists were driven by moral certitude and a sense of communal belonging. Yet they helped give rise to a process of state expansion that would lead to systems and forms of organization that are hard to reconcile with the lofty aspirations of the erstwhile campaigners. Far from promoting a charitable *communitas*, where a helping hand was held out to those who had temporarily fallen by the wayside, the control regime would become manifest in a criminal justice system of monstrous proportion. In the first decades of the twentieth century, when the instances of alcohol and drug control were created at national, and more critically, at international level, Christian charity was quickly replaced by the cold authority of the state. The international drug control institutions that had come into being in the early twentieth century very quickly rid themselves of the missionary zealots that had campaigned to bring them into being. Outside the public eye and accountable only to their governments, with little regard to popular opinion and no pretence of consultation, this small group of gentlemen created a complex set of international control organs.[1] Established first under the auspices of the League of Nations and subsequently the United Nations, it was staffed by dispassionate technocrats concerned primarily with the smooth functioning of their agency and the extension of its power.

They had counterparts at national levels, responsible for translating international conventions into a regulatory framework. These new bureaucracies of drug control, which in many countries included alcohol, were equipped with sharp teeth. They were supported by legislation prohibiting a range of activities involving different substances, and soon supported by specialized enforcement agencies. Perversely, their failure in stemming the distribution and consumption of the prohibited substances only added to their prestige and the urgency of their mission.

Politicians and drug law enforcement officials began to conjure images of an overwhelming danger, which they were combating with lamentably inadequate powers and resources. Some of the emerging leaders of the movement, like the notorious Harry Anslinger, the Commissioner for the us Federal Bureau of Narcotics (1930–62), proved adept at aligning responsibility for drug-related offences with stigmatized minorities. This allowed attention to be shifted away from the operational failure of enforcement, aligning the fear of drugs with the fear of ethnic minorities and marginal groups. In the us this was accomplished by associating Mexicans in the southwest with marijuana, Chinese immigrants in California with opium, and African-Americans with cocaine in the south.

This 'othering' of drugs and drug use remains a constant theme in the drug war and continues to colour the way illicit drugs are depicted as something foreign and abnormal. Drug control agencies in most countries of the world describe their function in terms of protecting domestic populations from an external threat. This threat, the drug, is depicted as coming from outside, and is often carried by physically distinct minority ethnic groups. Far less attention and prestige is given to the control of domestic production, and the economic principle that domestic demand is responsible for the supply in the first place is elided altogether. Physical conditions associated with stigmatized behaviour, in the words of one AIDS researcher, 'always begin in someone else's country'.[2]

Attributing responsibility for drug use and its related problems to ethnic minorities or immigrants furnishes both a set of grievances to fuel racist sentiment and a justification for discriminatory operational measures, such as racial profiling and targeted 'stop and search' operations. These aggressive policing methods serve to rationalize the victimization of a minority, as often 'repressive drug controls are a response to the drug user, not to drug use'.[3] Minority groups, such as the Chinese in the us, West Indians in the UK or Somalis in Sweden, are then stigmatized by association with a particular drug, whether opium, marijuana or khat, condemned as dangerous by the authorities and despised by the mainstream. Members of the community now provide a legitimate target for surveillance and control. At the same time they provide a screen to protect the control agencies from a rigorous investigation into their inability to keep the drugs out. These ethnically bonded drug trafficking networks, so goes the argument, organize the drug flow and can only be contained through the control agencies appropriating ever greater funds and powers.

These control agencies, and the state that gives them licence, do have a powerful impact on the character and configuration of drug markets. Yet they have failed spectacularly in suppressing the use of opiates, cocaine and cannabis, in spite of the significant allocation of resources. For the early church-based campaigners, taking up the issue of alcohol and drugs demonstrated the power of the 'social gospel', taking the bible to the street to fight for a better life in this world. But the movement reached not only downwards, but also to the commanding heights of government. By 1919 the prohibitionists had sponsored enough Congressmen and Senators to pass the eighteenth amendment to the Constitution prohibiting 'the manufacture, sale or transportation of liquors' in the United States. Employing the power of the state to enforce what was essentially a moral issue was contested from the outset, but also took campaigners and government into new territory.

It is important to recall that the state in the nineteenth century was far smaller and far less involved in the management of human affairs than a century and a bit later. The dramatic expansion of government, either in its totalitarian or its welfarist form, was yet to occur, and with it a more incisive understanding of the role of bureaucracy and the deployment of power. What should perhaps have been clearer to devout Protestants, learned in ecclesiastical history and the breach with Rome, was the vulnerability of any organization to corruption.

Alcohol and drug control agencies have from the outset been tainted with allegations of corruption and direct involvement in underground markets, with numbers of office holders deliberately breaking the very laws that they had been recruited and sworn in to enforce. Corruption, a problem as old as authority itself, is so rampant in the drugs enforcement field today because most drug offences are victimless crimes. In the absence of victims pressing charges against drug offenders, the level of enforcement is largely at the discretion of the police officers themselves. Ironically, in some situations tolerance of drug offences, deliberate oversight or even complicity may bolster the popularity and even efficacy of local officers. As officers get involved in a regular relationship, however, their ability to uphold law and order is dissipated. During the 1920s Al Capone, archetype and role model for any aspiring drug-smuggling mobster, had large sections of the Chicago police force on his payroll, precipitating the collapse of law and order in that city. At a more quotidian level, police officers are involved at lower levels in the drugs market. The citation from a US General Accounting Office Report illustrates some of the principle mechanisms: 'Since 1995, 10 police officers from Philadelphia's 39th District have been charged with planting drugs on suspects, shaking down drug dealers for hundreds of thousands of dollars, and breaking into homes to steal drugs and cash.'[4] There are multiple temptations for police officers:

- To use drugs themselves, particularly as they have easy access to confiscated substances.
- To use drugs as a means for obtaining confessions or of making arrests.
- To keep the financial benefits by either taking drugs for sale, or by keeping the cash found on people suspected of selling drugs.

There is no statistical information on the scale of any of these forms of abuse in any country. All that we know is that they are found in every police force in the world, and their prevalence is largely related to the ethical standards upheld by, and morale obtaining in, the force, the degree of oversight by civil authorities, and the level of remuneration for police officers.

A less eye-catching and subtle form of corruption derives from the lifelike properties of any institution with regard to expansion and self-perpetuation. This takes different forms in that organizations seek to hold on to their powers and resources long after their mandate has ceased to serve a useful purpose; after the social and cultural conditions that first prompted the bestowal of that mandate have totally transformed; after new knowledge shows the initial definitions to be false or inadequate; and after the identified responses have proven to be counterproductive.

Drug control agencies conceived towards the end of the nineteenth century, and reformed after the Second World War, illustrate the case of distortion and perversion, particularly when measured against the original objectives for which the regime was first put into place. Drugs, we recall, were deemed irreconcilable with the new model of 'enlightened' humanity triumphantly emancipated from church, crown and ignorance. Drugs were now threatening to engulf the seat of reason with the fog of inebriation, while addiction was set to break free will and impose a new tyranny. In order to preserve that essential and definitive human freedom, drug control advocates proposed a new compact designed to keep society drug-free. Governments were called upon to create instances of control, armed with powers of seizure and arrest, to thwart the evil machinations of profiteers and safeguard the sobriety of the weak of will.

Some hundred years or so later, the result has been an unmitigated disaster that failed not only in its original objectives of maintaining a drug-free society, but has given rise to a monster of Frankensteinian proportions. A machinery of control has been brought to life that is entirely divorced from the original intentions of applying a measured intervention to better secure the freedom of vulnerable individuals. Instead, a plethora of operational goals, often reduced to quantifiable indicators, has been brought in. A semblance of success is maintained by directing attention to tactical achievements, such as police seizure of a particular shipment, or the expansion of treatment facilities, and by continuously redefining objectives. All this has been accompanied by a growing appropriation of resources and the impingement of liberties.

Herein lies the critical problem for a mission that, in pursuit of human liberty, has brought in a system of controls that in their entirety have come to challenge the very freedom from the oppressive sovereign that the Enlightenment had supposedly heralded in. In order to assist the individual to release the hold of the addiction and self-actualize against the encroaching torpor of the drug, the regime has had to resort to controls that jeopardize the entire project. This is perhaps borne out by the two rare instances where drug control efforts have approximated success. Both the Taliban leadership in Afghanistan and the government of Singapore have succeeded in dramatically reducing the use and availability of drugs (albeit different classes of drugs). In each country, the notions of civil and individual liberty have been subordinated to greater values, such as religious purity or the moral hygiene of the city state. Draconian punishments, including the use of the death penalty against drug traffickers and users, and comprehensive surveillance systems, both electronic and through networks of informers, have achieved levels of abstinence that other countries may envy.[5] Sympathy for such tactics has been evinced by some of the more outspoken senior law enforcement agents in the US, most notoriously Daryl Gates, the former chief of the Los Angeles Police Department and credited with forming the first SWAT team and the Drug Abuse Resistance Education (DARE) programme. Giving testimony to the US Senate Judiciary Committee in 1990, Gates said that 'casual marijuana smokers ought to be taken out and shot because we are in a war.'[6]

A greater measure of operational success in restricting the availability of certain drugs and curtailing the prevalence of drug use is therefore within reach of our control agencies, although all hopes for total abstinence have to take into account the distorting factor of corruption. But any such success comes at the cost of sacrificing the very values of liberty, the rights to self-determination and of individual autonomy that the entire system of drug controls was created to preserve in the first place. The process is now well underway, with an ever expanding yet extraordinarily ineffective control apparatus that is diametrically opposed to the core values otherwise espoused by western democracies. In order to revive the ideal of the autonomous individual and the rule of reason, we need to review the costs and benefits of the control regime we have created, and the consequences for individuals and society at large. It is therefore necessary to revisit the purpose of the control mandate, assess the social and cultural conditions, look at the evidence behind the original definitions and examine the counterproductive consequences of some interventions.

Anthropological approaches to the study of drugs and drug addiction

Drug control is an area that at global, national and local level involves the cooperation of diverse groups of professionals. The original drug control conferences held at the beginning of the twentieth century were attended by physicians, chemists, diplomats, law enforcement officers and missionaries. As the system began taking shape, competencies were allocated to different international agencies. Since the late 1940s they have come under the umbrella of the United Nations and are now distributed among the World Health Organization (WHO), the United Nations Office on Drugs and Crime, the International Narcotics Control Board and UNAIDS. Each is fighting hard to protect its turf from intrusion regardless of anomalies and distortions. As a result the WHO holds the brief on alcohol and tobacco and the United Nations Office on Drugs and Crime oversees everything involving cannabis, cocaine and opiates, a division that does nothing to dispel the popular delusion that alcohol and nicotine are not drugs – that word is now usually seen as referring to substances that are illegal.

The tussle over funds and power between these agencies has been mirrored at national level, leading in most countries to the allocation of alcohol- and nicotine-related work to health departments, while the lead for the illicit drugs is taken by law enforcement. In France, for instance, during the 1990s public health agencies would set up drop-in centres where injecting drug users could collect clean needles. In many instances these were then confiscated and destroyed – often on the pavement – by police officers who were not informed about the scheme or disagreed with its objectives. With different agencies of the government rendering each other ineffectual, there was a growing realization that all drug-related activities needed to be coordinated more closely.

In the UK these efforts found their crowning manifestation in the Drug Action Team. A 'virtual body' created in the late 1990s at county or borough level to bring a shared sense of purpose to the anti-drug activities of the various branches of government such as the police and health services, local government, housing and social work agencies, and Her Majesty's Customs and Excise.

These so-called 'strategic partnerships' are also found in countries as diverse as Australia, Hungary and Switzerland, in recognition of the impact that drugs have on different areas of life, and the need for cooperation among different professionals. While drug strategies are becoming increasingly complex and interdisciplinary, the actual distribution of resources across activities and sectors remains highly skewed towards the criminal justice sector. In a recent analysis of UK drug policy the authors note the difficulty in accurately calculating expenditure on different policy strands. Money allocated to drug treatment, with contributions from different departments, has been estimated by the National Treatment Agency as totalling £508 million. More complex still is the fact that money spent from mainstream budgets, such as the costs of prosecuting a drug case, incarcerating drug offenders or dealing with drug arrests as part of routine duties, is not included. To account for supply-side interventions – prosecuting and punishing drug dealers and users – a crude estimate of £2 billion is provided. This is more, in other words, than what has been earmarked for the entire drug strategy, including supply reduction, and therefore raises the question of whether the government has got the balance right.[7] The drug strategy of Vancouver, the first North American city to pioneer drug consumption rooms where heroin users could find a peaceful and clean haven to inject, was based on the four pillars of prevention, treatment, harm reduction and enforcement. Yet, with reference to funding distribution, it has been described as 'three matchsticks attached to a tree trunk'.

In terms of resource allocation and the extension of powers, law enforcement agencies have been the greatest beneficiaries of the drug control regime brought into being over the past century. Inevitably this has resonated in the presentation and definition of drug issues. Drugs are widely regarded as a handmaiden of crime, a perception that has reinforced the assumptions of the control regime and its moral authority. In terms of representation, the drugs/crime link has served to elevate law enforcement officers into authorities not merely on the operational details of their work, but on the wider issue of drugs themselves. In consequence police officers have played a prominent role in the discussion of drug issues and in the formulation of drug policies.

There is little evidence that the campaigners of the temperance movements recognized the implications of drug and alcohol policing, with all its sordid implications of informers, the favour economy, the planting of evidence, deployment of violence and corruption. Their main concern was with addressing an abject social problem, fired by idealistic visionaries such as the evangelist Billy Sunday. After alcohol became prohibited, he promised the 'the reign of tears' would come to an end, 'the slums will soon only be a memory. We will turn our prisons into factories and our jails into storehouses.'[8] Rural communities in parts of America sold their prisons, soon to be superfluous institutions since alcohol was seen as the cause of most offending.[9]

Success in terms of legislative fiat, if not in the impact on social conduct, depended on patching together a powerful coalition of parties with overlapping interests. In the course of the nineteenth century the evangelical prohibitionists found a dynamic ally in the medical profession. Advances in scientific discovery with resultant benefits for public health over the course of the century had increased the prestige of doctors and surgeons, who were becoming increasingly assertive in claiming dominion over the human body and mind. This included the prerogative to dispense medicines. The ready availability of opiate-containing 'patent medicines' throughout Victorian England was a slur against the self-esteem of a profession seeking to 'place the patient firmly under the doctor's control'.[10]

To this day, medical professionals remain crucial in the definition of addiction as a disease, in the treatment modalities devised to cure it, and the classification of different substances according to risk. Though the law enforcement and the medical approaches concur on the problematic posed by drugs, they agree only on eliminating consumer sovereignty. In the UK medical practitioners have residual rights for dispensing heroin or cocaine to addicts. In Switzerland, the Netherlands and Germany diamorphine heroin has been introduced for the so-called hardcore heroin addicts who have been through and failed to complete successive treatments. But in most countries bureaucratic systems of regulation prevail that simply prohibit doctors from prescribing any of these controlled substances. In the US, where the most widely used drug in the maintenance of addicts is the synthetic opioid methadone, law enforcement officers and their concerns dominate in policy-making. While medical professionals do have a role in the treatment of existing addicts, they are also seen as a source of drugs diverted from proper medical practice into illicit markets. The use and abuse of prescription medicine, including the synthetic opioids oxycodone, fentanyl, hydrocodone, buprenorphine and hydromorphone, has prompted increased surveillance of medical practitioners. In 2006 the Drug Enforcement Administration (DEA) opened 735 investigations into doctors suspected of 'diverting' prescription medicines into illegal drug markets.[11] Some 71 doctors were arrested, and the implications of the ever tightening restrictions on opiate products for the management of chronic conditions are becoming painfully clear.

Tensions between the distinct objectives of combating addiction and managing pain are increasingly difficult to reconcile. The most severely affected are sufferers from chronic diseases like cancer in developing countries, where doctors find it difficult to obtain opioid-based analgesic because of regulatory and procurement impediments, and additionally run the risk of being accused of diversion. Some 89 per cent of global morphine consumption is therefore accounted for by patients in Europe and North America.[12]

The tensions between the members of this shifting alliance of different professional groups and bureaucratic elites have adverse consequences for the public at large, and contribute to the increasing disconnect between official policies and the reality of drug use among a sizeable minority of the population. To understand fully how this came into being it is instructive to recall the origins of the anti-drugs campaign and the precedent from which it derived, the fight for the abolition of slavery. In the struggle against slavery, the victims of this crime and the principal beneficiaries of reform were actively involved in the campaign; once the vision had been realized they shook off their chains to move on. In the case of drug control the search for an actual beneficiary to give momentum to the campaign has proved elusive. The prohibition of alcohol, opium, cannabis and cocaine early in the twentieth century was greeted with little rejoicing among the populations of habitual users 'liberated' from their addiction. Celebrations were confined to the lobbies themselves, not the ostensible beneficiaries in the closed saloons and opium dens.

In contemporary policy debates and consultation exercises drug users are marginalized or even excluded, unless they are recovering addicts who have renounced drugs. Accounts of the decision-making process preceding drug experimentation and recreational use are provided by theoretical models developed largely by anti-drug campaigners and taking the guise of impersonal processes. Terms like 'peer pressure', 'stepping stone' or 'gateway theories' and 'the epidemic' shift the focus from individual decision-taking to externalizing causal factors. Borrowing terminology, explanatory structure (the external pathogen) and prestige from medical science adds weight to the argument on the one hand, while stripping the drug-using individuals of their agency. Depicted as objects devoid of will or reason, they are propelled by cannabis through a gateway of spiralling drug use. First experimentation is not a positive decision but a failure to resist peer pressure. Each new user presents another infected individual, both victim and pathogen, of a spreading epidemic. And without unscrupulous drug dealers, preying on their gullible and impressionable victims, consumption would never occur in the first place.

The avid mix of metaphors and the constant shift of explanatory models is used to ward off criticism of the prohibitionist paradigm and avoid accountability. In order to explain the continuing availability of drugs in spite of years of increasing efforts to stem the supply, a modern demon is conjured, the drug dealer, 'merchant of death', 'slayer of youth' and 'enslaver'. Laying the responsibility for drug use at the door of individual agents satisfies both head and heart, while steering the discussion away from the underlying demand structure for drugs. It is an implicit plea for clemency for consumers, while identifying a scapegoat for both the social dilemma of drug use in general, and the failure of the control regime in particular.

Nowhere is that failure more apparent than in the process of 'normalization' around drugs such as cannabis or MDMA. In most European countries and North America these substances are now part of the repertoire of experience available to young people: across the EU between a quarter and a third of 16 to 24-year-olds admit to having dabbled with them. Their use is so widespread and in some areas spreading so fast that the analogous use of the term 'epidemic' approximates the scale of the phenomenon.

At the same time, it raises the question of whether behavioural patterns can be compared to the action of viral or bacterial pathogens. This particular redefinition of epidemic and human agency is relevant to control regimes of countries where the problem is drug use per se, and to which governments respond with obligatory treatment and/or penal sanctions. As a counterpoint to the idea of 'normalized' drug use, the term 'epidemic' evokes the magnitude of the problem in terms of numbers of drug users, and conjures by suggestion an external pathogen. In most instances of initiation, however, the user takes the drug voluntarily, knowing that it is risky. Usually instigated by friends and siblings, drug initiations form core experiences of identity development and social bonding. These aspects are glossed over by the catch-all term 'peer pressure' ubiquitous in the literature on drug prevention. Imprecise and highly suggestive, the term encodes a negative youth stereotype and hints at a non-volitional mechanical process.

Yet most of the young people who have engaged in drug-using behaviour have to overcome considerable internal and external obstacles. Aspects of immorality, danger and perdition have pervaded the public imagination for decades, fuelled by grossly exaggerated drug 'education' designed to instil fear and stereotypal media representation. In US government-funded films produced in the mid-1930s, such as *Weed with Roots in Hell*, *Reefer Madness* and *Assassin of Youth*, 'sexual inhibitions are shown to be lost as a result of drug consumption, where young people are driven wild and commit murder'.[13] While these gross distortions, easily satirized and reportedly popular viewing among stoned US teenagers in the 1970s, look like obvious propaganda pieces today, they have been replaced by equally powerful and images. TV campaigns in the US in the early 2000s showed a young woman frying an egg with the caption, 'this is your brain on drugs.' Most powerful and controversial, however, were the posters and TV adverts linking drug use with terrorism in the aftermath of 9/11, and shifting responsibility for the terror attacks onto unwitting recreational drug users.

This campaign, however ill-founded in substance, was considered successful by the Partnership for a Drug-Free America, a government-funded pressure group. Its president, Stephen

Pasierb, explained that an organization 'devoted to finding new, credible ways to reduce demand for illegal drugs'[14] celebrated that six out of ten polled respondents believed in the link between drugs and terror. Though the Taliban ran the most successful opium poppy eradication programme in the history of Afghanistan, and there is no suggestion of al-Qaeda involvement in any trafficking activity, the end – putting teenagers off drugs with scaremongering – justified the means.

Drug experimenters have not only to overcome considerable inner scruples, grapple with fear of unknown risk, and fly in the face of the law and social conditioning. They also have to negotiate a series of difficult relationships with suppliers and avoid detection by parents, educational authorities, the police and their peers. In most cases, then, initiatory drug use is not an automatic impulse or an involuntary response but the outcome of a rational and voluntary decision-making process. Taking that step in breach of the explicit decree of the authorities is perhaps a final testimony of the triumph of the Enlightenment, as individuals assert their right to control their own bodies.

Drug initiation remains one of the most under-researched aspects of the drug-use phenomenon. Getting to understand why and how people use illicit drugs requires an approach that is fundamentally different from the predominantly crime- and addiction-based perspectives and their hypothetico-deductive research paradigms.[15] Researchers working within the framework laid out by either medical or law enforcement practitioners embark from the hypothetical deduction that the object of their inquiry constitutes a problem that their findings are designed to help resolve. Worthy as this may be, it precludes the researchers from exploring, for example, the social benefits of drug use, or even the motivation of the informants who take a different view on the problems of the issue. Data is always gathered around established sets of variables and defined along established axes. In the case of the European Union, the indicators used include drug-use prevalence, drug-related deaths, the morbidity of problematic drug users, the number of problem users (addicts) in treatment and the number of drug-related incarcerations. It limits the information gathering to established sets of variables, predefined in accordance with prevailing views of the problem. In the case of drug research it has resulted in concentrating investigation on the problematic margin – the tens of thousands of addicts – leaving the broad band of millions and tens of millions of unproblematic or recreational users understudied and outside the analytical frame. The evidence that then is generated about a marginal population with often complex mental health profiles, low educational attainments, weak social support systems, and a high incidence of criminal records, are then metonymically used to speak for drug users in general.

From the premise that drug use is inherently problematic, much of the research then is decidedly 'action orientated' and aimed at alleviating addiction, crime, sex work or the spread of blood-borne viruses. The overwhelming urgency of these problems, particularly in an era of HIV/AIDS and organized crime groups, has occluded the fact that the populations concerned continue to construct their lives around the use of drugs, and seem to obtain benefits and meaning from them. In order to retrieve the humanity of these informants, research needs to look beyond crime figures and HIV status, to uncover trajectories into drug use, the meaning of intoxication, the symbolic role played by substances, and the importance of the identities derived from consuming these substances.

To capture the experience of drug use within the different social and subcultural contexts, new research initiatives are required that approach the issue not from the premise that drugs are a problem that needs to be eliminated, but a social phenomenon to be understood beyond a simple moral division into good abstinence and bad consumption. The study of social phenomena, many of which seem at first sight evil and strange, is the classical task of anthropology. The first generation of anthropologists concentrated on explaining the strange-seeming rites and customs of people encountered by explorers, missionaries and then colonial officials at the height of European imperialism. Prior to such systematic efforts, returning travellers had, through the emphasis of otherness in their narrations of polygamy, poison oracles, ghost dances and cannibalism, sought to underscore the irreconcilable difference of east and west, north and south. Anthropologists, by contrast, would attempt to set these practices in their cultural context and understand them with reference to their social function. In a departure from the arrogance of nineteenth-century colonialism, anthropologists would jettison the credo of European superiority by positing that every culture was as valid as any other. No culture could claim superiority in totality, even though there were different levels of achievement in technology and adaptation. In order to understand a particular set of beliefs or a custom, the anthropologist had first to set it in the context of the wider culture, and to dispense with their own, native moral judgement.

Known as the relative method, this allows anthropologists to establish intellectual proximity to the subject of investigation, create an 'inter-subjective' affective relationship, and embark on the phenomenological project of understanding the world from the subjects' perspective. In the study of substance use it is a prerequisite for relocating drug use from the confines of criminality and addiction, to the wider context of recreation, identity, subculture and youth. The practical technique is known as 'participant observation', in which the researcher mingles with the study population, making connection between different aspects of belief system and practice, to draw up an ethnography – or the description of a tribe or culture.

While the end product – a definitive work on an identified community – has come in for much postmodern critique, and may not be feasible in complex modern societies where groups are living in vast webs of interdependency, the required contact with informants in open settings is invaluable. First, it allows for the observations, analysis and portrayal of the phenomenon in question. Secondly, it allows for detailed examinations of processes and opinions of the individual involved, and helps to thereby restore both their agency and the meaning that they give to their activities. Thirdly, it provides a feedback loop on the activities of professionals and on policy outcomes.

Given the much stated importance of quality assurance and the prominence of performance-measuring management tools in the delivery of public services, it is interesting to note that the voices of the clients are conspicuously silent in the voluminous literature on drug treatment. According to two medical anthropologists, 'Individual clients removed from their social and cultural contexts are seen as objects to be controlled and measured. They are, in effect, transformed into passive figures upon whom treatment modalities are applied.'[16] Small-scale studies of drug users have produced important breakthroughs in the conception of the phenomenon and in assessing effectiveness of interventions. Yet, the main agencies responsible for the coordination of drug control activities, both at national and at international level, have shown themselves indifferent to the potential of such research, preferring to continue with prevalence surveys among school-children or 'rapid assessment studies' in neighbourhoods. It has been suggested that one of the reasons for the reluctance by control agencies to explore the meaning people attach to their drug use, is that it could end up justifying and legitimizing that use.[17]

When anthropologists do work together with medical researchers in interdisciplinary teams, differences of opinion soon arise over, first, the assessment of risks and, secondly, recommendations for interventions. In studies of street-drinking populations, for example, anthropologists would regularly down-play the adverse medical effects of chronic alcohol use, and point to the relative normality of such patterns of consumption within the particular 'culture'.[18] The terminology of cultural practice may not translate as well to patterns of behaviour among marginal groups, say, street-drinking groups of New England longshoremen, or needle-injecting heroin users in former mining communities in Yorkshire. But it preserves the notion that forms of regulation through culturally defined ritual, order and etiquette are found in all social settings. If interventions are to be effective in correcting social problems, these patterns of culture have to be understood. In the addiction field this is most pertinent with regard to lapse and relapse. The most difficult task is not so much to detoxify a problem user, but to maintain their abstinence once they return from the therapeutic setting to their former lives. Here an under-standing of contexts, cues, triggers, relationships and obligations is essential for assisting people along the road to recovery.

Anthropology has been crucial in providing information on the minutiae of cultural practices among drug users and drug control practitioners, for the development of targeted interventions and for generating an understanding of different phenomena beyond prison and clinic. It is also a reflexive exercise, first at research level, where the inductive methodology feeds continuously into the design and the conceptual framework of the research. Secondly, the information and insights generated from the field percolate upwards. This allows, for instance, for social processes that are explicit in other cultures but still have a vestigial or simply unrecognized function in the anthropologists' endogenous culture to be identified, as for instance in 'rites of passage'. In other instances, such as potlatch or taboo, they are assimilated as loan words. More generally, however, the reflexive impulse leads to a cultural critique, or the deconstruction of set assumptions and presuppositions. Anthropologists have been at the forefront in critically examining their own activities as an extension of colonialism and neocolonialism, taken to task their core concepts of self and Other, the meaning of tribe and ethnicity, the literary techniques and the practice of fieldwork. Yet, more generally, they have also contributed to the critical analysis of endogenous concepts of, inter alia, family and kinship, state and nationhood, religious practices and governmental institution, in the light of the alternative encountered in their fieldwork.

As an intellectual exercise it is useful to remove the ontological certainty upon which many assumptions have rested, and open the way for diversity and alternative ways of being. More practically, they have encouraged the development of informal alternatives in the economic, political and social spheres, and to redefine strategic objectives in the development context. One of the key principles of the discipline, 'to make the strange familiar and the familiar strange', is to generate critical thinking and explore alternatives. In the field of drug control a critical analysis of practices and a sustained challenge to their underlying assumptions are long overdue. Of relevance here is a method derived from Nietzsche's idea of social genealogy. It tracks the process of objects, ideas and institutions across time, to plot what has been described as the 'social life of things'.

There is a growing scientific and popular literature elucidating the role of food and drink at the heart of culture. It has become an anthropological truism that the transformation of the raw into the cooked is analogous with and often a material manifestation of the transformation of nature into culture.[19] Food, drink and the intoxicating substances that we will refer to as drugs are not simply a system of alimentation, but also a system of communication or, as Jack Goody claims, a syntax. Values are attached to substances that are ordered in a structure of corresponding meanings, which serves as a paradigm for understanding consumptions of other materials – thus 'taste' is extended to other forms of discrimination: 'Choice of foods and drinks [and drugs] and their manner of preparation is fundamental for the definitions, and indeed the creation, of social groups and classes.'[20]

Reconciling research, experience and practice

Armed with these diverse methods I will survey a number of issues that have been bundled together under the rubric of drugs, and draw on a range of sources from overlapping disciplines. One postmodern dilemma faced by any aspiring researcher is the sheer volume of extant material in any given discipline. In politically defined and academically diverse fields like drug control there is no hope of even approximating an adequate survey of the literature. The route taken in this book is therefore to look at a number of assumptions that are central to the drug control model currently used in the light of selected readings and professional experience in many different countries. Though many 'missions' do not fit into the classical anthropological format of extended field stays, cultural immersion and acquired language skills, what is lacking in cultural depth is partially compensated by the generation of well-targeted information. Working as a consultant on drug issues for different international organizations, I have had the opportunity to meet with key players in the drug control apparatus of more than twenty countries. I have observed activities in forensic laboratories, visited prisons and police stations, national drug strategy units and customs offices, drug treatment centres and psychiatric hospitals, courtrooms, schools and orphanages, cannabis farms, crack houses and drug street markets across the world. These insights will be used intermittently to support the central claims of the book.

1. Today's drug control regime was conceived to protect the core values of (a) reason from the intoxicating power of psychoactive substances, and (b) individual liberty from the

enslavement of addiction. After a century of institutional-
ized campaigning the methods employed have inflicted far
more harm on both these worthy goals than the substances
in question ever could.

2. In the course of implementing an ideal into policy and
   practice the original objective has been lost amid a myriad
   of intermediary goals. These have been reduced for the
   benefit of operational simplicity into negative values, such
   as abstinence from something, eradication and suppression.
   Taking on the destructive methodology of war, they have
   turned the substances in question into a problem that needs
   to be combated.

3. Drug control continues to operate in blithe rejection of the
   key epistemological insight that the knower is part of the
   knowledge, that the observer impinges on the experiment,
   and that every intervention distorts the phenomenon against
   which it is directed. Drug control has become dominated by
   vested sectional interests of professionals and agencies,
   depending for their privileges on the very perpetuation of
   the problem they have been created to correct. The system
   thrives on crises and will continue to expand into and
   destabilize new regions.

4. Drugs and the human penchant for drug-taking remains
   perversely ill understood considering the passions they
   arouse and the resources dedicated to controlling their
   production, distribution and use. Yet, such a deeper understanding is urgently needed as only an informed and
   rational set of regulations can ever contain the threats
   posed by political opportunists and the peculiar substances
   themselves.

2 The Pathology of Drug Use

Up to now the term 'drug' has been used loosely, referring sometimes to the range of substances controlled by national legislation
and international agreement, and at others to licit mind-altering
substances like alcohol. It is timely to come up with a working
definition of drugs, a word that is said to originate from the
Dutch 'droog' for dry goods – denoting the plant-based commodities, like coffee, cocoa, tea and tobacco, shipped by Dutch
merchants from Asia, Africa and the Americas to Europe in the
seventeenth century. The trade in these psychoactive substances
has been a key factor in the expansion of trade and establishing
social relations between different cultures since time immemorial.
At the beginning of the modern era the trade in these newly
discovered luxuries became pivotal to the genesis of the global
trading system. It is refreshing to think that the sprit of capitalism,
manifest in the globe-spanning enterprise of the merchant
adventurer, was driven by demand for tea and tobacco, substances
nowadays associated with downtime, rather than activity.

The irony of attaching the work ethic to new cults of idleness,
points to the dependent relationship of production and consumption and a new structuration of time with the coming of the
modern age. Time is increasingly controlled, with watches, calen-
dars and the organization of purposeful activity, along a series of
functional oppositions divided into work and leisure. The latter
is now marked not by the absence of work but the predominance
of consumption.

Drugs are the ideal commodity in that they meet no immediate
material need, such as nutrition or medication against physical
diseases. They afford fleeting experiences that transport the con-

sumer from the original state of sobriety, and engender a growing attachment, habituation and need, a point where the experience is to be repeated. With increasing refinement of product design and marketing the producers learn to calibrate the substance to a subliminal level and avoid any debilitating consequences, such as vomiting, loss of consciousness or intellectual incoherence. At its finest, the substance is so integrated into daily life as to become synonymous with pleasure, 'breaks', socializing and erotic encounter. As Oscar Wilde remarked, 'A cigarette is the perfect type of pleasure. It is exquisite, and leaves you unsatisfied. What more can one want?'[1]

It is the psychoactive quality that makes tobacco so exquisite, while the lack of satisfaction locks consumer and supplier into the perfect exchange cycle. Arguably, most ingested substances are mind- or mood-altering, if only by staving off hunger, and altering the human metabolism. Substances that we call drugs, however, belong to the higher end of this continuum; their psychoactive action is so intense that, in the words of Antonio Escohotado, 'they overcome the body', rather than being overcome by it in the form of nutrition.[2] Once again this needs to be qualified as it is perfectly possible for drug plants to have nutritious value. Poppy seeds are an ingredient in baking across Central Asia and Eastern Europe, and alcohol has long been integrated into European cuisine for both its mind-altering and nutritious properties.

The term drugs, as used in this book, refers to substances taken for the mind- and mood-altering action, for the stimulus, lift, hit, trip, relaxation or buzz. This emphasis upon effect also distinguishes the drugs we are concerned with here from the other non-nutritional dimension of drug use, also known as medication. Medical drugs, whatever their psychotropic side effects, are used primarily for their utility in redressing identified physical conditions. Once again, the boundaries are fluid. For many conditions psychoactive substances may be used to good effect. Opium and alcohol have been used as analgesics and disinfectants for millennia. It is perhaps that capacity to suppress pain that makes them so attractive to non-medical use. A more recent example is the use of LSD and MDMA in psychotherapy. Coca and cannabis are widely believed to have strong prophylactic powers.

And the use of substances like ayahuasca or ibogaine in their specific cultural contexts is often part of a ritual of healing. Finally, habitual drug use transforms the individual's healthcare requirements. Dependent drinkers need to maintain their alcohol intake, while problematic heroin users need to find the next bag to avoid 'becoming sick'. This is a vicious circle, with the addict taking for medicine the very poison that has reduced him to the state of physical misery and addiction.

These remain anomalies, as most of the people raising their glasses of wine, beer, spirits or kava, or puffing away on pipes, spliffs and fags, snorting lines of cocaine or popping pills of MDMA, chewing khat, betel nut or coca, and injecting heroin or methamphetamine, do so in the expectation of pleasure and not as a prophylactic against pain. The effect of the drug of choice, modulated by the expectations and attitudes of the user, what is also known as the set, and the situation where it is taken, the setting, can take different forms: intensely social and hyperactive or reclusive and quietly reflective. The contrast could not be starker between the crowded dance floor of an ecstasy-charged nightclub, and the solitary torpor associated with habitués of the opium den. All drugs will play out differently in the diverse environments where they are used, but they share a common feature in that they are used for their mind- and mood-altering effects, and the pleasure or relief that is expected to result from them.

In many cases drugs are culturally integrated, to the point where they are hardly recognizable as such. Alcohol provides one example of a powerful drug deeply embedded in different cultures. What the temperance movement and its first legislative triumphs in the early twentieth century demonstrates, though, is that societies can redefine their relationship with any set of substances. Established patterns of consumptions can be broken, drugs can be abandoned or substituted, and new forms of socializing displace ancient and hallowed habits. The arrival of tobacco, coffee, tea and cocoa in Europe over the course of the sixteenth and seventeenth centuries provide examples. All are substances that have been integrated into the rhythms of daily life and discarded the 'drug image'. Arguably, marijuana, cocaine and opium have also found a place in the cultural repertoire, though their integration into social life is impeded by the fact that they are under strict legal control everywhere in the world.

The rituals surrounding the drinking of tea, coffee and alcohol disguise the final definitive property of what constitutes a drug – they are habit-forming. In contrast to medication, which is administered until a cure has been achieved and no more, drugs are consumed repeatedly and perpetually. Occasions for use are determined, firstly, not by the individual's medical condition but his appetite, and secondly by the social setting and societal calendar. Integrated into the work/play rhythms of life, they often come to stand metaphorically for the free time and holidays during which they are consumed. For many consumers who would never think of themselves as drug users, holidays cannot be imagined without, or are even constituted of, the extensive and conspicuous consumption of these cherished substances. Where social convention or culture does not provide a framework to prescribe the pattern of use and restraint, individual users are vulnerable to the dictates of their appetite.

The social regulation of consumption, both through the informal culture of consumption and the law, is crucial for determining use, distribution and production. It is not helpful in defining what constitutes a drug. As substances become domesticated over time, they take on the appearance of comforting familiarity that belies their intrinsic pharmacological impact on human mind and behaviour. Hence, the working definition used here is that of a mind- and or mood-altering substance that is used for neither nutritional nor medical purpose, and is potentially habit-forming.

Drugs and crime

According to the Conservative MP Nicholas Hawkins, the issue is quite simple: 'The greatest cause of crime, as all law-abiding people know, is drugs.'[3] It is rarely either charitable or instructive to subject the rhetorical assertions of populist politicians to the rigours of scientific analysis. What merits the exercise in this particular instance, however, is that the Member for Surrey Heath encapsulated so neatly a widely held belief. It should be clear that

Hawkins was not referring to alcohol or tobacco in his use of 'drugs', but the range of substances controlled by law.

Unlike most other areas of crime, drug-related offences span different levels of activity and experience. First there is the shadowy world of organized crime, spinning a web of clandestine connections across the globe. With links to other forms of criminal enterprise, and alleged connections to terrorism, it challenges the very institutional foundations of the modern state. More immediate to most people's experience are the depredations of drug addicts. Fearless and pitiless from intoxication, and driven to desperate measures by their addictions, their spree of acquisition crime impinges directly on the lives of many. It has been suggested that over half of the total number of crimes committed in the UK are drug motivated.[4]

Substance is lent to these claims by a growing body of research among arrested offenders, made possible by breakthroughs in the drug testing technology, principally urine analysis. Adapted from a US model, the New England and Wales Arrestee Drug Abuse Monitoring (NEW-ADAM) system found that some 65 per cent of sampled arrestees had traces of drugs in their urine.[5] A cohort of problematic users undergoing treatment and subject to extensive research admitted to levels of crime that added further substance to the contention. These 664 recovering addicts admitted to an average of 436 crimes per year, totting up a tally of some 70,000 crimes between them.[6] Extrapolating from these reports, a team from York University estimated the social cost of class A drug use at between £9 billion and £16 billion, the bulk of it accounted for by crime and criminal justice.[7] It is not surprising therefore that the New Labour government committed from 1993 (before they were in power) to come down 'tough on crime and tough on the causes of crime', turning drugs into a key issue with an integrated, well-funded strategy led, for a time at least, by a UK Anti Drugs Coordinator.

The issue is given a further twist by the well-publicized use of violence among drug dealers. In both the UK and the US so-called 'turf wars' between rival gangs of drug dealers, debt collection and the enforcement of contracts among drug dealers constitute one of the main causes of homicide among young men, particularly from ethnic minorities. Even more dramatic has been the violence associated with drug trafficking in some of the key drug-producing and transit countries like Colombia, Mexico or Jamaica.

Drug crime typology

Against these serious contentions it is important to establish some clarity over the different types of crimes that are caused by drugs, and to get a clearer idea of the causal link. We therefore distinguish between the following categories of drug-related crime.

Pharmacologically induced crimes

This consists of crimes that are committed under the influence of any substance. They include a wide range of public order offences triggered principally by a lowering of social inhibitions. There is an invisible line separating boisterous from antisocial behaviour, largely dependent on social and environmental factors, and receptive to 'management'. The accompanying interpersonal violence often has strong ritualistic elements, which contains the damage to participants and bystanders. While the material damage is much more widespread, it comprises a fraction of the rising levels of vandalism that seem contingent to the proliferation of public and private property.

The most disturbing incidents of intoxicated violence come with the introduction of new drugs, whether methamphetamine, crack cocaine or alcohol. In one of the most chilling accounts of drug-fuelled frenzy, Euripides narrates the story of Pentheus, King of Thebes, who goes into the night to spy on the Bacchanalian rites near his city. Discovered on top of a tree by the wine-drinking revellers, he is torn to pieces and eaten alive. The killers include his mother Agave, who carries his severed head back to town thinking it belongs to a mountain lion. After this tragedy a temple is built to Bacchus, the god of wine, who teaches his followers to mix the wine with water and thus control its potency.

A more recent story of drug-induced personality change is *The Strange Case of Dr Jekyll and Mr Hyde*, written shortly after the introduction of cocaine to the medicine chest of Victorian Britain. The drug that unleashes Mr Hyde is the product of Dr Jekyll's own experiments. Yet,

> the spirit of cocaine lies both behind the description of its effects and in all likelihood behind the writing process itself. Stevenson was sickly and tubercular and his wife Fanny was a nurse with a keen interest in medicines, and his symptoms of 'nervous exhaustion' were among those for which coca preparations were indicated.[8]

The violent mood swings associated with the split identity provide a powerful account of addiction and reflect the anxieties about the powers and possible consequences of new psychoactives untamed by custom and convention.

Even more alarming was the introduction of new drugs into situations of rapid social change, experienced in the US, for example, in the expanding conurbations, such as Chicago, or the southern states after the abolition of slavery. During the 1880s cocaine was being used increasingly among African-Americans both as a performance enhancer on work gangs, where it often took the place of alcohol, and for recreational purposes. It soon took hold in the 'underworld' and was associated with a new wave of crime, including rapes and violent assaults allegedly committed under the influence or robberies necessary to satisfy the addiction. According to Colonel J. W. Watson of Georgia in 1903, 'many of the horrible crimes committed in the southern States by the coloured people can be traced directly to the cocaine habit.'

Yet the concrete evidence for this crime wave is poor, opening the possibility of explanations such as 'racial hypersensitivity'. This was a strong argument in the American South, where the white ruling class was watching the formally emancipated but structurally excluded and segregated black population with suspicion. It is difficult to assess if the alleged increase in criminal activity was the product of drug use stipulated by Dr Edward H. Williams in 1914: 'peaceful negroes become quarrelsome, and timid negroes develop a degree of "Dutch courage" that is sometimes almost incredible.' Or were these simply newly enfranchised citizens asserting their civil rights? As the legal framework of segregation was descending on southern states, 'extreme vigilance was exercised against Black assaults on Whites, above all sexual assaults on White women, which became a virtual obsession.'[9] This fear was played upon by political operators with their own agenda. For example, in pursuit of extending the powers of federal law enforcement agencies, officers such as the chief investigator for federal narcotic laws, Dr Hamilton Wright, were lobbying Congress: 'cocaine is often the direct incentive to the crime of rape by the negroes of the South and other sections of the country.' Federal agencies were vastly expanded in the early twentieth century in order to better control the trafficking and production of drugs. At state level, meanwhile, police forces pressed for, and were rewarded with, a bigger armoury in their fight with drug users, because, according to one sheriff, 'Those cocaine niggers sure are hard to kill.'[10] After the First World War cocaine largely disappeared from the US as a consequence of policing, the switch of many problematic users to heroin and, most importantly, the ready supply of licit alternatives in the guise of amphetamine.

In the 1970s, however, cocaine use celebrated a dramatic resurgence in the US with a very different symbolic status, initially at least. Associated with professional success and material wealth, it was totally dissociated from violence and aggression. Yet, as the drug moved downmarket, attitudes changed and law enforcement became more repressive. Backstreet chemists came up with a new product by heating hydrochloride in water with ammonia and ether. Known as cocaine freebase, it could be smoked for a much quicker, more intense rush. In the late 1970s it was replaced by an even simpler process, when cocaine hydrochloride was heated in a baking soda and water solution. When cooling down the brown crystals crackled as they expanded into the easiest and most powerful coca-derived commodity – crack.

Sold in small rocks, crack put the stimulating powers of cocaine within reach of new client groups. It was soon known as a 'ghetto drug', with its importation and distribution often controlled by African-American and Caribbean groups. The racial and social characteristics of these new consumer groups go a long way to explain the sentencing regime created in the US by the Anti Drug Abuse Act of 1986: 'The statute specified a mandatory minimum sentence of ten years for a violation involving 50 gms of crack cocaine, but powder cocaine required a full 5 kgs to warrant a comparable sentence.'[11] This disparity, known as the '100-to-1 ratio', has been justified by the association of crack cocaine with violence, and was upheld by Congress after challenge from the US Sentencing Commission in 1995. For many critics it provides another example of racially motivated legislation and law enforcement, as crack is popular mainly among black Americans and Latinos, while cocaine powder is mostly consumed by white Americans. Eliminating the crack/powder disparity continues to inspire US civil rights groups and drug policy reform more than ten years later, with submissions by the Drug Policy Alliance to amend the Drug Sentencing Reform and Cocaine Kingpin Trafficking Act.

Law enforcement agencies building a case for new resources, bigger guns and more sweeping powers often refer to the violence potential of new substances. It has engendered a new type of evangelism, as law enforcement officers carry the stark warning of impending doom to audiences on the brink of drug epidemics. The pattern is repeated with cyclical regularity. In the 1980s US marshals were warning brother officers in the UK and anywhere in the world of the unprecedented levels of violence triggered by the new drug called crack. So successful was this mission in establishing the meaning of crack that it has become a reference point in its own right; when, in the early years of the twenty-first century, a new cast of travelling officers were warning of the dangers of methamphetamine, it was conventionally described as the most dangerous drug ever seen – 'worse than crack'.

Evangelists, like journalists, may be prone to exaggeration in order to get the message across, but they can only succeed when the audience is receptive. Public apprehension over drugs and drug use cannot simply be reduced to decades of propaganda by the control agencies. There is a profound unease over the potential fallout resulting from the impact unknown substances can have on human behaviour. In the stories about the frenzied violence of the Bacchantes, of berserkers and coke fiends, we come closest to a deep-seated revulsion against drug-induced insanity. In the modern setting it presents the antithesis to Enlightenment rationality and control, as well as to the idea of public order.

Against this background of concerns it is therefore notable that in the UK, as in most of Europe, the drug most commonly associated with violence and implicated in more than one-third of all recorded assaults is alcohol.[12] It could be asserted that the use of opiates, MDMA and cannabis is in fact crime-reducing. Most pharmacologically induced drug crimes, that is crimes triggered by the action of the substance on the central nervous system and reducing levels of inhibition, are caused by alcohol, and only a fraction is attributable to the controlled drugs.

Acquisition crime

The type of crime that impinges most painfully on the public is committed by drug users in raising funds for drug purchases. Once the pattern of consumption spirals to critical levels, users face rising difficulty in funding it from legitimate sources. Long periods of intoxication impair their performance while their focus zeroes in on the drug at the expense of all else. At that very point of falling productivity, the users' need for drugs is increasing. The mechanism known as tolerance means that ever larger amounts of the same substance are required for achieving the same effect. Unable to pay for this growing habit from their loosening toehold in the licit economy, many users resort to criminal or socially unacceptable activities – crime and prostitution.

In Europe and North America the number of property offences committed to fuel alcohol or nicotine habits, by contrast, is minimal. Many drug-using offenders are also alcohol and nicotine users, and these substances do add an additional financial burden on overstretched budgets. But tobacco and alcohol products remain within reach even of the poor, in spite of heavy tax regimes on tobacco and alcohol. Still more cost-effective is cannabis, increasingly supplied from domestic sources, and competitively priced even in comparison to alcohol. The core reason for the desperate financial predicament of problematic drug users is the high price of heroin and cocaine. The cheapest retail unit of heroin trading in London early in 2007 was the £10 bag containing an actual heroin content so low that chronic users would need three or four of these just to stop 'getting sick'. Significantly larger quantities were needed for the sought-after euphoric effects. The costs rise further when the heroin is mixed with cocaine into so-called speedballs, with many users clocking up daily habits of between £100 and £200. This presents a serious challenge for people on the margins of the job market. Given that the UK population of problematic users is estimated to be between 250,000 and 350,000, the addiction complex is believed to be responsible for an enormous amount of property crime.

What seems extraordinary, then, is that keeping the costs of drugs high is the key objective of government drug policy centred on enforcement. Not merely in the UK, but globally, the principal aim of drug prohibition is not simply to prevent drugs from entering the market, as this has proven unworkable. Instead, the stated policy objective is to push prices up beyond the reach of most experimenters. The idea is to prevent early experimentation among vulnerable constituencies, principally the young. Where there is an existing population of users who suddenly find their supply is cut off and/or the costs are sharply increased, policy-makers face a dilemma.

US studies from the first wave of heroin use in the 1960s illustrate the workings of this mechanism. Sharper federal laws introduced in the 1950s led to the withdrawal of organized crime groups from drug distribution, and local heroin shortages hitting New York in 1961 resulted in panic. Prices tripled while the quality deteriorated, with devastating effect on the fledgling community of heroin users. Stealing from their families and each other, they would at best work in loose pairs, but mainly alone, adopting the motto: 'I have no friends, only associates.' According to Edward Preble and John Casey, the policy-induced temporary drought 'is responsible for major social disorder in the city today'.[13]

The actual dynamic of supply shortages leading to price rises, which in turn trigger increases in property crime, is not easy to demonstrate, owing to the absence of successful examples in supply reduction. Principles of demand and supply work with textbook efficiency even in the most underground of economies. When Australian drug markets experienced a sharp drop in heroin imports in 2000/1, a rapid increase in crime was registered, followed by a switch to methamphetamine.

The explanatory model is straightforward: demand for drugs like heroin is inelastic because addicts have no choice but to use.

This is, indeed, one of the main reasons advanced for controlling the substance in the first place. Constant demand against shortages in supply will lead to price increases and quality dilution. Debilitated by the dual effects of intoxication and addiction, the users are unable to meet rising costs legitimately and have increasingly to turn to crime. What makes this policy even more incongruous, for a government charged with securing the safety of its citizens, is the acknowledged impotence of enforcement agencies in preventing the inflow of drugs.

To restore a semblance of rationality, we need to recall that drugs are a cross-cutting issue, involving different government departments and professionals. From the outset the policy depended on alliances across disciplinary boundaries. Often, officials in one department rely on information provided by another, which they do not have the technical competence to interrogate or the remit to challenge. The fact that force continues to be employed in order to control illicit drugs is contingent on political developments. The underlying rationale of the entire regime has been the pursuit of public morality and public health. It is the basic incongruence between these noble goals and the enforcement-centred means employed that lies at the root of the crime wave with which society has now been burdened. Agency heads and policy-makers are all left in the throes of a dilemma: with every increase in drug-fuelled crime, the louder the call for additional resources to fight the supply chain, which in turn drives up the prices for the drugs, that then require a greater volume of crime for addicts to meet their needs.

Organized crime

With the growing effectiveness and sophistication of law enforcement, the stakes for drug market participants rise sharply. Amateurs like Howard Marks or holidaymakers coming home from Morocco, India or Peru give way to efficient organizations that employ technical expertise, instrumental violence and systematic corruption. The rise of organized crime groups in the wake of alcohol prohibition has become the stuff of Hollywood legend and turned Al Capone, the liquor bootlegger into an icon. Parallel developments triggered by suppressing the licit supply of cannabis, heroin, cocaine and MDMA remains too serious for light-hearted treatment by the entertainment industry. Yet the mechanisms have been analysed by criminologists, particularly with regard to the use of violence. Rising enforcement levels bring down the threshold of violence.[14] Policing techniques gain in sophistication, say through the use of informants, 'controlled deliveries', ever more complex entrapment methods and more intrusive means of surveillance. Coupled with escalating penalties, they have pushed the drug trade in the 'direction of becoming more security conscious, more prepared to use violence to deter informant and enforcement agents, and in general more brutal'.[15] Violence in the drug trade, then, is inherent neither to the pharmacological properties of the drugs nor the organized crime groups they attract. They are part of the knock-on effect of state-imposed sanctions and enforcement styles. In the US this is reflected in the increase in homicide rates during, first, alcohol prohibition and then the assault on drug dealing in the 1980s.[16]

The fight against organized crime has become one of the main objectives of law enforcement agencies in many countries. In the EU the transnational cooperation of police agencies and the judiciary is often justified with reference to growing public apprehension over organized groups involved in drug trafficking. The reorganization of law enforcement agencies in the UK to form the Serious Organised Crime Agency (SOCA) has been justified in part so as to better meet the threat of drug-trafficking syndicates. Dismantling such groups has become one of the key law enforcement performance measures. Vying with international terrorists and paedophile rings for the title of Public Enemy number one, the organized crime group has taken on an ontological dimension. It is widely believed that organized crime groups are out there, independent of policy and economic opportunity, and need to be tackled by well-honed law enforcement agencies.

Interestingly, this assumption runs against some of the prevailing models of criminological behaviour, as well as the evidence. Crime control strategies increasingly focus on prevention methods, including street lighting, security cameras and law enforcement visibility. These passive defence measures are intended to deter the large number of potential offenders who will strike when provided with the opportunity.[17] This marks an important conceptual shift in the typology of the criminal. Any of us could potentially commit an offence and might be tempted if the opportunity presented itself. Crime is no longer a dysfunctional quality that inheres in a marginal group of criminal types, but arises from situations in which people find themselves. The role of the authorities, then, is to prevent such opportunities from arising.

Drug policy, unfortunately, has achieved the very opposite by creating a market with dynamic demand and fluid supply chains to tempt anyone willing to take the risk. According to the conclusions of the most comprehensive study on drug traders in British prisons, 'barriers to entry for people with contacts operating in the market were small. No special skills were required other than a willingness to break the law.'[18] Some of these new entrants may have cut their teeth in some other criminal activity before they 'diversify' into the drugs trade.[19]

The profit potential of drug trafficking then provides incentives for players from diverse backgrounds. As long as the control regime continues to block legal commercial suppliers without eliminating demand, it creates an opportunity structure for criminals. As detection measures become more sophisticated, a perverse Darwinian impetus is triggered, wherein the weakest criminals are caught, leaving even wider profits for the remainder. This in turn spurs the demands of the criminal justice system for the appropriation of more resources and the imposition of harsher penalties to combat the growing danger.

With the level of entry for would-be drug traffickers so low, counter-trafficking measures may succeed in arresting and incarcerating ever growing numbers of traffickers, without effectively reducing the overall inflow of drugs. Vacancies in the supply chain are quickly taken up by opportunists, who have to find alternative ways of raising their start-up capital: 'some other money-making criminal activities, including armed robberies, are sometimes conducted specifically to fund Class A trafficking.'[20] It has long been argued that targeting drug traffickers has symbolic value at best, because the place of each trafficker taken out would be quickly taken up by newcomers. Once arrived, these would then need to first find their niche before establishing their position. What is yet to be widely recognized is the knock-on effect, that the war on drug traffickers generates serious criminal activity beyond the drugs field.

Corruption

In the UK and other developed countries with traditions of strong, centrally governed states, the threat posed by organized crime groups to institutions and the rule of law can usually be contained, although at high costs to individuals and communities. The situation is far more serious in countries with weaker systems of governance, where the impact of illicit drug markets can corrode the key institutions of the state. In Latin America governance has been jeopardized by drug-related activities in several countries, including Colombia and Mexico. The best-known example is probably Colombia, where the *extraditables*, a group of traffickers headed by Pablo Escobar, launched a double onslaught of terrorism and corruption that could only be met with sustained and continuing international support. Yet, while the Colombian authorities succeeded in smashing the Medellin and Cali cartels, this tactical law enforcement victory has had negligible effect on the overall outflow of Colombian cocaine. Instead of top-heavy, high-profile organizations, a myriad of smaller, more fluid groups have emerged, many organized as so-called Self Defence Forces, linked to the military and senior politicians – the very forces ostensibly fighting the war on narco-terror. The price for these 'successes' has been the heavy involvement of the US in Colombian affairs, and the compromise of some aspects of the country's sovereignty. Since 2002 the war on drug trafficking has morphed into a war against rural guerrillas, who have officially been redefined as terrorist groups, and become an end in itself. Plan Colombia is now a hybrid programme, supporting the Colombian government against a multitude of internal enemies. The main beneficiaries are the private US corporations contracted to undertake the crop eradication, training and surveillance activities and employing an estimated 800 US personnel. Inevitably, some of these US advisers have themselves become involved in drug trafficking. When caught, they are repatriated to be tried in the US since a bilateral agreement between the US and Colombian governments gives them immunity in Colombia.[21]

Corruption affects many countries well beyond the production areas of the key plant-drug crops. Circuitous drug trafficking routes plotted by ingenious drug traffickers across the globe have exposed the institutions of many countries to the risk of 'financial suasion'. When the carrot of cash and favours is backed up by physical threats to officers or their families, drug traffickers can determine court cases and infiltrate law enforcement agencies.

Drug-defined crime

While there is considerable public concern over drug-crazed psychopaths, prolific property offenders, the mafia, and bent coppers or judges, the vast bulk of law enforcement effort is targeted at those whose crime is defined by the status of the drug. That is people who commit no offence other than holding in their possession some quantity of the substance restricted by law to licensed medical or scientific purpose only. Many thousands of these are drug traffickers, transporting drugs illegally across inter-national borders, or drug dealers, either trading in bulk or selling directly to the end-user. Beneficiaries of innocence and addiction, these commercial operators are conventionally presented as the incarnation of modern evil, making profit out of other people's misery. Holding these couriers from mainly developing countries responsible for the drug problems of Europe and North America has been called the 'scapegoat strategy'[22] and is manifest in the rising number of foreign nationals held on long sentences in European prisons.

The rubric 'dealer' includes a wide number of operators en-gaged in highly specialized tasks. Drugs have to be sourced in bulk and broken up into smaller consignments: there is the cooking up (of cocaine powder into crack cocaine), the cutting with adulter-ants and the packaging; there are the lookouts and runners who deliver money to the head seller and the drugs to the customer; and, of course, there are the enforcers. Front-line services are often split into one end where the money is collected and another where the drugs are dispensed. One of the working principles of the trade is never to have the money and the drugs on you at the same time, in case of attack or, worse, arrest. Both are warehoused in the custody of trusted operatives in the neighbourhood, often by women or elderly people who themselves do not use.[23]

As we learn more about the internal working of the drugs economy it is becoming clear that the industry follows typical capitalist patterns, with concentrations of wealth at the top. Though the image of the drug dealer, sported by many protagonists themselves, is one of fast money and disposable income, it seems that only a fraction manage to rise above the poverty line. More representative for the vast majority of players is the experience of the street dealers in New York's Spanish Harlem hoping to cash in on the crack cocaine boom of the 1990s. When analysed soberly, dealers were performing one of the most dangerous jobs in the US economy, always vulnerable to attack from customers or rivals, arrest by law enforcement, and the temptation to smoke their boss's product. They were working in abysmal conditions in abandoned warehouses or on street corners, with no entitlements to holiday pay, no sick leave and no pension rights. The only benefit loyal employees of one 'firm' studied by Philippe Bourgeois could boast was the services of a lawyer for the first arrest.[24] When income is totted up over longer periods, including the lack of paid holidays and spells of imprisonment, they were just about averaging the minimum wage.

The cash-strapped reality of drug dealing is disguised by episodic conspicuous consumption and the large cash holdings individuals have on occasion. But even many of the most successful dealers are prevented from diversifying out of drugs by the lack of investment opportunities and financial skills. An even harsher picture of the exploitative nature of the drugs economy is provided by an economic analysis of a Los Angeles-based gang, the Black Disciples. The top twenty 'senior executives' were doing well with an annual income of $500,000. Below them were some hundred managers earning around $100,000 each. They in turn were controlling a workforce of about 5,300 officers and footsoldiers, who would make $3.30–7 per hour, and were taking home $700 per month. Below them still were some 20,000 unpaid gang members, who could be hired on a casual basis and were driven by the ambition to become a footsoldier.[25]

We should hold on to the fact that the majority of drug dealers are not only not rich, but also working in abject conditions at stark levels of deprivation. There is considerable scope for utilizing this well-documented fact in drug prevention 'education' aimed at some of the most vulnerable groups. That this is not done owes a lot to the tenacity with which the drug control community itself hangs on to the myth of 'Mr Big', the rich and powerful drug dealer. The entire mission looks far less heroic when it becomes clear that most of the adversaries belong to structurally excluded and systematically disadvantaged minorities struggling below the poverty line.

Many of the most aggressive sellers of drugs are not only poor but themselves addicted. They are the so-called 'user dealers', who finance their own habit by selling drugs. Driven by the immediate need of another fix, they will take far higher risks in dealing with strangers and in high-risk environments. These drug-dependent dealers are also believed to play a major role in recruiting new users, particularly in heroin-using circles, where they initiate novices into injecting. Reducing the number of drug injectors has been one of the main objectives of drug control policies across the EU for the past decade. Yet one of the most innovative initiatives to contain these problems was developed just outside the EU, in the unlikely setting of Switzerland, where in 1986 the government opened a number of 'drug consumption rooms' in Zurich. At first the idea was to provide a setting where drugs, though illicit, could be used safely. In the 1990s the scheme was extended to provide long-term heroin users, who had proved refractory to other forms of treatment, with heroin under supervised condition. This highly controversial scheme was motivated precisely by the dual objective of closing down open street markets and reducing the number of new injectors. The policy has paid off handsomely in both regards, with a drop in heroin prevalence and a fall in antisocial behaviour offences.[26] The policy provides, furthermore, an interesting reversal of the model described above, in that it used public health approaches to achieve law enforcement goals.

It is therefore important to re-examine the popular image of the drug dealer as the deserving recipient of penal wrath. Many are themselves victims of structural poverty and suffering the consequences of problematic drug use. Tough drug war approaches have succeeded in feeding large numbers of small-timers through the criminal justice system, but their position in a low-skill occupation is easily taken by a ready pool of replacements, who are socially conditioned into 'dissidence' and with few options in the legal economy.

Given the sheer scale of the drugs economy and the fragmented nature of supply at retail level, moral assessments are difficult to make. There are huge numbers of drug dealers operating along different principles. Many are selling dangerous substances with no heed of the consequences for their clients or communities, and get involved in other criminal activities. Others have little scruple selling to juveniles and will callously seduce drug-naïve clients into problematic habits. Yet immorality should not be equated with drug dealing. There are considerable variations in the modus operandi and the moral orientation of different dealers. Bourgeois renders a touching account of a group of street-level dealers in New York, who, satisfied after a good day's work, are closing down their 'shop' with all the eagerness to get home of employees from the mainstream economy.

Though the drug dealer has fired the imagination of the public for more than a century and served to justify law enforcement interventions across the globe, the vast bulk of resources, in terms of police officers and equipment employed for arrests, courts and probation services, and the growing prison estate, are dedicated to the pursuit of offenders whose principle crime is being in possession of a controlled substance. Particularly in the us, there is an evident disconnect between the official statements of senior policy-makers and what happens on the streets. Take the official line of former us Attorney General John Ashcroft, 'Federal law enforcement is targeted effectively at convicting major drug traffickers and punishing them with longer lockups in prison',[27] and compare it to the composition of drug-related arrests. In the period between 1980 and 1997 drug arrests tripled in the us, with 79.5 per cent of these for possession offences.[28] Moreover, increasingly law enforcement efforts have been invested in policing cannabis use. Out of a total of 1,538,800 drug arrests in 2000, 40 per cent were for marijuana offences, with only 41,000, or 6 per cent of the 734,000 total, resulting in a felony conviction.

In the us, the federal government does not consider cannabis a 'soft' drug to be distinguished from heroin or cocaine. There are significant variations at state level, with the recognition in twelve states that marijuana has medical uses, and tougher approaches in others. It is these state-level assessments of marijuana that make for a chequered arrest pattern across the us. Much higher rates were found in states employing deliberate 'stop and search' techniques as part of zero tolerance policing, for example in New York. In states like Maryland, by contrast, most marijuana busts were incidental outcomes of traffic stops, arrests for disorderly conduct and other patrol activities. Yet one common factor across the country was the large increase in police numbers against an overall drop in crime, and with the diminution of serious crimes, law enforcement agents 'are likely to turn their attention to nuisance crimes'.[29]

Equally in the UK, out of the 105,570 drug offences committed in 2004, 85 per cent were related to drug possession, 14 per cent to drug dealing and the remainder to production and importing/exporting. Though the majority of offenders were dealt with by caution, fine, or suspended or community sentence, some 11,270 people were sentenced to custodial punishment. Overall, drug arrests were down by some 21 per cent on the previous year, largely because of the downgrading of cannabis from Class B to Class C in January 2004.

The argument for maintaining powers of arrest for petty possession offences is that it provides law enforcement with a tool for unravelling other crimes. This does not stand up to scrutiny, however, as according to the US Attorney General only one in nine stops resulted in an arrest for another crime. Research in the UK shows an even lower yield, since 'arrests for possession offences very rarely led to the discovery of serious crimes'.[30] These low conversion rates raise serious questions about the motivation of the senior police officers lobbying so assiduously for the extension of powers of arrest. In a recent review of the shifting justification for cannabis prohibition, Peter Cohen summarizes the evidence from New York: 'The driving force behind the arrests of large and ever-increasing numbers of people for the possession of cannabis in New York City is not the actual use of cannabis or any possible increase in that use. The driving force is the local police department.'[31] Considerable benefits accrue from cannabis prohibition to individual police officers and the department at large. Officers get the opportunity to achieve arrest quotas and the opportunity to do overtime. The police department, meanwhile, can keep a large number of officers on standby and ready for deployment. In the meantime they are kept busy arresting, making official reports, placing in police custody, trying, fining and releasing more than 30,000 cannabis users.[32]

There are few practical benefits in terms of either public safety or criminal investigation to merit arresting drug users for their drug use. But it does bolster the power of police forces and allows individual officers to impose their own agenda on policing.

The thorny question of addiction

Working in the late 1990s with a US Drug Enforcement Administration agent stationed in Lagos, Nigeria, I was impressed by the account of his personal journey. Initially he had joined the police service for the adrenalin-charged excitement of kicking down doors. What was found inside those tenement blocks had then confirmed him in the righteousness of his mission: families subsisting on welfare cheques, neglecting their essential duties towards their children, all involved in a panoply of crimes, and morally inoculated to this depravity by the regular administration of drugs, licit and illicit. Many hundred arrests and several years later, his concern was shifting from taking down the user dealers to assisting them in their recovery. He had become more interested in treatment programmes both within prisons and without, and was now proud of every addict he had helped to start a new life free from drugs. This storyline is part of a genre frequently found in the autobiographical reflections on a life in the drug war by many law enforcement veterans. This may simply be the mellowing process, as the tough young guns mature into a more forgiving and avuncular middle age. Burnout and cynicism among staff are frequently encountered in law enforcement agencies, social care, medicine and other front-line services, where idealism plays an important role. After years of dedication, professionals realize that their individual efforts cannot change structural conditions, and they lose their motivation. In drug control, however, some officers come to believe that they are part of the very problem that they had thought they were combating. It was this thought process that led to the founding in 2002 of one remarkable American organisation: Law Enforcement Against Prohibition. Former and current law enforcement officers came together to campaign for an end to the war on drugs and a radical change to the control of currently illicit psychoactive substances. It does so by running public seminars, high-profile lobbying and media work.

Unlike this small band of 'brother officers', the DEA agent in Lagos had kept his faith in the overall policy. He had merely shifted his focus from fighting evil with violence to rescuing the fallen. As he was unskilled in the required techniques himself, all he could do was refer the arrestee to a treatment centre, often in person. Along the trajectory from 'custody' into 'care', the arrestee was transformed into a patient or, in contemporary parlance, a client, with needs, rights and a say in his or her treatment. As for the mechanics of the treatment process, how behaviour change is achieved and addicted bodies detoxified, this lay beyond the ken of my DEA colleague. All that he needed to know was that there was someone else to take care of the problem and, more importantly, that there was a genuine problem requiring a specialized form of assistance – the drug treatment. Most enforcement officers arresting drug users and suppliers have little understanding of the dynamics of addiction and treatment, and would not be expected to. In many countries, however, they do forge close working relationships that are supported by structural partnerships at strategic and policy level.

In the current drug control regime the notion of drug treatment is a crucial part of what the United Nations Office on Drugs and Crime has widely established as the 'balanced approach'. This reference to treating the problematic user conveys several key messages about both the problem at hand and the response of governments and intergovernmental agencies to it. Treatment and prevention provide a friendly gloss on a policy that devotes the vast bulk of resources to policing, prisons and paramilitary interventions. Beyond tokenism, the redemption of the drug addict provides the drug control system with a humanitarian alibi. It allows agencies such as the International Narcotic Control Board (INCB), a secretive council of government appointees, to declare that their punitive powers are wielded in order to 'reduce harm'. The treatment systems established and supported by governments give expression to the underlying reality of addiction, which, in turn, justifies the set of controls imposed by the regime in the first place.

The notion of addiction, then, plays a pivotal role in the drug control regime. In its popular form, the notion of addiction provides a set of explanations for the violent and antisocial behaviour of many different criminals and, secondly, a justification for criminalizing the producers and suppliers of the substance in question. While addiction is possibly one of the most important concepts in modern psychiatric medicine, it is not an easy one to define. With no objective boundaries, the condition is socially defined as a psychiatric disorder diagnosed with reference to symptoms, rather than an identified underlying pathology.[33] Increasingly applied to a range of compulsive behaviours, such as gambling, sex, shopping or video games, it belongs properly to the field of substance use and has its origins in the identification of alcoholism as a 'condition'. Records of alcohol-related problems date back to antiquity, but in the eighteenth century the concern shifted from the consequences of inebriation to the conditions that bring about chronic use. According to the historian Harry Levine, alcohol use was widespread and highly esteemed in colonial America: 'Drunkenness was a natural, harmless consequence of drinking.'[34] Though there were complaints about drunkenness, and some measures to control and penalize drunkards, they were not seen as a special group of deviants. Drinkers were said to 'love' drink, the consequences of which may be troublesome but not sinful. In the first formulations of alcoholism, a distinction was made between different patterns of use dependent on individuals.

The model of habitual drunkenness developed by Benjamin Rush included:

- the causal agent – spirituous liquors.
- the drunkard's condition was described as a loss of control over the drinking behaviour.
- the condition was a disease.
- total abstinence was the only way to cure the drunkard.

The proposition fell on fertile ground, as Rush and his followers succeeded in mobilizing a massive following. By the 1830s more than half a million people had pledged themselves not to drink any liquor. As it broadened, the demands of the movement became more forthright and its argument simpler. While initially the analysis had distinguished between drinkers and problem drinkers, who were weak of will and needed help, it now became committed to total abstinence from all alcoholic beverages. Many began to argue that controlled alcohol use or, in the phraseology of today's alcohol industry, 'sensible drinking' was impossible. One of the slogans in the US campaign for alcohol prohibition was: 'Moderation is a lie.' This idea is still upheld by Alcoholics Anonymous, but only with reference to recovering alcoholics.

In the mid-nineteenth century the temperance movement defined drunkenness first as a sin and subsequently as a disease. In the 1860s the first asylums were opened, both as an extension of Christian charity and a campaign for moral hygiene. Increasingly combative, the movement began to target the suppliers of alcohol as holding responsibility for the plight of the habitual drunkard. In the temperance literature the alcoholic is cast as a victim because of alcohol's wide availability and becomes an object of pity and sympathy, while anger and scorn is reserved for the moderate drinkers.

The early definition of habitual drunkenness has to be placed in the context of nineteenth-century ideas about deviance and mental illness. In the optimistic worldview of the Enlightenment, social problems were held to be solvable and all medical problems could be cured. Civil society did indeed have a duty to provide the means whereby cures could be sought. After all, social order depended upon self-control, as modern society had shifted the locus onto the individual: 'Madness has become a curable disease, the chief symptom of which was the loss of self-control. The asylum was construed as a place to restore the power of self-discipline to those who had somehow lost it.'[35] Asylums for habitual drinkers applied the same methods of treatment found in almshouses, penitentiaries, orphanages and all US institutions of the nineteenth century: moral treatment was administered to promote self-control through discipline, routine and hard work.

These developments were paralleled in Great Britain, where the Licensing Act of 1872 marked a major shift in emphasis designed for the better prevention of drunkenness. It introduced fines for being drunk and disorderly, and being drunk and 'in charge of any carriage, horse, cattle or steam engine', or in possession of a loaded firearm. Seven years later the 1879 Habitual Drunkards Act significantly expanded on these provisions, by establishing the powers for the arrest of habitual drunkards and their removal to a 'licensed retreat'. A further ten years on the treatment approach was abandoned for a more punitive approach: any offender who admitted to being or was found to be a habitual drunkard could be detained for up to three years.

What is remarkable about this shift towards intolerance over a 30-year period is that it was not prompted by changing levels in drinking. Alcohol use appears to have remained fairly stable, but public attitudes and the fabric of social life had changed significantly. According to one historian, in an increasingly mechanized age drunkenness was perceived as a risk.[36] The compassionate concern of earlier years had given way to a more vindictive approach, and drinkers as autonomous individuals were starting to be seen as responsible for their own predicament. It is against this background that the notion of addiction as a disease emerges. Norman Kerr, the Chairman of the British Medical Association's Inebriates' Legislation Committee, even proposed the compulsory detention of alcoholic inebriates on the grounds that inebriety is 'a disease, a functional neurosis'.

In the United States anti-alcohol activists were not content with extending police powers. In the 1880s the Prohibition Party was formed with the support of the Woman's Christian Temperance Union and achieved its first legislative success in 1881, when the state of Kansas outlawed alcoholic beverages, and other states followed. The campaign then began to concentrate on the evil effects of alcohol and its implication in industrial and train accidents, the power of the liquor trust, and the immorality of the saloon as a breeding place for crime, immorality and labour unrest. During the First World War it whipped up anti-German feeling to lobby for the closure of German-owned breweries, taverns and restaurants. As the focus became politicized there was less sympathy for the drunkard, no longer seen as a victim deserving of charity, but as a pest and menace to be dealt with. In 1919 the Anti Saloon League, working with both major parties, pushed the 18th constitutional amendment through Congress to outlaw the manufacture, distribution and sale of all alcoholic beverages. The 'Great Experiment' lasted until 1933, when it was repealed by the

21st Amendment. Its impact and the relative success and failure are still the subject of lively debate. What is beyond doubt, however, is that it provided a golden opportunity for organized crime groups across the US and in surrounding countries, from Canada to Mexico, and to the Bahamas.

With the end of prohibition alcohol-related medical problems resurfaced, and the definition of alcoholism as a disease experienced a renaissance. But now the locus of addiction was not the substance – alcohol – but the individual, vulnerable for a number of environmental, genetic or social reasons. Highly influential in the reconfiguration of alcohol as a disease was the work of E. M. Jellinek at Yale University. Although the model he worked with was far more subtle, he, and many like him since, colluded with the vulgarization in order to 'keep the alcoholic out of gaol and get him or her into treatment'.[37]

To this day, the introduction of the 'disease model' is widely considered as a progressive step, by freeing people struggling with the affliction of problem substance use from the moral opprobrium faced by earlier generations. Yet, as the idea of addiction as a disease was extended from alcohol to other substances that remain illicit, the progressive and emancipatory benefits have to be weighed against other consequences. As the idea of addiction as a disease is married with the fear of a particular substance, so it gives rise to the notion of the drug epidemic – the rapid spread of drug use independent from the decisions of rational individuals, resulting in a medical crisis on a society-wide scale requiring the protective intervention of the authorities. The dual notions of the addiction disease and the drug epidemic continue to provide key concepts in the conceptual foundation of the drug control regime. While buying some space for the individual afflicted, they provide an even greater function in providing a rationale for the control regime.

The difficulties with the terminology become evident when the 'official' definitions are analysed closely. According to the International Classification of Diseases 10 produced by the World Health Organization, 'addiction' is diagnosed when three or more of the following have been experienced or exhibited together:

1. A strong desire or sense of compulsion to take the substance.
2. Difficulties in controlling substance-taking behaviour in terms of its onset, termination, or levels of use.
3. A physiological withdrawal state when substance use has ceased or been reduced, as evidenced by: the characteristic withdrawal syndrome for the substance; or use of the same with intention of relieving the symptoms of withdrawal.
4. Evidence of tolerance, such that increased doses of the psychoactive substances are required to achieve effects originally produced by lower doses.
5. Progressive neglect of alternative pleasures or interests because of psychoactive substance use, increased amount of time necessary to obtain or take the substance or to recover from its effects.
6. Persisting with substance use despite clear evidence of overtly harmful consequences, such as harm to the liver through excessive drinking, depressive mood states consequent to heavy substance use, or drug-related impairment of cognitive functioning. Efforts should be made to determine that the user was actually, or could be expected to be, aware of the nature and extent of the harm.

The problems with this definition are recognized both within the field of addiction and the WHO itself. Firstly, only the third and fourth criteria are measurable in biological terms, while the other four criteria involve elements of cognition, which are less accessible and can hardly be measured. Secondly, the first criteria relates to the self-perception of users, which may vary significantly among different individuals, but also among different cultures, and relates to the crucial but poorly defined concept of 'cravings'. Thirdly, a case of addiction can be diagnosed if any three of the above criteria are met, potentially without any biologically measurable criteria. An addict is therefore someone so declared by a specialist on the basis of the client's subjective assessment. In consequence, 'a continuing difficulty in the neuroscience of psychoactive substances is that while most of the effects shown are directly measurable, drug dependence is not, both as it is currently defined and as it is generally understood.'[38]

The ICD10 does provide two important criteria with physiological manifestations: tolerance and withdrawal. Tolerance has some utility in tracking the drug-use career of a client and in building awareness on overdose risks for relapsers after periods of abstinence. It is the drama of withdrawal, however, that looms large in the mind of the addict and popular imagery of problematic drug use. The most acute and dangerous cases are found among alcoholics, where the sudden cessation of alcohol intake can have serious health consequences, and even be fatal. Coming off opiates has become a feature of modern fiction and filmmaking, with the process of 'cold turkey' portrayed as a contemporary version of purgatory. While the actual discomforts suffered during this period of detoxification seem to vary drastically between different clients, the difficulties with addiction arise after the completion of the detoxification process. Once the offending substance, alcohol or opiate, has been cleared out of the system there is no longer a physiological dependence. How then, without this overt biological drive, can addiction be explained? Putting the problem differently, how can one become addicted to substances where abstinence does not lead to physiological dysfunction?

In spite of dramatic advances on mechanisms of the neurological action of drugs, the overlapping branches of science studying the pharmacological action on brain and body are still working on explanatory models of addiction. Treatment practitioners rely, therefore, on alternative methods of analysis, perhaps reminiscent of a bygone age of medicine as an art. The notion of 'psychological dependence', then, so richly suggestive and yet so imprecise, takes the analysis from the solid ground of measurable withdrawal to the fuzzy world of cravings, triggers and higher beings. It is not surprising that the most successful movement in dependence recovery is built on religious principles and is highly evangelistic. The initiation of each new member of Alcoholics or Narcotics Anonymous opens with a statement marking both identity and belonging: 'My name is . . . and I am an alcoholic.'

The absence of hard measures to counter the compulsion to use, together with the cravings and triggers prompting the addict to indulge once again in spite of their best intentions, does not detract from the material reality of the ordeal. The addict loses control over their reward-seeking behaviour, with the search for and use of the drug of choice displacing all other concerns. As they spiral downwards in their dependency, addicts are compelled to use even against the expressed desire not to. The psychosomatic action becomes manifest in the anticipation of use during purchase and preparation. Passing a place where one once scored, going up to a bar and pouring a drink, or handling a needle and syringe can all produce physiological symptoms such as sweating, increased heart rate and swallowing.

Individuals with problematic patterns of substance use face extraordinary problems of temptation and relapse long after their last session of use. There has been no shortage of responses to this problem, with a range of service providers offering different forms of treatment. In most cases the problem lies not so much in moving the client from intake towards abstinence. While clients engage with treatment, particularly residential facilities, they are often able to control their habits. It is upon return into the community, revisiting old friends and past haunts, that they are most liable to relapse.

Structural arguments indicating, for example, the ecology of certain environments, or the impact of poverty and social deprivation, are persuasive in explaining particular cases but fail to address the key problem – why are some individuals affected and not others? This is critical with regard particularly to substances like alcohol and cannabis, which are widely used and associated with a full range of problems, but acute instances of addiction are found in only a minority of cases.

The explanatory models for addiction range widely from scientific variations on the AA notion to deconstructions of the entire idea. In the former it is argued that some people are genetically programmed to develop addictions, a quasi-scientific revision of negative preordination. The implications for policy and treatment are profound: it would mean the first would have to be applied in accordance with DNA status, while the latter would presumably be superfluous.

While more research is being conducted to generate evidence, the opposing idea, that addiction is a social construct, also has some adherents. This derives from the notion of 'addiction' as a collusive alliance between treatment specialists and the drug user. It provides the former with a living and the latter with an alibi. Containing a kernel of truth, like many conspiracy theories, it picks up on the institutionalization of some problem users, who after spells in clinics, care homes and prisons have internalized their own case, and the deliberate manipulation of substance use by some offenders and their legal representatives. Some offenders use their substance dependency and the power of addiction to renounce responsibility for their own offending behaviour: 'It wasn't me, it was the drugs.'

At the same time, it is realized that different substances inspire dependency of very different degrees of intensity. The consensus in addiction medicine has identified nicotine as one of the most powerfully addictive substances, yet in the UK at least it is never implicated in any form of criminal or even antisocial behaviour, other than the not inconsiderable nuisance of unwanted smoke to members of the public. Alcohol was the *ur*-substance of problematic use and has been problematized by religious leaders and social reformers. Yet alcohol use has a venerable tradition as a religious sacrament and social lubricant, and is deeply embedded in many cultures. Other substances under control, particularly hallucinogens like LSD and MDMA, and also cannabis, have only limited habit-forming powers. Far more critical, by contrast, are opiates and cocaine. Yet even here care needs to be taken, as we know of established cultures of opium consumption without widespread addiction problems, both from antiquity and different Asian societies.

Even more pertinent for current concerns is the well-documented case of American soldiers stationed in Vietnam during the 1960s and '70s.[39] It is estimated that 75 per cent of troops were smoking cannabis regularly, while amphetamines and barbiturates were also widely used. One in five soldiers was also using heroin, of high quality, cheap and readily available. There are stories of GIs at the end of their tour of duty handing over their last heroin stash to incoming soldiers at the airport. Concerned by the debilitating effects these levels of use would have on their reintegration, the US Army began to screen and then follow up returning soldiers. After discharge from the army only 7 per cent ever used an opiate again, and less than 1 per cent felt that they had become addicted again. One way of explaining this easy transmission from an intense level of consumption to abstinence lies in the social context. The soldiers had been removed from their familiar environment and freed from social and behavioural constraints. Finding themselves in a war zone they had to manage intense emotions of fear and long stretches of boredom. Drugs were readily available, of excellent quality and cheap. Drug use, moreover, was sanctioned by the peer group. Back in the US these conditions were reversed. The soldiers returned to their familiar environments, where fear and boredom were replaced by security, routine and meaningful lives. In this setting drug use was no longer socially acceptable, drugs not easy to come by and the experience potentially unpleasant.[40]

Around the same time the US experienced what has been called its second cocaine epidemic. It is important to grasp the speed of this development. In 1957 the chief of the Federal Bureau of Narcotics, the notorious Harry Anslinger, had declared that cocaine addiction had disappeared from the US. A decade later it was said to be everywhere, and by the 1970s cocaine paraphernalia had become fashion items. The image of cocaine was so positive that successful young men would wear golden spoons on a chain around their necks. With a cachet of high life and glamour, cocaine was in a different class from heroin (junk) or cannabis (pot). It fitted into the 'American lifestyle' and could be reconciled with the work ethic.

These positive associations were loosened as cocaine use extended across new social groups. With wholesale prices dropping from $60,000 per kilo in 1980 to $15,000 in 1988, cocaine became increasingly accessible. Ingenious backstreet chemists had meanwhile managed to refashion the product and take it right downmarket, creating a smokeable form of cocaine, freebase, and then the ultimate ghetto drug, crack. At this point law enforcement agencies were taking cocaine seriously and consumption among the white middle classes was falling dramatically. Social attitudes shifted, the golden spoons disappeared, and hundreds of thousands of recreational cocaine users reverted to more conventional psychoactive pleasures, like alcohol. The vast majority achieved this transition without coming anywhere near a drug treatment centre.

Individualizing the problem

Most conventional forms of drug treatment concentrate on the individual user by addressing either imbalances within the body of the individual through chemical interventions, and/or his or her psychological well-being through different forms of psychotherapeutic intervention. One widely used technique is Motivational Interviewing, which rests on the assumption that addiction problems are primarily problems of motivation.[41] Of central importance to motivation are human relationships, which in treatment terms places emphasis first on the 'therapeutic alliance' between therapist and recovering addict, and secondly on the so-called 'aftercare', referring to an ongoing engagement with recovering addicts after the completion of the core part of the treatment. Positive relationships, such as family and lovers, work and self-help groups, are conceived of as 'protective factors'. Opposed to this are negative relationships, usually former drug-using associates, who are one of the gravest relapse triggers for recovering addicts. Further testimony to importance of relationships is the success of 'therapeutic communities', groups of recovering drug users living together, often in rural settings away from the temptations of drug markets.

The importance of relationships has been highlighted by some practitioners to argue for an anthropology of addictions, because the problems encountered are cultural.[42] The argument follows from the success of mutual self-help groups, such as Alcoholics Anonymous and Narcotics Anonymous. Participating in any capacity is a predictor for maintaining abstinence, both for people obtaining help and the helpers, since 'altruistic behaviour in groups was a curative factor'.[43] Helping others, therefore, is one of the best ways of helping oneself, because it provides individuals with meaning, which is construed from shared understanding, shared values and common goals.

We also recall the lack of community among problematic users, who have no friends but only associates. Often the position of the most problematic users is correlative with a range of other factors: chaotic families, care homes, poor educational attainments. Much of the theory about the dysfunctionality of drug use is misguided when applied overall. But it has valid application for describing problem drug use. Indeed, many problematic drug users have histories of offending behaviour, sex work and poor social relationships that precede their introduction to illicit substances. These can easily become a complicating factor in a wider constellation of problems, particularly if dependencies develop. The best protection for the users themselves and their communities is for consumers to develop their own safeguards, measures of control and rituals of reducing the harm. Ironically, a policy that drives users underground only serves to reinforce their self-image as criminals, and to lock the most vulnerable of users into a pattern of perpetual consumption.

Implications for the treatment sector

The prevalence of the disease model has important consequences for the treatment sector and clients. Treatment delivery is predicated on the notion that addiction has a biological aetiology that is not as yet fully understood. Once activated, addiction is irreversible and malignant and the only hope of arresting the disease is by total abstinence. As there is no known cure, the afflicted person will always be vulnerable to relapse, which explains why former users carry the cachet of 'addict' many years after their last drug-using episode. It also means that a person who has once had this illness can never get well, so addicts are never recovered but always recovering.

The medical model, therefore, typecasts the addict and defines the relations of power and dependence between client and practitioner. It also implicitly prioritizes certain modes of intervention. The more closely drug treatment is aligned with conventional medical treatment, 'the more congenial it is to the mainstream medical community. Consequently, inpatient treatment is valued and promulgated assiduously; it has the requisite hospital trappings and mystique.' Equally the use of a prescribed drug 'fits well with the conception of how one ought to treat a disease and who should treat it'. Since 1964 methadone maintenance has evolved into the single largest modality for the treatment of heroin addiction.

These biomedical approaches to addiction continue searching for the key to the disease process in the hope that, once the aetiological mechanism is uncovered, a medicinal 'magic bullet' will follow as a cure, much as occurred in the case of tuberculosis after the aetiological role of the tubercle bacillus was established.[44] Until that treatment comes onstream everything is a stopgap, including the cost-intensive provisions like inpatient rehabilitation, methadone maintenance, detoxification, therapeutic communities and drug-free outpatient therapy. Given the poor returns on these modes of treatment, most biomedical practitioners in western countries allow for the employment of so-called 'talking therapies'. While the multitude of treatment approaches and theories included under this rubric have notched up some successes, they continue to be viewed with suspicion and are often described as mystical and unscientific.

Nevertheless, having some variant of talking therapy available for drug addicts is convenient for the physician who, in the absence of a biological cure, needs an out. It allows the medical professional to extricate himself from a patient with an illness that medicine cannot cure. According to some theorists, the achievements of medical approaches to the treatment of addicts are risible:

> The barebone facts about the mainstream therapies of substance addiction that have become associated with the medical model are first, that most addicted persons will not enter the programmes; second that of those who do enter, most drop out; third that of those who complete programmes most soon go back to abusing drugs (they relapse); and fourth, that the usual types of therapy employed – detoxification, counselling, inpatient rehabilitation treatment, outpatient drug free therapy, methadone maintenance, therapeutic communities – all seem about equally effective (or rather ineffective).[45]

Regardless of outcome efficacy, defining the addictions as a medical rather than a moral problem has the attraction of placing the addict into the care of the health service instead of the criminal justice system. While the latter invests resources in punishing the perpetrators for their criminal actions, the former seeks to treat the patient of the underlying problem. Problematic users of any psychoactive substance tend to present with a host of health problems that have to be treated separately. Needle injectors, particularly, may suffer from abscesses, collapsed veins, bacterial endocarditis, thrombophlebitis, hepatitis and HIV. These conditions are all consequences of the underlying pathology, the discussed addiction complex, which is often associated with the substance of abuse.

Attributing the property of addiction to any particular substance does, however, raise as many questions as it seeks to solve. After more than half a century of research and promises of new insights from genetics and neuroscience, we are no closer to finding a biological aetiology of addiction. In the meantime, the condition itself remains difficult to define, impossible to measure and varies from case to case. It provides a smokescreen for problematic users and different categories of offenders, a livelihood for many professionals and a foundational myth for the control regime. Yet it also describes a set of behavioural and physiological problems applying to patterns of consumption of substances both illicit and licit. While it is used to justify the sanctions against, say, opiates and cocaine, it also applies to sugar, chocolate and many other food items. It is associated with forms of consumption, increasingly problematic in a post-scarcity, consumer-driven society, as well as with certain patterns of behaviour.

3 Possible Benefits of Drug Use

According to the literature produced as part of the Home Office Updated Drug Strategy: Fighting Drugs to Build a Better Britain, the issue is clear – drugs provide a threat to individuals, families and communities, and need to be fought by the powers of the state. It is one area of policy where the main political parties are in accord. The Conservative opposition unfortunately missed the opportunity to set out a real alternative in its 'landmark' social report 'Fractured Britain', wherein drug use is identified as one of the ailments causing cracks in contemporary society. Sadly, the report makes no mention of the vast volume of recreational drug use that is routinely reported in government and scientific publications. Studies by the Prime Minister's Strategy Unit, the Ministry of Science and Technology, and the Annual Reports by the Northwest Public Health Observatory all attest to the scale of drug use free from medical complication or crime. Instead, the emblem of the drug user is the injecting heroin addict, who has been let down by a government intent on preventing the spread of HIV. Quoting the idiosyncratic speculations of a maverick sociologist that the HIV threat was exaggerated in the early 1990s,[1] the report critiques the policy of harm reduction and the provision of clean needles to injecting addicts, and the prescription of methadone. This policy is sharply attacked for simply swapping an illicit drug for a licit one, when the object of the exercise should be abstinence. The reasoning in the document illustrates the process of policy-making based on the uncritical acceptance of prohibition. Reducing drug use by coercing addicts into treatment and discouraging young people from experimentation are the proposed activities towards achieving the overriding policy objective: the reduction of drug use as an end in itself. His message is propagated by a number of religious groups including diverse offshoots of Christianity, most branches of Islam, and more obscure cults like Scientology. In the literature pushed through my letterbox by proselytizing sects, drug abuse is regularly cited as an index of worldly corruption, followed by a vision of an otherworldly future that is blissful, clean and sober.

There is an alternative vision of human progress, however, facilitated and possibly triggered by the pursuit of altered states. According to some scholars, the relationship between humans and mind-altering substances has had a far more benign trajectory than suggested by evangelists and drug warriors.

Drugs as a contributing factor to human evolution

As a point of departure, proponents of this position point to anthropological data on plant-based mind-altering substances found with few exceptions, such as Inuit groups in Alaska, across human societies. Not only is the recreational consumption of non-nutritious intoxicants an almost universal feature of human cultures, but it usually enjoys a privileged position at the heart of ritual and religion. When chewing betel, sipping maize beer or ayahuasca, or smoking tobacco or opium, the user is not simply engaging in some animalistic feeding pattern, but comes close to the very essence of what it means to be human. Far from providing a sinister threat to culture, drugs are the essential ingredient to make it happen. As sacrament in religious ritual, or lubricant in social process, each society's drug of choice enjoys a place of privilege.

This is not merely the outcome of progress, a material benefit of the post-scarcity society. According to some theorists the interrelationship between humans and plant-based drugs provided the foundation for these attainments. The most prolific and poetic exponent of this theory is the late cultural anthropologist Terence McKenna, whose work over 25 years spanned a range of issues relating to illicit drugs. A member of the growing New Age ayahuasca cult, McKenna linked the use of mind-altering plant-based substances to a theory of social evolution that was complex, daring and highly speculative. What it lacked in material evidence, it made up for by providing an overarching theory with a confidently posited rationale for the pursuit of altered states. And it takes the reader on a speculative journey to the mists of time.

Towards the end of the last Ice Age, when the receding North African jungles were giving way to grasslands, a branch of our tree-dwelling primate ancestors swung off their branches to take up a life out on the open steppe by following the herds of ungulates and eking out any food items they could. These early hominids were low down in the food chain and, left to scavenge, were probably out of necessity more experimental in looking for alternative food sources than other, more successful species. The argument for this vulnerability has built by combining archaeological evidence with insights from psychoanalysis and primatology. Comparatively weak creatures, early hominids held a dual status as both predator and prey, which has been used to explain the origins of war and religion in the sacralizing of violence on the early plains.[2] How this vulnerable creature managed to rise to the top of the food chain has mystified evolutionists for two centuries. There is fossil evidence to track the change, particularly the expansion of the human brain, which tripled over the three million years, and which eventuated in the rise of *Homo sapiens* around 100,000 years ago. While evolutionary theory has made great advances in tracking this development, there is very little other than speculation as to what caused it – the causal link between the walking ape and man is missing from conventional evolutionary theory.

A reinterpretation of the relationship between humans and mind-altering substances provides an interesting alternative. The early hominids needed to experiment with foodstuffs and came across the dung-loving (copraphilic) mushrooms growing in the droppings of the ungulate herds traversing the African plain. The mushroom's psilocybin – a psychedelic alkaloid of the tryptamine family present in many species of fungi – when eaten at low levels would have imparted a noticeable increase in visual acuity, especially edge detection. These 'chemical binoculars' would have provided a clear adaptive advantage to hunter-gatherers. Taking in larger quantities, however, they had a more significant effect by catalyzing consciousness and the capacity to reflect on the self.

The experience may also have contributed to another development as 'human language forming ability may have become active through the mutagenic influence of hallucinogens'.[3] The psilocybin activates the areas of the brain that are concerned with processing signals. One of the suggested processes in the early development of spoken language is effected through the blurring of boundaries between the senses, or synaesthesia, which produces the ability to form pictures in another person's mind through the use of vocal sounds.

This is described in the analysis of the three working principles used in ethno-biological nomenclature summarized by Brent Berlin in his speculative account of how early cultures would have established systems of classifying the animals around them.[4] First of all would be onomatopoeia, calling an animal by a sound it makes, such as the cuckoo. Secondly animals are named after some observable feature such as a colour. The third organizing principle, sound symbolism, is derived from synaesthesia. These are names that express properties of the named animal, and are unconsciously recognized by humans. In this process vowels and consonants are linked so as to represent the visual and tactile properties of objects, such as size or shape. The reasoning behind this is supported by the experiments devised by the Georgian psychologist Dimitry Uznadze and developed by the German psychologist Wolfgang Koehler, the founder of Gestalt therapy, in the 1920s. Subjects were asked to assign the nonsense names *maluma* or *takete* to two drawings: with 90 per cent consistency people were found to select *takete* for the angular drawing and *maluma* for the circular one. The experiment has been repeated in different linguistic and cultural settings, always with the same results, supporting the claim of the universal relevance of the model.

In the context of hallucinogenic experience, the synaesthetic interpretation, the combination of impressions from different senses, has been described by Gordon Wassoon, the banker and mycologist who retired from the world of finance to study hallucinogenic mushrooms. Wassoon believed that mushrooms were the basis of Soma, the wonder drug of the Indian Rig Vedas, and was a pioneer of ethnographic fieldwork methods. In his account of his experience when eating hallucinogenic mushrooms at a Mazatec ceremony in Mexico, he reports that: 'We felt ourselves in the presence of ideas of Plato ... at that moment our visions were not false or shadowy suggestions of real things, figments of an unhinged imagination. What we were seeing was, we knew, the only reality, of which counterparts of day are mere imperfect adumbrations.'[5]

If hallucinogenic experience through the synaesthetic merging of sense data facilitates cosmic insight and generates new forms of expression and creativity, it should be remembered that the uttering of the spoken word is, in the cosmologies of many peoples, the source of creation. The power in naming is not merely the allegorical expression of dominance, such as that of humans over all creation. It is also one of the ways of creating reality, in the Foucauldian sense of discourse of truth and power.

If hallucinogenic experience then, lies at the foundation of spirituality, it also provided for the division of labour and special-ization. The new experience gave rise to a new sensibility that became manifest in the figure of the shaman who, once able to harness the energy unleashed by the drug, could activate new and hitherto unimaginable sources of power including, possibly, the determination of the calendar, by scheduling social and sexual activity in accordance with the lunar cycle that also determined mushroom availability. With the conscious alignment of human events with the motion of the nocturnal heavens we have the origin of ritual.

Man/mushroom symbiosis

In evolutionary terms, the facility of language and the increased visual acuity and sexual activity all combined to provide the mushroom-consuming humans with a significant adaptive advan-tage. Yet the relationship may well have been symbiotic, with both species gaining from their cooperation. Human intervention in the environment, primarily through deforestation and the exten-sion of the savannah, vastly expanded the habitat for ungulates. In addition, humans began to domesticate cattle, which in turn increased the requirement for new pasture. These creatures, wild and domesticated, covered the expanded savannah with their droppings in which the mushrooms could flourish.

The relationship may have gone beyond the organic function-ality of adaptive advantage. The psychoactive alkaloids in the mushrooms could have been exopheromones, chemical messengers that cross species lines and are used by the hallucinogenic plants to transfer information to primates and thereby facilitate the encounter with the transcendent other – and a perception of nature as being alive and intelligent.

Plant-teachers and entheogens

There is another dimension to this relationship, in which the plant is a teacher. The hallucinatory experience is seen as a transfer of wisdom from the plant to the human user. Similarities in sound be-tween 'psychedelic' and 'psychosis', and the range of often pejorative connotations with pop culture, raised the need for a new term to be used in the serious exploration of substance-induced transcendental experience. In the late 1970s the neologism 'entheogen' was derived from the Greek *entheos* ('god within') and *genesthe* ('to generate'). These combine into 'that which generates the divine within'.[6]

One of the best-known accounts of the ritual application of entheogens, either ethnographic or fictional, is that of Carlos Castaneda's encounter with a Navajo shaman by the name of Don Juan, who initiates him into peyote use. The work of Castaneda has suffered from allegations that much of the material was fiction rather than ethnography; critical analysis has uncovered discrepan-cies in the sequence of events described in the texts, and he has been accused of plagiarism in his accounts of shamanism. These points of criticism notwithstanding, some of the observations from his fieldwork, and the accounts of the human–plant relationship, are strong descriptions of basic entheogenic principles. He estab-lished four concepts in the teachings of Don Juan that have been found in other texts on plant teachers and are worth recording:

1. The initiate aims to become a man of knowledge, for which he has to undergo an apprenticeship, as the one of Carlos Castaneda himself. This is made up of learning and self-discipline, and moral challenges, as the apprentice has had the option to become a *diablero* or black sorcerer.

2. The man of knowledge has an ally, a 'power capable of transporting a man beyond the boundaries of himself'. This could be either the datura plant, also known as Devil's weed, or psilocybin mushrooms. The ally is powerful, unpredictable, violent and could enslave a man if he does not learn to tame it.

3. The ally has a rule that is inflexible; there is no room for individualism or innovation. Knowing the rule opens a non-ordinary reality, as experienced when taking the drugs, and being able to manipulate it.

4. The rule is corroborated by a special consensus, which is the interplay between the benefactor or guide into the knowledge and the apprentice.[7]

In his later writings, Castaneda's accounts lose their authority as the shamanic power attributed to Don Juan becomes increasingly incredible. It has been alleged that all the work was a fiction, and that the figure of Don Juan was a creation of the author. From the detail Castaneda provided about the teaching, and the descriptions of encounters and rides into the hills to go mushroom picking, we can assume that at least some of the field scenes were authentic and their findings remain valid in themselves, although the interpretation may be open to argument. Moreover, the figure of the teacher is plausible, even if the character of Don Juan is a composite of various senior men Castaneda did meet and talk to. When we refer to the structural analysis of the human–plant relationship, we find that the four components throw some light on the evolutionary scheme we have been looking at. Again the psychedelic experience is valued as positive and constructive to self-realization. The benefits include attaining greater powers in the 'non-ordinary' world. The idea of the non-ordinary as a plateau for human endeavour with an alternative ranking system, and a distribution of prestige, fits into the picture of marginalization. Among Native American rural poor in California, the possibility of achieving status and powers in a virtual world is attractive and persuasive.

It is hard to say where exactly Castaneda's radicalism lies, other than that taking hallucinogenic mushrooms was central to his study. The perspective is still that of the human consumer using the powers inherent in the plants for their individual purpose. McKenna, by contrast, looks at the relationship as a two-way flow. He attributes intelligence and agency to the plants, because 'Hallucinogens [are] repositories of living vegetable gnosis that lie, now nearly forgotten, in our ancient past.' According to McKenna's brother Dennis, an ethnobotanist, the ayahuasca plant is communicating, through the user, a warning from nature to humanity about the imminent destruction of the natural world. Other scholars take a more cautious line, sidestepping the question of human–plant relationships by maintaining that the 'educational value of entheogens comes more importantly from the social practises into which their uses have traditionally been incorporated.' The experience is crucial in stimulating wonder, awe and existential understanding. But the importance lies in the impact they have on social and cultural practice.

Given the lack of empirical foundation for this theory of the missing link, it is appropriate to reflect on the context and contemporary influences. The poignancy of prevailing values in scientific modelling is apparent in the theory of social evolution. In the nineteenth century the theory of nature was one of 'red in tooth and claw', where relentless competition ensured survival only of the fittest. It could be argued that this projection of social theory was the zoomorphism of Victorian cultural arrogance and its US equivalent of Manifest Destiny. Nature and society were held up as mirrors, with Malthusian visions of the war of all against all transposed onto the lawless jungle, where might rightly prevailed.

Writing during the 1990s at the height of the Archaic Revival, Terence McKenna suggests that nature is better conceptualized as a dance of diplomacy. Referring to the ancient Greek notion of Gaia, the world may be thought of as an organism with interconnected components communicating with one another through the release of chemical signals. How strongly scientific theory is affected by values and aesthetics becomes clear from the offence caused to contemporaries by the Darwinian suggestion that man descends from apes. McKenna adds mischievously that our generation will have to accept that these apes were stoned apes.

Ironic, provocative and counterintuitive, the argument for the positive contribution made by psychoactive substances to the course of human evolution remains speculative and juxtaposed. It is as much a series of indices of New Ageism as a contribution to palaeontology. For something approaching material evidence we need to look at Richard Rudgley's examination of the archaeological record.[8]

Material evidence from the archaeological record

While refraining from cosmological speculation and evolutionary modelling, Rudgley looks at a wealth of archaeological evidence from the Upper Palaeolithic period (45,000–8,000 BC) to establish the central role of drug use. He introduces the idea of sacred or initiatory rites around the use of drugs to freshly interpret the cave paintings and engravings in the Dordogne region of southwestern France. Distributed over some 130 recognized sites, most notably Lascaux, and spanning many millennia (34,000–13,000 BC), these depict a bewildering collection of animals and geometric signs. There are several established schools of explanation, including, for instance, the suggestion that the depictions of animal tracks and herd formation were the teaching equipment of a prehistoric academy for the instruction of young hunters. This theory, no doubt influenced by the personal work experience of institution-based scholars, has been challenged by ethnographic accounts from contemporary hunters and gatherers. These suggest that in most hunting societies knowledge is transmitted not in the theoretical environment of the classroom but through firsthand observation and participation, with the young accompanying the hunt. Moreover, the gloomy atmosphere of the cave is hardly appropriate for technical instruction. It is much more likely to have served a ritual and religious function, as a setting, for instance, for the rites of initiation.

Rites of passage are characterized by the unveiling of the mysteries, as neophytes are introduced to formerly forbidden secrets, often related to the story of the group's origins. The process combines the tuition of special knowledge with tests of mental and physical stamina, the learning of tribal lore with acts of courage and perseverance. During the entire period the young men and women are sequestered into a secluded site with special spiritual qualities. Initiation grounds are the origin of the sacred space so manifest in today's religious complexes, churches, temples, mosques and other places of worship, which mark a difference between the sacred and the profane. Rudgley suggests that this was the function of the painted caves, to enhance the experience of mystery and wonder of the neophytes, who would make out the shapes and colours on the cave walls in the flickering light of a fire and by the heightened sensory awareness induced by the herbal stimulants they had ingested or imbibed. According to David Lewis-Williams and Thomas Dowson, 'the visual system generates a range of luminous percepts that are independent from light from any source . . . because they derive from the human nervous system, all people who enter certain altered states of consciousness, no matter what their cultural background, are liable to perceive them.'[9]

These visual percepts are sometimes called phosphenes or form constants, and are included under the generic term 'entoptic phenomena', of which there are six basic forms. Laboratory research has identified three stages in the experience of entoptic forms. Initially the images appear alone and cannot be controlled; in the next stage the subject embellishes the entoptic form, until in the final stage there is a shift from entoptic forms to hallucinatory iconic forms. The geometric entoptic images are universal, while hallucinatory iconic images derive from the subject's mind and culture. To substantiate that point, Lewis-Williams and Dowson compare rock paintings by San bushmen in the Kalahari and the Shoshonean Coso of the California Great Basin, to mark their similarities.

Rudgley draws the parallel between these and prehistoric cave paintings. He suggests that these prehistoric caves were ideal sites for inducing trance states that would have included the perception of entoptic phenomena. It is these entoptic forms that are represented on the cave walls together with the animals, a pastiche of images from the inner and the outer eye. We do not know how these early humans achieved these visual percepts, but we deduce from the presence of these abstract cave paintings, and from our interpretation of the use of the caves, that they were reaching an altered state.

Once again, the argument is highly conjectural, in that a state of drug-induced altered consciousness in the context of initiation provides an explanation for the purpose and origin of the cave paintings. What the role of psychoactive substances was is guess-work. Yet, there is a rich seam of archaeological evidence to suggest that cultures of the Neolithic and early antiquity had a selection of psychoactive materials at their disposal. These include braziers used for the burning of opium from different sites in France and, most persuasively perhaps, the so-called skeuomorphs (the borrowing of shape from one material to another) from Cyprus and eighteenth-dynasty Egypt (1550–1295 BC). He argues that these base ring juglets were produced in the shape of an opium poppy capsule and contained poppy juice.

The archaeological record, then, supports the argument that, during the period stretching from the Neolithic to early antiquity, drugs were known to and used by many different cultures. To what degree they were implicated in religion, ritual and art remains subject to speculation, as does their continuing contribution to the evolutionary scheme.

Paradise found and lost

There is, then, a school of thought at the intersection of anthro-pology, archaeology, ethnobotany and evolutionary theory where psychoactive drugs are assigned a privileged place in human devel-opment. Far from being corrosive, pernicious and destructive, drugs facilitated the special relationship between species during an evolutionary stage described as the 'partnership society'. This notion, adopted from the religious scholar Riane Eisler, posits that human social formations were inherently cooperative and their political structure matriarchal.[10] McKenna gives it a time, around 12,000 BC, and a place – the central Sahara – where the partnership blossomed into a Garden of Eden, the loss of which forms a perennial theme in the human imaginary. Accordingly, language and complex religious ideas emerged in the game-filled, mush-room-dotted grasslands of Africa. Steadily expanding beyond the carrying capacity of their terrain, this system became a victim of its own success. The response was, firstly, migration beyond the fungal-producing African plain into new environments where other psychoactive plants were used as substitutes. And even in

Africa, climate change effected variations in the availability of mushrooms. In the ritual context mushrooms would have been substituted by other substances, perhaps fermented mead, where their use was more symbolic, and which were then replaced by the symbols themselves, as is the case with the world religions today.

The second response lay in the domestication of animals and plants. The emergence of agriculture in the early Neolithic period spelt the end of the ease and abundance of the roaming horde, which, according to Marshall Sahlins's seminal work on hunting and gathering societies, spent a minimum of time at work and a maximum of time at play.[11] With it notions of toil and labour were introduced into human society that played into the new value systems of competition and were framed within the new political form of patriarchy, or what Eisler calls the 'dominator style'.

They are partly defined by two phenomena that gain shape in that period and have been with us since: the temple complex and the creation of a professional priesthood exercising control over gods and the fruits of human labour. Dispensing powerful sacred substances is often a key to their power. This brings about an alcohol/warrior nexus, documented from early antiquity and vividly relayed by Homer, that forms a constant theme in European history until the present.

4 How Drugs Have Shaped History in the Modern Era

The discussion of prehistorical drug use and the possible benefits of the plant–human relationship in evolutionary terms is, of course, entirely speculative and at times deliberately provocative. As there are no possibilities for either verifying or falsifying these propositions, their main role is as a corrective to the extraordinarily one-sided development that has led us to a position where drug use is construed as dangerous, pathological and deviant. This ignores the material evidence we have to document the use of psycho-actives across the length and breadth of the globe and over vast swaths of recorded history. They are woven into the cultural fabric of diverse civilizations, play a privileged role at the centre of religion, rite and ritual, and bind cultures into complex exchange relation-ships. It is remarkable, then, that current research plays down the constructive contributions of this range of substances.

This is particularly so in the us, where the National Institute on Drug Abuse (NIDA), which controls an annual budget of just under a billion dollars, is the principal body for organizing research funding and the dissemination of findings. Yet in spite of its claims to the highest scientific standards, the work of NIDA suffers from fundamental flaws in direction. Funds are provided for research into the physiological problems caused by the use of the most popu-lar illicit drugs in the us. Over the years, NIDA funding has become a showcase for policy-led evidence generation, and has abandoned any attempt to find medically or socially useful applications for illicit substances. The research never challenges or moves beyond the presupposition that the substances under investigation are dangerous, their use inherently problematic, and the altered states obtained with their assistance an altogether negative experience.

As a result, the proposition that marijuana, one of the most widely used substances in the US, has medical benefits has been ignored by the nation's most generously funded drug research institute. Knowledge generation is therefore circular, amassing new detail on, say, the function of neurotransmitters, the limbic system, and the reward mechanism, but with no insight into the thorny question of why some individuals establish complex relationships with these different substances and what function they play in human society. Neurotransmitters are the chemical messengers that transmit signals across different parts of the brain and are often related to moods and feelings. They move around a set of brain structures that are known as the limbic system (and include the hippocampus and the amygadala) and control emotion, behaviour and long-term memory. It is believed that human behaviour is trained by the release of neurotransmitters such as serotonin, dopamine or norepinephrine, which will positively affect mood and feelings and provide an incentive to repeat the behaviour. It is a premise of the thrust of the overall research effort that the substances listed in the schedules have no constructive role to play, and the term used to describe their consumption is *abuse*.

We therefore have to turn to social sciences to develop a better insight into the role of psychoactive substances in society and history. From the first foundation of the 'social' as a separate 'science', thinkers have contributed to the explanation of medical phenomenon by looking not merely at factors within the physiology of the individual. One celebrated and highly relevant example is the French sociologist Emile Durkheim's analysis of suicide, which demonstrated the social dimension of the condition and attributed a rise in suicides to periods of social crises.

In other words it was not the individual's fault or failing that explained his or her particular pathology, but the social and cultural context. This insight can be transposed to the analysis of consumption patterns, particularly with regard to illicit psychoactives and, further along the continuum, also to food. We can learn from social historians that the availability and provision of food crops was determined not simply by optimal conditions for cultivation, but cultural preference and political regulation. Until the nineteenth century, for instance, the diet of large tracts of Christian

Europe was determined in good part by the injunctions of the Church. The proscription of meat on one day in three, for instance, had significant alimentary, cultural and political consequences. Unable to use animal fat for cooking, northern Europeans were importing vegetable oils from the Mediterranean, until these patterns became ingrained in culinary practice and continued under their own momentum.[1] This illustrates how a particular cultural preference, derived from the early Christian churches proliferating along the Mediterranean rim, where oil-producing fruit and fish were plentiful, assumed the form of a universal principle. It could be argued that the current injunction on opiates and coca, as developed by North American and European officials, is equally a reflection of cultural predilection, assuming universality by dint of a spurious claim to 'science'.

The religious restrictions on food consumption have a cherished antiquity, serving to distinguish Jew from Gentile or Brahmins from members of lower Hindu castes. Food is defined in equal part by utility and culture to provide both nourishment and meaning. In totemic societies the distinctions are at their clearest, in that each individual is under a regime of food restrictions in accordance with the totem ascribed to them at birth. As patterns of consumption then are inextricably wound up with identity, they set a challenge to the authorities in more complex societies. On the one hand there is the need to accommodate diversity, on the other the will to control and the temptation to exploit. More complex still is the tendency of cultural entities to morph, and of individuals to traverse cultural boundaries. Consumers lose no time in making new foods their own. Within a couple of centuries the South American potato became an Irish staple and, fried in chunks, an emblem of French and English culinary identity. In most cases, these processes of acculturation are 'naturalized', with consumers losing the sense of the otherness of the respective items, even where they have to be imported from exotic locales.

It is not only foods that become assimilated over relatively short periods of time. The mystery, which originally helped to render enjoyment so exquisite and refined, is stripped off the substances as they become familiar. With familiarity the substances lose much of the 'peculiarity' that, according to Andrew Sherratt, characterizes psychoactive substances in different cultures.[2] In many cases, particularly with largely unrefined, plant-based substances, the psychoactive dynamic is no longer recognized. During the advanced state of a substance's trajectory in a host culture, the consumers' identity is construed around the form, dosage and the mode of consumption, not its exotic provenance or psychoactive action.

To illustrate the importance of drugs in culture and history, we should therefore review the introduction of a number of peculiar substances into European cultures early on in the modern period. It has been argued that without their discovery and commercial exploitation the historical development that followed would not have been possible. Over the past four centuries they have become integrated into European lifestyles to a point where they are no longer recognized as either exotic or as drugs. Their transformative effect has been due precisely to the respective properties that define coffee, tea, tobacco and cocoa as 'soft' drugs and sugar, in the words of Sidney Mintz, as a 'drug food'. The changes to European society associated with their consumption, and the consequences for the economies of three continents, were far beyond the expectations of the first transatlantic navigators.

The European quest for spices

It is significant that European exploration of the Atlantic oceans in the late medieval and early modern period was motivated by the quest for spice. A set of substances that are contingent to and often overlapping with the psychoactives were a catalyst to enterprise and adventure at this critical point in European history. They may both have medical properties, be used to flavour food or, as with nutmeg, for example, combine both functions in one. What needs to be recognized is that economic interests were driven by the search for luxuries, not staples.

The role of spice in the pre-Columbian era has fascinated historians, perhaps precisely because of the high point of contrast. For the majority of pre-modern households, spices like pepper, cinnamon or cumin were special treats enjoyed only on high days and holidays. Highly prized and rare, they were well beyond the reach of the masses. Hence, the use and measure of spice itself served as a marker of social distinction. Exchanged as gifts among the aristocracy and granted as reward for loyal service, they had political and economic roles well beyond the kitchen and the hospice. Heavily spiced meals were a form of conspicuous consumption asserting the social status of the host. As tastes remained unrefined, prestige attached to excess rather than moderation.[3] Heavily spiced food during the late medieval and early modern period is best understood as a form of potlatch – the wilful destruction of objects of value to establish social status.

In the later medieval period, from the eleventh century onwards, social differentiation accelerated across northern Europe. A section of the population emerged from agrarian life, where there had been little to distinguish noble from peasant, with both wearing similar clothes and eating the same kinds of food. At court the aristocracy found interests beyond war and horsemanship in beautiful objects and elegant manners. Such a refinement of taste was paralleled by the citizenry of the burgeoning towns, where spices began to figure strongly as symbolic markers of the good life. In the medieval imaginary visions of paradise were replete with descriptions of the fragrance of cinnamon, ginger, nutmeg and cloves. In the material world, meanwhile, the profits of the spice trade became manifest in the opulence of Venice, the power that controlled the spice trade. This is the background to the long-distance adventures of European explorers in the fifteenth and sixteenth centuries. The discovery of America was a by-product and unintended consequence of this quest and hunger for spices, which would ultimately change both European palate and larder completely. Not long after the sea route to India had been established, the spice trade tapered off in Europe. First, spices constituted a falling portion of international trade and were soon overtaken by other goods of value. Second, there was a shift in the palate, favouring more moderately seasoned food. And the evocation of paradise, a stock theme for poets, musicians, troubadours and bards throughout the Middle Ages, vanished with the discovery of the New World: 'The paradise that the Middle Ages had sought became secularized as the land of unlimited possibilities.'[4]

The coming of stimulants in the early modern era

If there were no spices in the Americas, there were other agricultural commodities to quickly take their place. First, substances like cocoa and tobacco, which were unique to the New World, spread via European middle men to the rest of the world. Tobacco, particularly, was propagated at an astonishing rate, assimilated into local cultures of consumption and integrated into social life. Cocoa followed at a slower pace, and then suffered some upsets in social status following the French Revolution.

If the first wave of explorers discovered new delights for the enjoyment of the European elite, it was the colonists who produced the quantity demanded by a dramatically expanding market. In the process the settlers developed systems of production that could be adapted to other tropical agricultural commodities. It was based on forced labour supplied at first by captured native Americans, then transported European convicts, until from the mid-seventeenth century onwards a regular supply of men and women could be secured from West Africa. With labour, capital, technology and markets in place, coffee and sugar could be produced in massive quantities and under European control. Only tea remained in the hands of the original producers, largely because the Chinese state had the central organization and the power to prevent the exportation of seedlings by European traders. This made tea the last of the five key drug commodities that spawned the first age of globalization. By the mid-nineteenth century, however, China had itself sunk briefly into the status of a semi-colony and tea plantations were established in India.

Why drugs?

Why then do I group tea, coffee, cocoa, tobacco and sugar in the same category as heroin and cocaine? Surely there is no equivalence between a friendly cuppa and a needle? Nobody has ever overdosed from coffee, so how does one strike a comparison? There is no doubt that the psychoactive effect of Europe's favourite soft drugs is far more moderate than that of the refined pharmaceutical products that have gained such notoriety in the twentieth century. A more appropriate comparison should be with coca and opium. The former is quite benign in its leaf form and could theoretically have found a market in early modern Europe, were it not for the chemical fragility of the plant. The psychoactive alkaloids disintegrate after a few weeks, which in the days of wind-powered maritime transport ruled it out for export. Yet, with regard to potency, impact and effect, coca chews are not that unlike coffee and tea, in that they are all stimulants that energize the central nervous system. This is in marked contrast to opium, a central nervous system depressant and the original narcotic, in that it sends the user to sleep. But over the past twenty years the major drugs of concern, particularly in the US, have been stimulants, even though the official terminology co-classifies all illicit substances as 'narcotics'.

Discussing homely substances in the same breath as evil poisons raises the original debate on definition and description: what is a drug? Psychoactive effect, the stimulation or depression of the central nervous system was one, addiction and the absence of nutritious value the others. Tea, coffee, cocoa and sugar may not produce dramatically altered mental states or conjure hallucinations, but they all impact on the function of the body. One of the attributes of 'drugs' is that they are habit forming, leading to regular consumption, even to the point where life is organized around satisfying this need. Over a period of several centuries tea, coffee, cocoa and tobacco have insinuated themselves into the very fabric of European social life. The early morning caffeine fix has become so acculturated as to be hardly recognized as the chemical stimulus that it is. Chocolate has become a regular childhood treat and a secret adult indulgence. Few other substances can simultaneously evoke images of innocent delight and wretched cravings. The combination of cocoa, milk and sugar has an addictive hook few other combinations can match. While cocoa and sugar do not match all the criteria listed for 'drug', since they are mood- rather than mind-altering and have some nutritional value, there is enough overlap to merit inclusion.

The powerful effect of the habit-forming properties of sugar is borne out by the extraordinary history of sugar production. All of Europe's new soft drugs were imported at exponential rates during the early modern period. But sugar, the substance that registers the most dramatic rates of increase, provides foundation for an entire political economy. During the seventeenth and eighteenth centuries Britain, France, Holland, Spain and Portugal were almost incessantly at war over a handful of colonies in the New World. The main prize was not the vast continental hinterland of either North or South America, but the islands of the Caribbean, known at the time as the 'cockpit of Europe'. By the time that Britain wrested Jamaica from Spain in the eighteenth century the main product of these tiny possessions was sugar. The significance of sugar lies not merely in the importation figures, which are shared with the exponential leaps registered by other commodities during the heroic period of modern capitalism. The search for profit drove many an enterprise into the dramatic exploitation of natural resources all over the world. For native peoples, the custodians of the land, the consequences could be devastating. They frequently disappeared from history,[5] to be followed by animal resources as these too, in the course of unregulated exploitation of the fur trade in North American forests or the cod fisheries of the North Atlantic, were pushed into extinction. But sugar production pioneered the processes that would, in the nineteenth century, lead to industrialization in terms of capital concentration, the development of technology and the regimentation of labour. The need for labour bound the western part of Africa into the global economy, unleashing, in the words of one historian a 'tidal wave to cross the Atlantic and hurl itself against a 20 mile stretch of the West African coast', which for several centuries would become the slave emporium of the Atlantic economy.[6] The profits of the production and commerce of Europe's new soft drugs contributed significantly to the capital accumulation that cemented the seaborne empires of Great Britain and a handful of western European countries.

The three beverages were originally imported from different continents, respectively coffee from Ethiopia, tea from China and chocolate from Mexico. Coffee came to Europe via the Islamic countries. It is first recorded in Venice in 1615, arrives in Paris with a Turkish embassy in 1643, and reaches London in 1651. These dates 'for the new drug . . . refer to its first rather clandestine arrivals rather than to the beginning of a popular taste or public consumption'.[7] The process of 'extensification', the spread of consumption from centres of privilege like the court, followed within decades. In the process, the formerly exotic substances became domesticated, integrated into national traditions and adapted to social settings and the rhythms of consumption. European powers also took over control of production, and by 1712 coffee shrubs were being grown on plantations owned by the Dutch East India Company in Java, reached the French Antilles by 1723, Jamaica by 1730, and Santo Domingo by 1731. Soon European colonists and merchants were controlling the production and the trade in these new commodities.[8]

It is notable that it was the trade in these luxuries, not everyday staples, that consolidated national and international trading networks. Mercantile capital, the bourgeoisie that controlled it, and the trading networks of modern commerce formed around the 'drug trade', not the provision of victuals. Up until the nineteenth century, rural England was supplied more regularly and reliably with colonial commodities than with domestically produced staples. And it was around the boycott of slave-produced sugar that civil society set the first challenge to the state, by calling into being the most powerful activists of the capitalist era, the consumer. The anti-slavery campaign was pivoted on the boycott of sugar products, but not on any of the other colonial produce, say cotton, coffee or tea. Campaigners all over England were now drinking their hot beverages as they came. It is ironic that today both the drug control interests and the reform lobby trace their origins back to the anti-slave trade campaign. In the case of the former there is a historic link, in that the original anti-opium campaign consciously emulated the anti-slavery campaign, though it was, of course, overshadowed by the alcohol-orientated activism of the temperance movement. In the case of the reform movement, the parallel is drawn between a campaign for liberty and freedom against an oppressive and exploitative system then and the call for the reform of legislative provisions harming hundreds of thousands of drug users, farmers, peddlers and couriers against the authoritarian instincts of states and the entrenched interests of the beneficiaries.

Drug control efforts continue to be bedevilled by having to account for the popularity of the very substances that wreak such damage to individual health and social welfare. Most explanations are therefore mechanical – peer pressure, stepping-stone theory, pushy dealers – ignoring the preferences, experiences and intentions of consumers. In a similar vein most economic historians sidestep the question why these soft drugs became so popular in the seventeenth and eighteenth centuries. Yet the success of tea, coffee, sugar, cocoa and tobacco in European markets is not only of historic interest, but crucial for understanding the popularity and spread of the illicit drugs used with equal enthusiasm and consistency in the UK and other European countries today. In the stimulus of caffeine and the energy boost provided by sugar, modern Europeans found something that furthered their aspirations much more effectively than the substances hitherto available. The combined effect of wakefulness and strength accorded with the values of an emerging bourgeoisie bent on fashioning a lifestyle from the product of their labour. As so often in the history of consumption, the new product established itself by usurping the place of another and slotting into its place. Tea and coffee, prepared with the addition of indispensable sugar, were taking the place of alcohol and sparked off one of the longest running culture wars in Western civilization.

Many accounts of medieval Europe suggest a continent swilling in alcohol, where beer soup was a staple and intoxication was a permanent state, with the differences only a matter of degree. In southern Europe wine consumption was estimated at around a litre per head per day,[9] while in Germany beer had become an essential part of the diet as another 'drug food'. While alcohol in general and beer in particular were of nutritional significance, drinking and drunkenness also played an important ritual function. Across Europe elaborate customs had become established, like drinking to someone's health, clinking glasses, the obligation to return another's toast, and drinking bouts, not to contain the impact of alcohol, but to achieve inebriation.

From the early medieval period onwards preachers and princes attempted to contain the thirst unleashed onto Christendom. Yet it was the Church that had established the sacred use of wine, following the assertion in scripture: 'Hic est calix novum testamentum in sanguine meo' ('This cup is the new testament in my blood'; Luke 22.20). And it was the monasteries that propagated the cultivation of vines up the river valleys of the continent.

There were moralist concerns over the controlled use of alcohol while other psychoactive substances were prohibited as instruments of Satan. The worldly powers also saw their authority jeopardized by the inebriated revelries accompanying popular festivals and particularly carnival. The danger of excitable tempers being whipped up by demagogues in the class-stratified, highly exploitative societies of late feudalism was forever lurking. The ambiguity of alcohol at the time of the Reformation is exemplified by Martin Luther, who shares on the one hand in a carnivalesque *joie de vivre* in celebration of 'wine, women and song', while at the same time condemning the 'demon alcohol' in adherence to the emerging Protestant work ethic. The intellectual changes fashioned by the Reformation and Renaissance changed the relationship between man and alcohol, just as it changed ideas of the relationship between man and God. Of possibly even greater consequences were the changes it effected in relations between men, organized along lines of class and status. The key drivers for change, the urban bourgeoisie, were intent on differentiating themselves from both peasantry and urban poor on the one hand, and from the aristocracy on the other. Drunken revelries were not the preserve of the popular masses alone, since the aristocracy too indulged in alcohol and other pleasures of the flesh.

It is against this background that the assertions of the urban middle classes and the new cult of sobriety have to be seen. The power of the rising class was anchored in crafts, trade, commerce and the written word. In contrast to their rural cousins, they were no longer working under the open sky but in workshops and offices. Their labour required concentration and application that was difficult to maintain on a diet of beer soup and a drip-feed of wine. These were the people who embraced the cult of the new stimulants that became both a performance enhancer and a symbolic gesture in the assertion of new values. As James Howell wrote about coffee in 1660, 'whereas formerly Apprentices and clerks used to take their morning's draught of Ale, beer or wine, which by the dizziness they cause in the Brain made many unfit for business, they use now to play the Good-fellows in this wakeful and civil drink.'[10] It was upon these humble aspirations that the mass market for coffee and tea was built. The coffee pandemic in London, a city of some 600,000 people, was manifest in the

3,000 coffee houses that had sprung up by 1700. They were giving the taverns, of which there had been some 1,000 in the preceding century, a run for their money and accelerating social change in the process. While traditionally inns and taverns were places of rest and recreation, coffee houses became centres for business. They served as editorial offices for the incipient newspaper trade, as shipping and insurance brokers, as trading marts and recruitment offices.

This process of urban growth and the rise of a new class of merchants, craftsmen and scholars, who were tied to neither land nor lord, was happening all over Europe. Tea and coffee provided the right psychosomatic stimulus to support their aspirations: 'coffee functioned as a historically significant drug . . . it spread through the body and achieved chemically and pharmacologically what rationalism and the Protestant ethic sought to fulfil spiritually and ideologically.'[11] The new beverages could be adapted to fit into existing customary slots for consumption, as there were both designated times and places for drinking. Once in place it was possible to abstract symbolic content to promote sectional ideals, such as property, domesticity, family life and work, celebrated in 'The Winter Evening' (*The Task*, Bk 4), William Cowper's 1785 eulogy to tea – 'the cups, that cheer but not inebriate'. Less romantically, they provided a lifeline for a new urban underclass made up of the rural poor who, dispossessed by the enclosure of public land in the eighteenth century, were flocking into the towns where new industries were springing up. They became hooked on the fast foods of the day, commercially produced bread dunked into a hot mug of sugared tea. The first generation of proletarians rose to work on stimulants and retired on a powerful new form of inebriants, distilled gin. There is much information on the gin crisis of the eighteenth century and the first public health campaign, supported most memorably by William Hogarth's iconic pictures. Gin, as the infamous advertising slogan – 'drunk for a penny, dead drunk for tuppence' – promised, was only one side of the coin; sugared tea was the other.

The new soft drugs spread across Europe and its growing overseas colonies with astonishing speed. By the late seventeenth century tea came to rival coffee in the Netherlands and, most of all, England, where it 'extensified' in spectacular fashion. This meant that consumption spread out from the elite across the social spectrum, to become embedded as a performance enhancer, medicinal drink and an essential for recreational gatherings across class boundaries. The 'rate of transmission', with every new user recruiting more than one into consumption networks, was as fast as that of any of the illicit drugs of today. But this not only relates to consumer behaviour, for government policy is also analogous. The heavy hand of the state came down to manipulate the importation and distribution in its favour by imposing tariffs and restricting the free movement of goods. By restricting the licences issued to traders and ports of importation, import duties and excise taxes were relatively easy to collect, even though it distorted trading patterns: the East India Company, for instance, held a monopoly over tea imports during much of the eighteenth century.

The government had to weigh up the benefits of convenience with the overall need for revenue, which rose incessantly during this period of almost continuous military conflicts. One short-term measure was to declare tea a dispensable 'luxury' that could support high levels of taxation. This was hypocritical and ingenious, as the very social and economic transformations that were spurring England into ascendancy had by then made tea (and sugar) a necessity for many working people. As policy it was a disaster, economically counterproductive and inflicting misery and pain upon coastal communities. In the late 1750s, with excise duties climbing up again eventually to reach 119 per cent, the contraband economy took off. There were smuggling networks along all coastal areas, stretching into the retail centres inland. The response by the state was ruthless. Troops were sent to occupy some of the most notorious port towns, and there were public hangings and deportations. To economists in the heyday of Adam Smith, it was clear that these measures were doomed to fail as long as the demand for affordable tea created the opportunity. It was a clear example of the market triumphing over the will of the state. The situation was remedied when William Pitt the Younger became Prime Minister in 1783. Redefining tea as a necessity, he slashed the duty to 12.5 per cent and replaced the loss of income to the exchequer with the introduction of the window tax. In due course the revenue collected from tea exceeded the pre-reduction levels.[12]

It was too late, however, for maintaining the integrity of what historians have called the 'first British empire', as the North American settler colonies hived off from the 'mother country' to form the United States of America, today predominantly a nation of coffee-drinkers and home to Starbucks. The fuse had been lit, of course, by the duty slapped onto a cargo of tea. In Britain, meanwhile, the smuggling networks disappeared virtually overnight. It is instructive to think about the destiny of nations in relation to drugs and the drug trade. During the eighteenth and nineteenth centuries, relations between three of the most powerful empires of the time revolved around the trade in mind-altering substances. Britain, having lost one empire in North America over a trading dispute involving one drug, would recover new ground in the Far East following a dispute over another.

Opium in China

Throughout the eighteenth century Chinese tea exports had been rising, from 28,000 pics (a unit of some 60 kg) in the period 1720–30, to 172,000 during the period 1780–85.[13] Since Chinese markets proved resilient towards European exports, however, trade flowed one way and Chinese suppliers had to be paid in silver. Britain then, as the US today, was running a perpetual trade deficit with China. The implications became acute towards the end of the century when the country was facing a formidable adversary in Napoleon, and successive governments were becoming concerned about the outflow of resources. The export of opium from British-controlled India was a neat way to conserve precious bullion.

Opium had a long history of use as a medicine in China, where the poppy had been cultivated on a modest scale. Price, custom and marketing arrangements contained the spread and use of opium. In recent years historians have tracked the journey opium took through Chinese society from its birth as a recreational item to its old age as a social icon. The first transformation can be traced to the sixteenth century, when 'the medicine to aphrodisiac metamorphosis was opium's genesis of lust and luxury; it is what anthropologists call diversion, that is the diversion of a commodity from a specified path.'[14] Once again it is important to note that a cultural space had been created with the consumption of tea and tobacco. Not only did this create the sensibility of punctuating time with the recreational consumption of a non-nutritional substance, but also a cult of beauty around all the different utensils needed.

Tobacco had already habituated Chinese consumers to the practice of smoking and the importation and cultural integration of foreign drugs. Less than a century after its introduction tobacco had become 'naturalized' and was grown extensively in provinces such as Fujian. The cultivation and nationwide participation in the recreation of smoking and the culture of smoke, *yan wenhua*, was modelled on and thriving alongside *cha wenhua*, the culture of tea. A pattern had been established for opium to follow. In the eighteenth century opium spread through the brothels of China's extensive sex industry, and was promoted by soldiers and officials in contact with south-east Asia and Taiwan. Visitors to south-east Asia, a region with a much older history of culturally integrated opium use, and participants of the Taiwan conquest came back with habits and memories of smoking to accelerate the spread of opium. By 1729 the governor of Fujian, Liu Shimin, wrote to the emperor that 'the opium smoke is like an epidemic there. We should punish the traitors who possessed and sold it illegally.'[15] Little notice was taken, and when George Leonard Staunton visited China as part of a British embassy in 1793 opium smoking was so endemic as to appear indigenous to him.

The accelerating consumer trend depended first on the participation of a growing urban population and the availability of opium. Socio-economic trends within China had accelerated the move to urban areas, thus creating centres of demand, while British traders would guarantee the supply. A trickle of Bengali *patna* opium carried in British vessels had been reaching Chinese ports since the eighteenth century. The quantity exported exclusively by the East India Company rose gradually from 15 tons in 1773 to 75 tons in 1773. But in 1834, when the exclusive trading rights of the East India Company were terminated, individual traders, most famously William Jardine and James Matheson, stepped in. Four years later some 1,500 tons were being imported. As foreign traders ignored attempts by the Chinese government to control the inflow and movement of this unwanted cargo, stronger measures were resorted to. In 1839 Commissioner Lin Zexu confiscated opium belonging to British merchants and flushed it out with water. The British government took the position that this amounted to the destruction of private property and demanded compensation. When this was ignored British forces invaded China in what became known as the First Opium War; this was followed by a further conflict (1856–60) conventionally referred to as the Second Opium War. Strictly speaking neither war was about opium but the principle of property, which happened to be opium, but the principal consequences were the British occupation of Hong Kong, the establishment of British trading rights, including the trade in opium, and the recognition of the extraterritoriality of British subjects.

There is a wonderful inconsistency in Britain fighting wars over import controls in successive centuries: the one fought in the American colonies over the right of government to impose levies, the other in China to deny a foreign government precisely that same right. Tea and opium formed a commodity chain spanning three continents, and became inscribed into the economic production patterns of the consuming nations. Tea, as a performance enhancer, helped to stimulate British workers into the productive action that helped the country gain ascendancy. The favour was repaid with the stupefying gift of opium, which assisted the declining power of the Celestial Kingdom on its slide into oblivion.

Within another half century or so the British government position changed once again. Reluctantly at first, British officials played a key role in negotiating successive international treaties early in the twentieth century that gave frame and foundation to the global drug control apparatus. For the officials and campaigners who called this system into being, China has become what Mike Jay has termed the *locus classicus* of the opium problems.[16] The story of social catastrophe told so eloquently by foreign missionaries and frustrated nationalists, and the successful containment following the introduction of stringent controls, form the foundational myth on which the entire edifice of treaties and controls is built.

These assumptions have been attacked in a recent analysis of Chinese documents against the prevailing histories drafted from the records of foreign observers, principally missionaries. These trace the origin of the opium scare to the missionary movement to whom 'opium was an extraordinary and gigantic obstacle to receiving the gospel'.[17] Within China, however, the turn against opium was motivated by different reasons. Initial resistance to opium imported by British traders from India was motivated by concerns over the balance of payment. For the first time in its history China was running a negative trade balance with the West. Two defeats in the opium wars rammed home the conviction that China was quickly losing ground to Europe, America and later to Japan. A dramatic social overhaul was needed for the country to catch up, hence the Chinese of the early twentieth century chopped off their pigtails, discarded their robes for western-style clothing, and traded their opium pipes for cigarettes. The cigarette was short, snappy and symbolized the modern machine age. By the 1930s, remarked Jean Cocteau, 'Young Asia no longer smokes [opium] because "grandfather smoked".' This process was aggressively promoted by western companies such as British American Tobacco, which claimed to be combining business with humanity by 'weaning the Chinese . . . from opium and teaching them to smoke North Carolina cigarettes'.[18]

The problem, it seems, was not so much about opium but who was smoking it. According to Zheng Yangwen, 'when men of letters smoked, opium was culture; when the poor began to inhale it became a social problem.' In the 1830s opium use signalled worldly knowledge and sophistication, but by the end of the century it had become ordinary; another decade on and it symbolized Chinese weakness and inferiority. As often happens, the unintended consequences of this shift in cultural values, reinforced by political action, had a high number of casualties. After opium was banned, morphine and heroin took over. During the 1930s tens of thousands of opium smokers were rounded up 'without any regard for the logistical and humanitarian problems engendered by strict prohibition'. Within a short time opium offenders accounted for one-third of all incarcerated offenders. Treatment provided a charitable gloss to the intervention, but the moral definition shared by both the Chinese government and the missionaries, of the addict as someone lacking in will power, ignored the widespread medical use of opium: 'Opium smokers died in detoxification centres because the authorities failed to treat the ailments for which opium was taken in the first place.'[19] In other words, people were being penalized for self-medicating their sickness.

As the opium houses closed down many dependent users and the sick switched to morphine, now injected with the hypodermic needle. Administered under extremely unhygienic conditions, the massive uptake in imported morphine and heroin ensured that 'Opium prohibition contributed to social exclusion, drove drug consumption down the social ladder and . . . to a significant extent government policies purporting to contain opium actually resulted in creating a "drug problem".'[20]

Only in the European colonies, including Hong Kong, Singapore, Vietnam and Indonesia, did opium smoking continue under the auspices of the administration. These countries predictably escaped the depredations of morphine and heroin injecting. Controlled opium smoking provided affordable medicine, a pleasant pastime for the populace and an important source of revenue for public coffers until the 1940s. As American troops evicted Japanese occupation forces from the vestiges of European colonialism in Eastern Asia the lights went out for the last licit opium smokers. Cigarettes and penicillin, the recreational and medical drugs of the modern era, rendered opium obsolete. It would resurface in the form of heroin, now distributed via criminal networks and taken clandestinely under often deeply unhygienic conditions.

Shaping the modern world

The production of, commerce in, and desire for different drugs have been instrumental in shaping the modern world. They have motivated the seaward expansion of European countries, the founding of settler colonialism and, with the development of the plantation complex and the formation of mercantilism, fostered the beginnings of industrial capitalism. Much of this is counterintuitive, as the origins of capitalism and modernity are often attributed to puritan abstemiousness. Since Max Weber much has been made of the Protestant work ethic and deferred gratification as a driving force in the rise of the bourgeoisie. It is rarely acknowledged that it was the search for habit-forming and mood-altering luxuries that shaped our era.

The history of Europe's favourite soft drugs provides a number of important parallels for the analysis of contemporary drug control. It first demonstrates the powerful function of the market in spreading new consumption patterns and in establishing substances within cultures. It shows how substances become associated with groups, values and lifestyles to attain symbolic status. The processes of replacement and popularization, with new substances fitting into established categories of consumption and moving across the social pyramid via different mechanisms of propagation, are also well established. We then see the intervention of the state, which is principally concerned with issues of control and revenue, and, stemming from this, the conflict between state and market. Organized crime then forms in response to opportunity occasioned by state interventions, to flourish or wane not as a result of effective policing but by a correction of policy eliminating the distortions. The main consequence of aggressive law enforcement is to drive up the level of violence among the illicit market participants and the surrounding communities.

The case of opium provides a fascinating parallel, in tying Indian producers and Chinese consumers to the benefit of British intermediaries. The single most significant commodity, opium, was subject to regulation as much for economic as for public health reasons and would trigger British expansion along the Pacific rim. Government attempts at controlling the trade would succeed ultimately at enormous social costs, involving large-scale violence and the suspension of political and civil liberties. These drug trading networks were linking Britain and Europe, the Americas, Africa, India and China into a global trading network long before the term globalization was dreamt of. The form and status of the drug in question was adapted in each setting, however. Europeans added milk to their hot beverages and sugar. The Chinese took their opium in designated parlours where the smoker could lie down. In both markets, the packaging and presentation of products – tea, coffee, tobacco or opium – emphasized the exotic.[21] At the same time, the ritualization of the habit and the familiarity of brands suggested a homely comfort.

To the consumer the experience was simultaneously an affirmation of belonging and a flavour of the world beyond. In the process of drinking, smoking, eating or all three, he/she constructed him/herself as a member of a given society, while at the same time exhibiting aspirations to a wider world. But in the case of psychoactive substances image construction is even more complex, in that the evaluation by one social group may lead to the rejection by another. Social contradictions can be projected onto the substance, and then develop a dynamic of its own. This process is particularly notable in the most successful drug of the twentieth century, cannabis.

Globalizing plant-based drugs: cannabis

Nigeria's most notorious musician was the late Fela Ransome-Kuti, whose venue, the Shrine in the Ikeja neighbourhood of Lagos, became not only a place of pilgrimage for music lovers, but a centre of resistance to the successive military regimes that ran and ruined the country during the 1980s and '90s. Scion of a family of high achievers, Fela was a consummate rebel, whose lyrics provided a caustic commentary on the political rulers and a much needed pressure valve for the population. His performance was equally a choreographed spectacle of alternative values. Invigorating the West African tradition of polygamy, he would invite his many wives on stage to provide backing vocals, building up a chorus of some 33 women.

Equally demonstrative of a rejection of post-independence respectability was his conspicuous consumption of marijuana. There was much smoking during session breaks and, later on, increasingly during actual performances. Many of the fans followed his example, with thick clouds of marijuana smoke building up over the open-air venue and sparking off conflicts, arrests and interrogation by the Nigerian Drug Law Enforcement Agency. African nationalist though he was, believing that modern-day Nigerians were all too quick in jettisoning traditions in pursuit of material wealth, Fela was not drawing on the rich Yoruba culture, or on any of the country's 250 other ethnic groups with distinct languages and traditions, when enjoying his herbal cannabis. In

Nigeria marijuana is widely known as 'Indian hemp' and has only been known of for half a century. The story has it that units of the West Africa Frontier Force, recruited in Nigeria and Ghana, were stationed in India during the Second World War and took part in the Burma campaign. After the end of hostilities, when shipping was scarce and the repatriation of other units was given priority, they spent a long stretch in India getting to know different parts of its culture, including the sacramental and recreational use of cannabis. Taking seeds home with them, some veterans began planting in the late 1940s, particularly in the southern states. With a ready network of ex-combatants to organize distribution, a supply network was quickly set up and by the 1960s Indian hemp had become a regular feature in popular culture. In the short stories and novellas that are known as the 'Onitsha market literature', which were among the most popular forms of entertainment before the advent of videos and TV, Indian hemp is often used by the darker figures of the plot, thieves, prostitutes and corrupt police officers. But Fela and many of his followers were inspired by a different set of associations. Their role model was the spliff-toting Jamaican musician Bob Marley, who became something of an icon for African nationalists on three continents. The marijuana spliff, the matted dreadlocks and the attitude of casual defiance travelled across the Atlantic as symbols of a transcontinental black identity based on difference and rebellion. This did not translate into an uncritical approval of drug use per se. While never a puritan, Fela would not extend his tolerance of human foibles to the synthetic substances making an entry into Lagos during the late 1990s: he would tell his fans to 'go fuck prostitute, have a piss, drink *ogogoro* [distilled spirit], smoke *igbo* [cannabis], but don't take *gbana* [heroin]!' Another injunction was 'no Jones-ing!', meaning no cocaine use.[22]

This distinction between good marijuana and bad cocaine is also found in one of the heartlands of marijuana use, contemporary Jamaica. There is a widely held view that marijuana is a natural product, and therefore not a drug. The implicit definition is that a substance must be processed in some way before it transforms from herb to drug, although it is not clear whether, on the one hand, drying marijuana leaves qualifies as a form of processing, or whether naturally occurring fermentation rules alcohol in. In any case, some Jamaican marijuana users have taken the celebration of marijuana even further, by elevating it into a sacrament of the syncretic Rastafarian religion.

Possibly modelled on the Christian ritual use of wine in the consummation of Mass, it is nevertheless part of the overt rejection of Protestant and Catholic forms of Christianity, associated with the tarnished past of slavery and subordination. In Jamaica and across the English-speaking Caribbean, marijuana, known as ganja, is associated with Africa. Like the dreadlocks, adopted in the 1950s from the independence fighters of the Mau Mau rebellion in colonial Kenya, ganja has become a symbol of a black identity and a positive evaluation of the African past. The actual historical events are of lesser importance here than a higher order of mythological truth.

There is a long tradition of marijuana use in Eastern and Southern Africa, but the linguistic and archaeological records suggest that it was introduced from India and popularized across trading networks from the coast into the interior.[23] Moreover, in West Africa, the cradle of much of the population of the Caribbean today, cannabis was unknown until the mid-twentieth century. There is, of course, every likelihood that cannabis grew wild in Africa long before the use of bhang or ganja was imported from across the Indian Ocean. But the only culture of cannabis consumption of endogenous origin has been recorded among the Twa – or pygmies – of Central Africa. The Twa are credited for their superior knowledge of flora and fauna in the lore surrounding a different African drug, iboga,[24] and may have been enjoying this fruit of the forest long before the arrival of the first Bantu migrants.

In all likelihood, ganja was taken to the Caribbean by Indian indentured labourers, who were shipped across in the late nineteenth century after the abolition of slavery created a sudden labour shortage in the sugar plantations. Significantly, ganja use remained the preserve of the Indian settlers in the colonies of Guyana and Trinidad and Tobago, where the populations were large and self-contained. A much smaller number of Indian migrants found their way to Jamaica, where they became integrated with the majority population of African descent, facilitating the crossover of ganja use. Whether African or Asian, ganja came to symbolize a cherished aspect of the non-European heritage of the Caribbean. The early efforts by the colonial authority to suppress it[25] only served to underline the cosmic scheme in which a corrupt material world of Babylon would persecute anything that was liberating and beneficial.

This Rastafarian argument continues to have a strong resonance in ganja-smoking circles the world over. It is interesting to note, however, that the audiences of Fela Kuti in Nigeria and of Bob Marley in Jamaica were looking at each other for cultural affirmation when clenching their spliffs. Today, the link between marijuana, political opposition and cultural alternatives remains most vibrant in the Caribbean. This owes much to the prevailing sense of exclusion, disempowerment and economic dislocation among many of the population, and is also subject to significant regional variation, with much lower use patterns in Barbados and Grenada, for instance, than in Jamaica and St Vincent. Yet across the Caribbean, the call for freeing the herb still has a political ring to it, even though its most glamorous and universally appealing advocate has long passed away.

The contrast with the situation in Europe could not be greater. Cannabis has certainly had a meteoric career, rising from the unknown to the quotidian within the course of a century. It also provides a further instance of the familiar pattern of elite use and subsequent extensification. The first record of recreational cannabis use becoming established in Europe stems from the mid-nineteenth century, when it became popular among a bohemian elite in Paris. The Club des Hashischins provided an opportunity for cultural luminaries, including Charles Baudelaire, Alexandre Dumas, Théophile Gautier and Eugène Delacroix, and their patrons to dress up in oriental clothes and consume large amounts of mind-altering substances, in the name of exploring the workings of the mind. This followed in a tradition of auto-experimentation by European scientists from Sir Humphry Davy, who discovered nitrous oxide or laughing gas, to Sigmund Freud's experimentation with cocaine. The purpose could be a happy combination of research and recreation, and in clear contrast to the laboratory-based efforts of today. The Parisian *hashischins* were less concerned with the wider application of their discoveries, but were playing instead with a novel psychoactive muse. An early realization of the clash between the languid sensuality inspired by the drug and the productive ethos of industrial capitalism was summed up by the poet Baudelaire in his dictum that 'no government will allow this drug'.

Yet the French and other European governments did allow cannabis to spread right across the nineteenth century. They were just as happy for opium, and its new derivatives morphine and heroin, to be sold over counters by pharmacists and apothecaries. Cocaine and coca were coming into vogue with advances in chemistry and improvements in transport links, opening new fields of opportunity for pharmaceutical companies and Andean exporters alike.

Recreational use of cannabis, on the other hand, remained largely unknown throughout Europe. When an Egyptian delegate suggested at the third drug control conference in Geneva in 1925 that the list of substances to be brought under control be extended to cannabis, European delegates complied out of solidarity. The controls subsequently introduced in the series of drug control conventions organized under the auspices of the League of Nations were, as far as the UK and most European countries were concerned, of a pre-emptive nature. There was little incidence of cannabis use and yet legislation was introduced that curtailed the rights of citizens and criminalized forms of behaviour long before these had become problematic. This was a perverse inversion in the formulation of legislation, in that laws were framed in anticipation rather than in response to social problems.

The heavy hand of the state is even more in evidence in the US, where marijuana control became the mission of ambitious law enforcement agencies in search of a remit, and a tool for criminalizing and controlling minority populations. One of the greatest challenges of the 'noble experiment', as the prohibition of alcohol between 1919 and 1932 has been called, was oversight of the control apparatus. Even more challenging was the orderly dismantling of agencies created for a single purpose, once that had been removed. Just like armies in wartime, these agencies had been armed, trained and sanctioned to use violence. Unlike armies, however, they were employed against their own people and fighting on home ground. What made matters even more sinister was that they were exposed to little risk to themselves and were quick to establish contact with their adversaries in low places. The symbiotic relationship between enforcers and breakers of the law is as old as criminal justice itself. The revolution in the modern state machinery and the meteoric rise of bureaucracy has created a high-risk dynamic of organizational self-perpetuation and expansion. The legion of police officers and prosecutors building a career on the persecution of alcohol and its purveyors faced an existential threat when the 21st Amendment consigned alcohol prohibition to history. They were quick to join a new crusade: the campaign against marijuana stepped right into the vacuum, promoted by a cynical alliance of vested interests. US drug control cannot be separated from the mercurial figure of Harry J. Anslinger, chief of the Federal Bureau of Narcotics from 1930 to 1962, and an accomplished propagandist. He brought his genius to bear on the fabrication of stories about marijuana and its attendant dangers, culminating in the classic propaganda film *Reefer Madness* (1936).

It is apparent that the concerns for public health, which had in part inspired the early campaigners of the Temperance Society, had finally passed into irrelevance. Controlling the three prohibited substances (opium, cocaine and cannabis) had become predominantly a law enforcement issue, though only vaguely related to crime control. There was no relationship between the three substances and crime, other than those defined by their status, in spite of the claims of the propaganda machine. It could even be argued that it was precisely the all too obvious corruption of government agencies, the abuse of authority and betrayal of trust that motivated the countercultural embrace of marijuana in the 1960s. It was during the opening of what in the US is known as the 'culture wars' that marijuana moved from the minority margins into the mainstream, a process paralleled with national variations in most western European countries. By the 1970s cannabis was established as an accoutrement of an alternative lifestyle choice and continued to grow in popularity right into the 1990s, when it became 'normalized' as yet another item available to consumers.

Countries with rigorous control regimes, such as the United States, Sweden and the United Kingdom, have seen dips in cannabis consumption over the past twenty years. Inevitably politicians and the public relations departments of the respective national control agencies hailed these as proof of policy success. With the same inevitability, however, the figures have begun to climb once more after several years. In the UK, where cannabis use peaked before falling off only in the aftermath of the vaunted reclassification of cannabis from class B to C, it is still too early to tell. The subsequent return to class B by an ailing government in the spring of 2008 is unlikely to have any impact on consumption trends. The link between trend shifts in the use of cannabis or any other drug, for that matter, is perhaps quite independent from actual government policies. So-called 'drug education' has at best had only a marginal effect in persuading young people to desist from drug use, although this is a notoriously difficult outcome to measure. More important than interventions on the supply and campaigns on the demand side may be the ineluctable sway of fashion in determining the popularity of psychoactive substances. In the late 1970s and early 1980s cocaine enjoyed a splendid revival, followed during the 'decade of dance' by a craze for MDMA. Somehow cannabis found a complementary role, detached from the hippy subculture with which at one point it was inextricably bound up. More significant still was its spread into other areas of life beyond the weekend world of clubs and partying. In much of western Europe cannabis has completed its migration from counter-culture into the mainstream, with a symbolic status akin to pop music – holding on to vague pretensions to subversion and rebellion, while remaining entirely conventional.

5 Redefining the Issue: Symptom of Decadence or Development Problem?

During the 1970s the countries troubled by drugs and drug-related problems were only found in North America and Europe. These were the societies with youth cultures and protest movements, with the political freedom for lifestyle experimentation and the wealth to allow for new patterns of recreational consumption to emerge. Drug use was an inverted sign of industrial democracy status, an index of moral decline following the triumph of materialism. Conservative commentators at the time associated drugs with other pathologies of modernity, like vandalism, homosexuality and terrorism. In some ways these jeremiads are a regular feature of both economic prosperity and social diversity and remain the stock-in-trade of moral entrepreneurs, political pundits and cultural critics. In the US the Evangelical movement, partly rooted in the Puritan tradition, has long thrived on the condemnation of particular aspects of sexuality and cultural difference. In the more secular societies of western Europe different anxieties emerged over the virility of the nation and its capacity to wage war with its youth, who were in thrall to debilitating drugs. The devastating fallout was demonstrated by the experience of American GIs stationed in Vietnam, where the use of marijuana, barbiturates and opiates was endemic and an acceptable form of behaviour.

Political elites in all western countries were concerned over the subversion of traditional cultural values and the erosion of social structures that followed from the cognitive disconnect between the pre- and post-war generations. During the 1950s and '60s a generation of young people emerged as a social entity with an identity, a lifestyle and a worldview distinct from their elders.

Riding the crest of an economic boom, they were free of the cares and fear of scarcity that had haunted previous generations of the industrial era, and were simultaneously more idealistic and self-indulgent. The use of illicit drugs played a crucial role in signifying difference and carving out new identities. Linked to a wave of political protests, mass drug use was tantamount to the rejection of established values and tradition, and thereby jeopardizing their continuation into the future. Forceful interventions by governments and the agencies of the state, while inflicting significant collateral damage among those precious young people, could therefore be justified as a defence of the nations' heart and soul.

As drug use during the 1960s and '70s was, in the perception of commentators and policy-makers, as well as among the consumers of 'our generation', a youth phenomenon, it was difficult to condemn the perpetrators. The full force of social wrath therefore fell on the evil minds orchestrating the drug trade and seducing young innocents. The fall from innocence was attributed to the dealer, who was conjured as a figure of hate, the object of opprobrium and the alleged target of intervention. It also prepared the way for political arrangements in some European countries, including the Netherlands, Germany, Belgium, Spain and Portugal, which today allow consumers to escape criminalization by a system of 'civil offences', such as fines and warnings, while harsh penalties are meted out to suppliers.

Notwithstanding these harm reduction responses, in most jurisdictions moral and political principles have been severely distorted by harsh, 'rights'-infringing measures that have been introduced in order to save people from themselves. When these are young people lacking in experience and maturity to safeguard their own interests, the state steps in, *in loco parentis*. As drug control was originally motivated by health concerns, there were precedents, an aetiological rationale and a vocabulary drawn from psychiatry. Yet in that context they had always referred to exceptional cases, remarkable for their rarity; never had the analysis been applied to a broad social phenomenon. Only with the war on drugs did democratic societies allow for the mass incarceration of citizens as a therapeutic measure for health damages they had inflicted solely upon themselves. The array of criminal justice interventions, with arrest, trial and punishment, conflated the logic of punishment and cure by bringing the drug-using offender under the control of the state.

The second response was to shift the blame for drugs and drug use onto outsiders. Drug problems, so the official representations of the 'threat' maintained, were the product of drug pushers, entrapping young people at the school gates. They were supplied by criminal organizations with international connections. 'Othering' the drug problem allowed policy-makers to address widespread fears of crime and nascent xenophobia, while deflecting from the inherent problems of drug demand and growing popularity. It also provided a target and a logic of intervention, formulated in terms of 'supply reduction', that could inform operations and provide set objectives. The formula by law enforcement agencies was that arrests and seizures would drive up the price for drugs, and put them out of reach of consumers, particularly of young people. Drug squads and dedicated drug control agencies, such as the Drug Enforcement Administration, were formed on the assumption that a tough crackdown on suppliers and markets would ruin the market. Lessons from the history of alcohol prohibition, it seems, were conveniently forgotten.

The other two problems with the formula lay in the untested assumption that, because most drug users in the 1960s and '70s were young people, drug use per se was a youth phenomenon and therefore temporary. This equivalence of youth and drugs is perpetuated in much of the official drug literature circulating in the US and other countries, where the drop in drug-use prevalence among older age groups is referred to as 'maturing out'. Ironically, this was inspired by much of the 1960s sociological literature on deviance, where drug use was depicted as part of a rebellious rite of passage, a youthful error devoid of malign intent but full of risk. As long as drug users are young people then the penal regime of law enforcement and courts is roughly in line with other forms of paternalist authority and guidance. Inversely, the occasional instances of non-youthful drug users can be explained as anomalies whose arrested development is perhaps a consequence of their drug use. In either case, interventions are not only justifiable, but a moral responsibility of the authorities.

These policy-driven theories of intervention take little note of much of the ethnographic evidence on the use of opiates and various hallucinogens from around the world. Opium smoking in India and South-east Asia, for instance, kava drinking in Polynesia, the use of ayahuasca among Amazonian Indians or psilocybin rich mushrooms in Mexico were the preserve of adults and controlled by elders. There was nothing inherently juvenile to consuming these substances that would lead to an organic process of maturing out. Moreover, according to accounts from all these diverse settings, the very problems attendant to the use of psychoactives were contained by the social controls put in place by an experienced set of users. Once again, the very definition of the issue as a problem of substance and the othering of 'drugs' has blinded observers to comparable data from the use of alcohol, tobacco, and also so-called junk foods. These are consumed across the lifecycle and controls are put in place to protect immature users. Instead of drawing on these parallels, the drug control complex has imposed a total prohibition, which is upheld by increasingly intrusive measures of electronic and chemical surveillance, such as drug testing in schools and the workplace, sniffer dog patrols on public transport and decoding of closed-circuit television footage.

A further problem with the original formula of 'pricing drugs out of the reach of potential users' has been the tremendous rate of economic growth enjoyed by western countries. These advances have driven down production costs while raising disposable income even at the lower end of the economy. Supply-side interventions based on cost calculations of half a century ago have simply not managed to keep abreast of the spreading levels of prosperity. As a result drug prices have been falling dramatically in spite of ever more dramatic control efforts. In the 1970s cocaine was an icon of the nouveau riche and compared to champagne: twenty years on champagne is sold in supermarkets and cocaine snorted by working men in the toilets of public bars. Heroin, meanwhile, has become so cheap that by the early 2000s recreational users in Europe could afford once again to 'chase the dragon' – that is smoking heroin instead of injecting it intravenously.

These developments were unthinkable during the first phase of mass illegal drug use in the 1960s and '70s. Many social anxieties and the apocalyptic fears of a Cold War turning hot were projected onto cultural phenomena at home, such as popular

music, youth culture and drugs. Ubiquitous and spreading inexorably, it was compared to an infectious disease, an analogy that
has become assimilated into the discourse on drugs. The epidemic
model once again fulfils several important functions: it removes
responsibility from the social and political environment; it strips
the individual user of voluntary agency and denies his/her right
to take decisions; and it suggests an intrinsic malevolence to a
process that was seemingly random. For drug use and addiction –
the terms were often used synonymously in the 1970s when all
use was believed to lead to addiction – could strike anywhere.
Whereas many of the other contemporary issues from racial
tensions, labour strikes, and the assertions of feminist women,
were the consequence of sectional discontent and often stirred by
sectarian agitators, drugs were being consumed right across the
social spectrum. Unlike any other issue at the time, drug use pen-
etrated the best defences that families could build up around their
children, who now had the disposable wealth, the social freedom
and the services of a dynamic market economy to supply them
with a set of vices beyond the comprehension of their parents.
For many Europeans, the dilemma was encapsulated by the story
of Christiane F. and her friends from Bahnhof Zoo, selling sex
and injecting heroin in the toilet of a Berlin railway station, with
sometimes lethal consequences. How could the life of a nice girl
from a good family, with all the advantages provided by an
advanced economy and a comprehensive welfare system, end in
such squalid misery? Social commentators were united in claiming that this could not have happened to previous generations,
and was geographically confined to western Europe and North
America. Drugs, in short, were the scourge of the contemporary
West, a *Zivilisationskrankheit* unknown to those still struggling to
meet their material needs.

It is interesting to note that in what was then known as the
'second world' commentators heartily agreed. The prosperity of
the capitalist West was dismissed as 'decadence' and drugs were
identified as a key indicator. According to William Butler, 'the
official Party line was that narcotism and addiction were inherent in and endemic to the capitalist world.'[1] There was little
awareness of drug use in the Soviet Union and the drug control
measures derived from 1920s legislation aimed at the 'economic

crime' of selling a commodity for profit without a licence. With alcohol clearly distinguished as a licit substance and therefore not a drug, it was possible to claim that drug problems were negligible. The Soviet Union also provided a model for successful prohibition – closed external borders, highly restricted internal travel, total surveillance, minimal civil rights and maximum law enforcement powers.

Drugs in developing countries

Countries in the Third World up until the 1990s also had a clear sense that drug abuse was a western problem and not a domestic concern, and felt no need, therefore, to adopt the prophylactic methods of either the western or the communist bloc. An example of how cultural stereotyping can render groups of experts blind to health trends occurring under their very eyes is provided with reference to HIV/AIDS by James Chin. In 1985 the author ran a seminar modelling the problems of AIDS with African health researchers and epidemiologists in Swaziland. A passionate argument ensued, with some of the participants insisting that AIDS was a western disease of homosexuals and drug addicts and of no relevance to Africa. According to back calculations, there were at that very time between one and two million people living with HIV across the continent.[2]

African countries during the 1980s were just as vehement in rejecting suggestions that drug use was spreading among their populations. Once again, this was a western problem that did not affect their people, who were simply not as morally corrupted as the wealthier westerner. The drug control community during that time was not so much concerned with drug use in developing countries as with drug production and drug trafficking. The main production areas for all the three plant-based substances – opiates, cocaine and cannabis – were in developing countries, and the threat was seen to be emanating from them. The imagery and language of threat are now well established, and used to illustrate the publications of national and international drug control agencies. These show production sites in particular regions with romantic monikers such as the 'golden crescent' or the 'golden triangle', and are then transported along indicated routes such as the 'Balkan route' or the 'silk route' towards consumer markets.

These 'threat scenarios' resemble the anti-Chinese agitation along the American west coast in the nineteenth century and the hysterical reportage on the white slave trade, with reports of Chinese opium peddlers luring white women into opiate dependence and worse, the dual degradation of promiscuous and interracial intercourse. The more recent location of drug problems as originating in source countries has created new stereotypes by identifying certain minority groups as drug traffickers or dealers. The operational consequences include ethnic profiling by law enforcement agencies, and the forwarding of the war on drugs into producer countries. It helps to continue the myth that drugs – like HIV/AIDS – 'originate in someone else's country' and so, in another exercise of economic illiteracy, justify the destruction of the production sites. So far this has had little success in securing the ultimate objective of reducing the availability and price (one of the measures of availability) of drugs in what were then called 'consumer countries'. But it has led to the expansion of drug production sites into new and hitherto unaffected areas, such as Colombia for coca leaf, and the proliferation of drug trafficking routes. One of the most notable consequences, rarely remarked upon in policy forums, has been the import substitution effect in North America and parts of Europe, which now supplies most of the cannabis available in local markets, once the preserve of North African, Middle Eastern and Latin American producers. A related issue and topic of ongoing discussion among the medical community and the public at large is the expansion of the pharmaceutical industry and the concentration on anti-depressant, performance-enhancing and lifestyle drugs. These developments not only blur the boundary between medical and non-medical use, they also put the use of plant-based substances into a new context.

Back in the 1960s and '70s it was assumed that most producer countries were principally involved in export. Their domestic markets were underdeveloped because mass drug abuse was one of the costs of advanced development, a stage that had yet to be reached. Interestingly, the same was often said to apply to democratic government, which, according to the prevailing development theory at the time, was one of the benefits of 'progress'. There has been a dramatic revision on both issues over recent decades. During the 1990s, democracy, governance and the rule of law, which had hitherto been thought of as luxuries afforded by material prosperity, were redefined as the necessary conditions for economic development. Considerable efforts have since been invested in building up governance mechanisms, promoting democracy and embedding the rule of law. In a parallel development, problematic drug use is no longer considered a symptom of post-industrial decadence, but an impediment to development. Countries around the Third World have been exhorted to put drug control mechanisms into place not only to stop the out- or through-flow of drugs to the so-called 'consumer countries' but also to curtail domestic consumption.

According to experts, drug abuse is now a global problem of enormous proportions. Some 3 per cent of world trade, it is claimed, is accounted for by the trade in illicit drugs, which in sector terms is third only to oil and arms. The organized crime groups controlling this trade dispose of resources well in excess of the wealth of smaller or poorer nations. Fortunately, international agencies have been created to support national governments in their efforts to fight the drug 'barons'. Working closely with the national agencies in the leading developed countries, they have created an organizational infrastructure for tackling drug problems globally. Since these agencies themselves are relatively young, their activities opaque and the objectives and overall rationale not stated with quite the desired precision, their activities continue to attract only modest public attention. To a growing number of historians and political analysts studying this select club of gentlemen,[3] the opaque methods used, the appropriation of funds and the acquisition of power by stealth has given rise to concern. The agencies concerned with drug control, such as the International Narcotics Control Board and the United Nations Office on Drugs and Crime, have used the image of the UN as a benevolent organization to promote activities that can be questioned in the context of human rights. The imprisonment of drug users, for example, 'violates the inherent dignity of persons, the right to be free from cruel and degrading punishment and the right to liberty'.[4] The use of punishments disproportionate to the gravity of the offence extends from the blanket use of incarceration for drug possession and petty dealing, to the application of capital punishment for drug distribution and importation in countries including China, Egypt, Indonesia, Iran, Kuwait, Malaysia, Saudi Arabia, Singapore, Malaysia, Thailand and Vietnam. Most disturbing, perhaps, has been the Chinese authorities' custom of celebrating the UN's International Day Against Drug Abuse with public executions of drug offenders. In 2001 some 50 people were executed at mass rallies, at least one of which was broadcast on state television.[5] The emphasis on law enforcement to suppress use, distribution and production has put drug control at loggerheads with public health objectives. Over recent years the policy of so-called 'harm reduction' has emerged as a battleground between proponents of zero tolerance and advocates of a measured approach aimed at reducing the harms associated with drug use, rather than drug use itself. With injecting drug use having become the major mode of transmission for infectious diseases, most seriously HIV, in Eastern Europe and Central Asia, the refusal of both agencies to support simple strategies like needle exchanges, diamorphine prescribing and drug consumption rooms has severely compromised the effectiveness of health agencies. At the heart of the problem is a 'reluctance to deviate from a situation where the secondary harm caused by drug control policies often seems to exceed the primary harm of drug use itself'.[6] The 'collateral damage' of the zero tolerance to drug use has prompted professionals and policy-makers all over the world to rethink their approaches on drug issues. It is therefore disturbing that agencies working with a global remit and charged with the promotion of health-related matters, as well as the respect and observance of human rights,[7] have compromised these key objectives.

6 International Drug Control: System and Structure

A series of international agreements were arrived at in the first part of the twentieth century to impose tight restrictions on the production, distribution and use of the three plant-based drugs and their derivatives. Special agencies were created to monitor adherence to the treaty provisions, and agencies established in different branches of the international agencies – first the League of Nations and from 1945 the United Nations – were charged with lending technical expertise in relevant areas of pharmacology, medicine and law.

The key functional commission for drug control that is of relevance today was established in 1946 as the Commission on Narcotic Drugs (CND) within the Economic and Social Council (ECOSOC). It has oversight over the United Nations Office on Drugs and Crime (UNODC), an agency with the primary task of assisting Member States with the ratification and implementation of the drug control treaties. The UNODC also provides secretarial functions for the INCB, established in 1968 and responsible for overseeing the implementation of the UN drug control conventions. The INCB inherited a number of tasks from the Opium Control Board of the League of Nations in the 1920s and '30s, which, in addition to monitoring treaty adherence, are to ensure the availability of drugs for medical and scientific purposes.

At the beginning of the twentieth century international agreements had been non-binding and drug control had been a voluntary measure exercised by each national government as it deemed fit. It was an international policy issue of interest primarily to the US, which had jointly with the Chinese government organized the first conference in Shanghai in 1908. Discussions centred on controlling the production of and trade in opium before including other substances. Bringing cocaine into play, it has been argued, was a negotiation ploy by a British delegation concerned with protecting the Indian opium industry. The us representatives were unfazed and simply incorporated cocaine and coca in the discussions, to the subsequent dismay of Andean countries.

Restrictions on opium and cocaine became binding only after the First World War, when they were built into the Versailles Treaties and adopted by all signatory states. Permanent offices were established at the League of Nations in Geneva to ensure that countries would honour their treaty obligations. In 1925, at the behest of South African and Egyptian delegates, the list of controlled substances was extended to cannabis. The response by Stephen Porter, the leader of the American delegation, provides an illustration of the level of expertise and competence on which these decisions were taken:

> The very carefully prepared statement of the Delegate of Egypt, together with my own knowledge on the subject, have satisfied me that we are under obligation in this Conference to do everything we can to assist the Egyptian and Turkish people to rid themselves of this vice. We are asking them to help us destroy the vice of opium, coca leaves and their derivatives, and I believe that this is a good time to practise a little reciprocity.[1]

Though the us was not a member of the League of Nations, it actively participated in and supported the drug control aspects of this international agency. During the Second World War, moreover, the International Opium Board decamped to Yale University in Connecticut. When the League was resurrected after the war in the form of the current United Nations, us diplomats were quick to include drug control as one of its remits, took a major role in drafting the international conventions, and saw to the formation of a supervisory regime in the form of the International Narcotics Control Board.

The first significant international treaty was the 1961 Single Convention on Narcotic Drugs, which bundled together the various pieces of international legislation that had been drawn up under the League. The treaty was complemented in 1971 by the Convention on Psychotropic Substances, which brought a range of pharmaceutical substances under control. The 1988 Convention against Illicit Traffic in Narcotic Drugs and Psychotropic Substances added new powers to crack down on global drug trafficking. As of July 2007, some 183 states are party to the first and second of the three conventions, and 182 to the third. These treaties form the architecture of international drug control, severely restricting any signatory state's room for manoeuvre on developing national or local drug policies. Deviations from treaty obligations as interpreted by the independent INCB can lead to sharp reprimands. The governments of Canada and Switzerland, for instance, have been sharply rebuked for opening up drug consumption rooms where drug users can inject their own drugs under clean conditions, and the UK was told in 2003 that the downgrading of cannabis from class B to class C was having 'worldwide repercussions . . . including confusion and widespread misunderstanding'.

While the board is restricted to naming and shaming wayward members, a more proactive role in the implementation of drug control measure has been played by some of the governments with 'experience' in the field and by dedicated UN agencies. The United Nations Fund for Drug Abuse Control was established in 1971 and folded into the United Nations Drug Control programme in 1990. Renamed the United Nations Office on Drugs and Crime (UNODC), it runs a host of projects from surveying poppy cultivation in Afghanistan, to providing technical assistance with drug prevention education in the Caribbean, to assisting Central Asian countries in introducing drug control legislation. It has a global mandate and seeks to cover all things related to drugs. While the agency can encourage member states to sign up to the conventions, it has only a limited arsenal of incentives and sanctions to press its case home.

The European Union, on the other hand, heavily promotes accession to drug control treaties among developing partners, and has made it a pre-condition for some of its development partnership programmes. When countries are seen to be in breach of their treaty obligations, however, it is the US that steps up to the plate with a series of heavy sanctions and penalties. Since 1984 the us has been running an annual certification system of countries that have been identified as producing or transiting drugs. Their governments and government agencies are assessed as to how strictly they apply the treaty provisions and how well they cooperate with the us drug enforcement authorities. Failure can result in the loss of us development cooperation funds and, more critically still, loans from the international financial institutions in which the us holds a share – the World Bank and the International Monetary Fund. In many UNODC field offices a close working relationship has developed with us embassies, which as part of the us State Department have to deal with drug issues. In consequence, the UN drug control officers can borrow a set of teeth in their negotiations with developing country officials.

The UNODC began to develop a coherent, forward-looking strategy during the 1990s, at a time of dramatic shifts in the international balance of power, and an avid interest in new security risks. During the middle of the decade drugs in general and drug trafficking in particular became identified as actual threats to global stability. This shift in perceptions opened up new opportunities for a global organization with the requisite expertise and mandate. In the early 1990s an intergovernmental advisory group was tasked with studying the drug control system in order to counter the 'strong movement aimed at showing that the international drug control regime . . . had failed and that legalization was the only solution'.[2] The group, comprised of officials employed by international control agencies and who arguably held a vested interest in the continuation of the regime, concluded that the legal provisions were sufficient but that it needed greater resources and some technical adjustments to be effective. These findings were taken to the Commission of Narcotic Drugs (CND), which in turn recommended to the UN Secretary General that he convene a Special Session of the General Assembly (UNGASS) in New York in 1998. In the build-up, countries like Mexico, Australia and Peru sought to use this opportunity for a comprehensive and critical review of existing drug control arrangements. They were, however, outmanoeuvred by the hardline member states, including the us, collaborating with the drug control agencies INCB and the United Nations Drug Control Programme in charge of organizing the event, and their requests were sidelined. Under a new Executive Director, the UNDCP presented an ambitious plan called Strategy for Coca and Opium Poppy Elimination by 2008 (SCOPE).

The conference opened with a clear statement reiterating the zero tolerance approach to dugs, and backing away from any suggestion of compromise on the issue of legalization:

> Drugs destroy lives and communities, undermine sustainable human development and generate crime. Drugs affect all sectors of society in all countries; in particular, drug abuse affects the freedom and development of young people, the world's most valuable asset. Drugs are a grave threat to the health and well-being of all mankind, the independence of States, democracy, the stability of nations, the structure of all societies, and the dignity and hope of millions of people and their families.[3]

This was followed by an elaborate ten-year action plan to 'mobilize resources . . . [for] the elimination or substantial reduction of coca leaf, opium poppy and cannabis cultivation by 2008'.[4] Though the delegates baulked at the cost of some US$3,894 million, they agreed on the programme's principles and gave the agency the go-ahead. Ten years on, prices for all three drugs are cheaper in the main markets than at the time of the conference, and in Afghanistan a bumper opium harvest has just been brought in.

Coming up towards the end of the so-called strategy, a major effort has been made by the UNDCP and its supporters to avoid an independent, external evaluation of the process. Charitable observers may invoke *force majeure* as the collapse of the Taliban regime was unforeseeable and well beyond UNDCP control. Yet a better understanding of the dynamics of drug production and, particularly with reference to cannabis, a realization of the futility in setting targets without production baselines should be expected from an international agency. More critical questions could be raised over the propriety of a UN agency striking up so close a working relationship with a pariah regime. Yet in 1999 and 2000 the UN was providing the Taliban government of Afghanistan with technical assistance and the promise of financial support to achieve reductions in poppy cultivation. It has also been working closely with the government in Burma. Both regimes were widely denounced for grave human rights violations and internationally isolated. Yet this UN agency chose to engage in pursuit of a very specific goal. The questions as to why UN agencies concerned with the education of children or maternal health care were withdrawing from a country, while those working on drug control remained, were never satisfactorily answered. There was a nagging suspicion that this was allowed mainly because Afghani and Burmese drug production was affecting western countries, which meant that UN agencies prioritize the needs of 'donor nations' over the supposed beneficiaries in the developing world. A further question was whether it was the proper role for the United Nations to encourage the use of force by non-democratic regimes against their own populations. This is a strongly contested issue, since it poses a point of departure in the history of the organization that has not received the attention it deserves.

Finally, the assembly itself and the ambitious goals wrapped into the slogan about a drug-free world had all the hallmarks of a fund-raising event. With little core funding from the Secretary General, the UNDCP was and remains dependent on voluntary provisions by member states. Launching an ambitious programme was a glorious attempt to set the agency and its management on a different footing altogether. The 'drug-free world' came with a price tag of just under US$4 billion.

Unfortunately for the organizers, little of this was forthcoming and UN member states, while signing up to these lofty goals, decided to keep their money and control over most operational aspects at national level. Its grandiose scheme thwarted, the UNDCP slid into an organizational crisis, losing qualified staff, technical capacity and organizational integrity. There were allegations of mismanagement and misappropriation of funds, an investigation by the UN Office of Internal Oversight into irregularities in recruitment and the awarding of contracts, a series of resignations including the Executive Director, and finally a reorganization. In 2003 the agency was rebranded as the United Nations Office on Drugs and Crime, and came under the management of Antonio Maria Costa, an official from the International Bank for Reconstruction and Development.[5] He inherited, among other things, a ten-year programme that had been built on untested premises and outlined unattainable goals, with no coherent strategy. The activities of the agency, while having little impact on the actual level of global drug use, are contributing to the very anti-democratic and human right-violating activities that the UN was once created to avert. It has done little to understand the domestic needs of member states but endorses and promotes the aims of its major donors, principally the US and the EU and its member states, who appoint its senior officers and second many of its staff.

UNODC in context

The US State Department and the foreign ministries of the EU member states are primarily concerned with protecting national interests, which they translate in operational terms into control of the inflow of drugs into their own countries. They may support so-called demand reduction projects in partner countries, but then mainly in the framework of development cooperation, and even then as an afterthought. One member of the Drugs and International Crime Department at the UK Foreign Office admitted, 'we like to spend one dollar in ten on the demand side, to show our partners that we are also concerned about their problems.' Most bilateral cooperation, however, is about supply-side interventions and will typically comprise training programmes for law enforcement officers, the provision of equipment from aircraft to drug identification kits, or judicial cooperation to strengthen legislation. This involves the despatch of jurists who help recipient countries in drafting laws on drug control.

The United Nations, however, has to address the needs of each of its member states. It therefore has a responsibility to deal with the problems of drug use in the producer and trafficking countries. Indeed, the UNODC is a one-stop shop where all drug policy requirements can be met by a single organization. It provides assistance in all areas and encourages members to identify their needs and outline the strategies for meeting them in the drug control master plan.

Putting these measures into place and helping countries avoid decertification by the US, with the attendant set of economic sanctions, is of course conducive to development. In effect it is not so much the drugs, but the absence of appropriate drug control policies that are an impediment to achieving development goals. Such circular reasoning lacks the credibility for so fundamental a claim, and is not enhanced by the imposition by a single, powerful member state onto the policy of an intergovernmental organization. The UNODC does recognize that countries have different needs, depending on their stage of development, their history and culture. There are significant concessions, for example, to the use of drugs within traditional settings. The 1997 World Drug report includes a section on traditional use and allows that in many cultures some form of the substances that are currently under control have been used in a non-problematic and culturally integrated fashion. This caveat is followed with the unsupported claim that recent developments have overtaken these traditional forms of consumption, eliminated the control systems of custom and culture, and replaced them with problematic patterns of use. A prime example would be the use of opium in countries of South-east and Southern Asia, where the traditional opium pipe has been replaced by heroin, which is either smoked on silver foil or injected intravenously. There is no discussion as to how these developments are in fact a response to the repression of the opium trade, so well documented across Asia. Most importantly, there seems to be no room for the organic development of patterns of consumption. Instead traditions are lodged firmly in the past, while all contemporary manifestations of drug use are by definition problematic. For the drug control body, then, there are two pairs of concepts: traditional/integrated versus contemporary/problematic. The report pays lip service to the right of cultural autonomy manifest in diverse traditions, but moves on to interpret these as historic that have been overtaken by the malaise of modernity.

There is of course a further dimension to this, in that historic use may also have been problematic. There is strong evidence to suggest that the use of alcohol among native peoples in Northern America, Australia and parts of Africa was indeed problematic.[6] Equally, opium use in China was highly contentious. But one does not need to venture into either the developing world or stray into illicit substances, as the favourite drugs of Europe and North America, alcohol and nicotine, have been the topic of discussion and controversy for centuries. Indeed, as we covered earlier, the origin of the contemporary drug control movement lies in the campaign against alcohol. Yet the UN's ten-year strategy towards a 'drug-free world' makes no mention of alcohol. In the official documentation by the UNODC alcohol and nicotine are not even referred to as drugs. This is in part due to the internal politics of the UN, where responsibility for alcohol has been assigned to the World Health Organization. Excluding the demon drink from its remit is more than a question of turf war. It also reflects the cultural conventions of the most powerful member states, in which both sets of substance are culturally integrated and promoted by powerful economic interests.

In operational terms there are further difficulties with regard to societies without literary traditions and no external records of use. We have a growing body of evidence, for instance, that cannabis use is endemic among the Twa or pygmy people over large parts of Central Africa. It is not clear whether this is the product of cultural transmission, which seems to be the case in most parts of sub-Saharan Africa, or indigenous: '[cannabis] smoking is on the list of Twa practices and behaviours . . . relating to the particular talents and the stronger appetites and greater capacities, compared to the Tutsi and Hutu, that make them specially and distinctively Twa.'[7] There is a strong likelihood that cannabis was naturally occurring in Africa before the custom of *bhang* drinking was imported from across the Indian Ocean. The Twa have a more detailed knowledge of the local flora than any other people, and may well have been familiar with the plant's psychoactive properties. If non-problematic cannabis use is socially embedded among this particular ethnic group, what entitles a national government to introduce prohibitions, particularly when other psychoactive substances like alcohol will still be available? Given that the Twa are a marginalized group within the Rwandan state, politically dependent and economically exploited, is it right for international agencies to press for the criminalization of ancient customs, and to furnish the authorities with the equipment to enforce it?

It is that issue of enforcement that lends such frisson to the issue of drug control. It is one thing to ratify treaties and bring in legislation, but quite another for these new powers to be applied.

For the UN family, the move into drug control is a major departure from such headline activities as disaster relief, immunization campaigns or education projects, which are unequivocally welfare-orientated and empowering. With drug control, the prestige and the moral authority of the UN is being used for something that is inherently controversial.

All drug control is by definition repressive and disempowering, with force being applied against individuals for the greater good and, in the case of the user, their own good. More critically still, the international community condones the appropriation of power by governments with questionable records on governance, corruption and human rights. The UN drug control conventions, reinforced by advocacy by both the INCB and the UNODC to get member states to sign up to them and introduce the requisite legislation, rests on an assumption that these governments are the best representatives of the interests of their people. This may be a tolerable fiction when international agencies work in the field of education, rural development or health care, where the actual project inputs are benign. It becomes dangerously naïve when the specific content of the work is to extend the powers of the state, to beef up the capacity of law enforcement and paramilitary agencies and to enhance the capacity of the state to injure, kill, arrest and imprison its citizens. This is particularly so in countries troubled by inter-ethnic or religious conflicts and/or with no traditions of civil rights.

There is considerable evidence that structural abuses of drug control powers occur in countries with rigorous systems of scrutiny. In the US, for instance, the number of African-Americans imprisoned for drug offences is ten times the number of Caucasians, even though prevalence surveys testify a higher level of drug use among the latter. If this can happen in a large and vibrant democracy, what do we expect from other, less transparent and responsive political systems that UN officials are dealing with? Interestingly, neither the UNODC nor the INCB has set up any mechanism for monitoring the abuse of drug control, or even of engaging with member states on sensitive issues. It is up to civil society organizations like Human Rights Watch or the International Harm Reduction Association to publish lists of countries executing drug offenders. Antonio Maria Costa, the head of UNODC, has admitted in private that he opposes the use of capital punishment, but he is still to come out on public record. For an officer of an organization founded to promote human well-being this would appear as something of an omission. It may be argued that intergovernmental organizations have no business interfering in domestic issues. This sounds hollow, though, when coming from an organization that is assiduously advocating changes in the legislation of countries and the cessation of existing cultural forms for dealing with drugs.

7 How Drugs Became a Development Issue

It is time then to substantiate the assertion that drugs are a development impediment. The first thing to note is that non-traditional, illicit drugs have arrived in the recreational marketplace, with many developing countries now reporting rising incidence of drug consumption. To some extent this is simply a matter of reclassification. Officials responsible for returning the annual monitoring reports to the INCB, or who have been charged with the brief on 'drug abuse', may simply have taken a fresh approach to looking at well-established cultures of consumption, such as chewing coca leaf in Andean countries, smoking *ganja* in Jamaica, drinking *bhang* in India, or chewing khat in Yemen and Saudi Arabia. Alternatively, new scientific evidence may have come to light suggesting new risks and dangers, or changes may have occurred in the patterns of consumption as a result of social processes, such as urbanization, the reconfiguration of families or the dissolution of power of traditional authorities and customs. The alarm over drug trends may also rest on the simple availability of data. Behavioural epidemiology has made great strides over recent decades and has only recently been rolled out in developing countries. Problematic drug use, in other words, may have been around for many decades, but public health sentinels are only responding now that the data has become available.

There is a different argument about the spread of drug use drawing on the analogy of an epidemic to suggest the dynamics of a quasi-natural force. In the absence of a constructive theory of drug use, this remains powerfully suggestive, particularly in policy circles working at a social distance from cultures of illicit drug consumption. But it also links with one of the key operational premises of the control regimes, namely, that drug problems are created by criminal suppliers. It presupposes that people would be 'drug free' if they did not have the opportunity to take them, and that consequently the best protection for society lies in patrolling the borders and policing the distribution networks in order to prevent drugs from surfacing in the first place.

The appearance of drugs like cocaine and heroin well outside the traditional culture zones where these or analogue plant-based drugs were used in the past goes to support this model. One example would be the sudden popularity of heroin along the coast of Kenya, where it is known as Brown Sugar. The Swahili communities have long-established trading links with the Gulf and India, where heroin can be sourced. The original demand for heroin, however, did not come from indigenous users but European, and particularly Italian, tourists. Kicking off in the early 1990s when heroin prices in Europe were still high, tourists found the heroin peddled along Kenyan beaches cheap and of good quality. Within a couple of years a number of local people, usually in contact with tourists, emulated the pattern of use, acting as a bridge group into the wider community. Coastal cities like Mombasa and Lamu now have a local heroin scene with all the attendant problems of acquisition crime and the transmission of blood-borne viruses.[1]

The influence of tourists on local drug use is also found in Jamaica, which has one of the most dynamic drug tourism economies. Since the 1970s Europeans and North Americans have been drawn to Montego Bay and Ocho Rios by the promise of sun, sea and pungent ganja. In the 1970s, however, there was growing interest in cocaine. While Jamaica is not a coca producer, it was easily brought ashore by plane or go-fast (high-powered speedboat) from the Colombian or Venezuelan coast less than 1,000 miles to the south. Popular with holidaymakers to begin with, it soon developed a local market. Some of the peddlers started using it themselves, as did girlfriends, beach boys and the various hustlers providing all manner of licit and illicit services demanded by tourists. When kitchen chemists began mixing powder cocaine with bicarbonate of soda to cook up crack, the local market exploded. In Jamaica and other Caribbean islands, crack is widely regarded as an import by white – North American or European – tourists. It is often compared unfavourably to local ganja, which in the opinion of many aficionados is not a drug but a herb. Conspiracy theories abound over the suppression of the naturally occurring cannabis with origins quite distinct from the European heritage, as part of the ongoing domination of the white man. One island story recorded in both St Vincent and Dominica tells of local cannabis droughts during which crack remains available and cheap.[2] In St Vincent this dates back to 1998, when local police and international security forces supported by US naval vessels eradicated Vincennian ganja fields during Operation 'Weedeater'. Marijuana disappeared from the market and some of the less scrupulous dealers began plying a new trade in crack.

The official position on crack's arrival and pervasion of Caribbean societies offered by national drug councils and enforcement officers points in a different direction. According to this, Colombian drug cartels were exploring new transit routes for US-bound cocaine shipments during the 1980s. Continuing to this day, and part of a tradition of smuggling as old as the European presence in the region, these operations follow similar patterns.

Deliveries are run at night to avoid detection by marine and air patrols, before making landfall somewhere in the islands. Once landed they are warehoused by trusted partners, before being moved further up the island chain, or directly towards US or European end markets. In each island the Colombian cartels have been linking up with operators, some of them hardcore criminals, others simply opportunists. In the first instance payment is made in US dollars, but subsequently partly in cash and partly in kind. Island crime groups then take the cocaine to develop the local market, which can generate a new source of income and a power base.

This pattern has been observed in other transiting routes. During the 1980s heroin and cocaine became popular first in Nigeria, and then in South Africa. There was no geographical logic to either country emerging as a transit route, but trafficking syndicates set up bases in both and began to cover their running expenses by developing a local market. In drug control parlance this is known as the 'spill-over' effect and provides one more argument for raising capacity among local enforcement agencies. This goes in step with another observed phenomenon known as the 'balloon' or, less flatteringly, as the 'sausage' effect. According to this, pressure applied to any particular drug supply route will only push the bubble somewhere else. It is possible to close down the Mexican overland route into the US, say, but that will only reroute the drugs via the Caribbean or West Africa. As international efforts against drug trafficking have been stepped up over the last fifteen years,[3] the organizing syndicates have responded by developing ever more intricate supply routes involving an increasing number of countries.

In each of these, trafficking has left a footprint as some drugs spill over into local markets. The sudden appearance of a crack cocaine problem in countries like Ghana or Surinam can rightly be explained as being supply led. Local users did not create the trade by their demand, but responded to the opportunity of use once cocaine and heroin were being supplied. But it is also testimony to the failure of supply control, because the peripheral drug markets that have emerged and keep emerging along the trafficking networks are a by-product of enforcement efforts that have succeeded in plugging one particular hole, but have failed in stopping the in-flow.

In the main importing countries in North America and Europe prices for cocaine and heroin have been dropping down steadily, while purity remains level. In the US the average price for one gram of cocaine bought at retail level in 1981 was $544.59. In 2003 it had fallen to $106.54. Across the European Union, in spite of considerable variation in policy and market dynamics, the overall trend has been downward. Over the period 1999–2004 overall prices have fallen by 22 per cent while demand has risen steadily.[4]

These are the clearest indicators that supply controls have failed. It is arguable that it is only a matter of time before all possible entry points have been secured. Law enforcement budgets will have to be increased to cover every seaport and airport with extensive screening devices. Until this vision is costed and exposed as Utopian, supply-side controllers can continue relocating into new bases of operation. One region of intense activity over recent years has been the former Soviet Union, with thriving domestic markets, a vigorous supply network via the 'silk route', and a dynamic organized crime scene. Africa, which was explored in the late 1990s,[5] promises a new 'last frontier' for the 2010s, after which China may come into play. In the meantime established routes like the Mexican connection, or the Balkan route along which heroin flows from Afghanistan into Europe, continuously adapt and resurface. In the face of the seeming intractability of the approach, many law enforcement agents have concluded that supply will not resolve drug problems unless there is a reduction in demand.

Crime and corruption in developing countries: assessing policy responses in the English-speaking Caribbean

By accident of geography, the countries of the English-speaking Caribbean lie in the transit zone between large drug consumer markets in North America and Europe, and the main production centres in Latin America. As a result, they have experienced some of the fallout from both: the aggressive and ruthless intrusion of drug traffickers, and the heavy hand of the powerful drug-importing states. The struggle between traffickers and law enforcement is being played out against the backdrop of entrenched indigenous patterns of substance use, licit and illicit, that have since become implicated into the policy formulation, and a sense of unease about changes in the wider political and economic macro environment. Traditional allies in the US and the former European colonial powers have been relinquishing their commitment to the Caribbean region since the end of the Cold War. The 'arch of democracy', as the Eastern Caribbean is sometimes known, did lose much of its geopolitical significance and concomitantly such measures of special treatment as privileged access for its agricultural products to European Union markets. In the region it is further marginalized during hemispheric negotiations between the Latin American bloc of developing countries and the two English-speaking countries of the developed north.

Developing countries that have become centres of drug trafficking operations face a number of instant crime control problems. First is the question of capacity – are the defences adequate for meeting the threat? In the English-speaking Caribbean, for instance, governments became alarmed over the looming threat of drug trafficking during the 1980s, when they measured their own slender resources against the might of the drug cartels. These, it was feared, had the financial resources and the firepower to overcome national security forces and launch full-scale military assaults on the island states. For sceptics the fate of nearby Colombia provided a grim example.

In the 1970s Colombian-organized crime groups had moved into prominence in the Latin American cocaine export trade to the United States. Over the years the heads of the different 'cartels', such as Rodriguez Orejuela in the city of Cali, or the Ochoa family, the Lehder brothers and, most infamously, Pablo Escobar in Medellin, amassed spectacular fortunes. This made them targets for left-wing guerrillas who would kidnap family members and hold them to ransom. The trafficking groups rallied together to form a defensive alliance and strike back at the kidnappers. Soon after, they were again to find a common cause when the United States embassy began submitting requests for key figures to be arrested and sent to the US to stand trial on drug trafficking charges. The cocaine traffickers organized themselves into 'Los Extraditables' and began lobbying the government to refuse these extradition requests. In the first instance they sought a political solution, using the numerous senators and deputies on the pay-rolls of the different cartels to block the requests. At one point there was even a proposal to use their cocaine export earnings to pay off Colombia's foreign debt. As US pressure increased relentlessly and the government began to show signs of giving in, the traffickers sought to reinforce their position by violence. Politicians, high-ranking police officers and judges were being assassinated in broad daylight. Nothing could demonstrate more clearly the weakness of the state and the power of the cartels. In the end it backfired, swaying large sections of public opinion and galvanizing government agencies to build up their capacity by bringing in foreign support. Under the so-called Plan Colombia, the US agreed to a comprehensive assistance programme, including military equipment, technical advisers and financial support. In a bloody, chaotic campaign the kingpins were brought to heel, the big cartels dismantled and many traffickers, including Pablo Escobar in 1993, killed or imprisoned. By the early 2000s the threat of the 'Extraditables' had been eliminated. Successful as the operation was in shoring up government powers, it was an utter failure in stemming the outflow of cocaine into US and other markets. Not only had Colombia become a major producer of coca leaf for the first time in its history, but cultivation and export were often carried out by the very security forces and paramilitaries that had been armed and trained to combat the cartels.

During the early 1990s, however, the outcome of the struggle in Colombia and the Caribbean still looked uncertain. Caribbean governments were therefore responsive to the prodding by the UNODC, the US and the EU to move drug control up the agenda. The sense of alarm about the growing power of drug cartels is well encapsulated by the warnings of the West India Commission, who concluded that, 'nothing poses a greater threat to civil society in CARICOM countries than the drug problem; and nothing exemplifies the powerlessness of regional governments more'.[6] This working group of senior politicians from across the Caribbean Community and Market (CARICOM) drafted a report that was critical in swaying governments in that region to engage with the drug control programmes suggested by their main bilateral partners as well as the UNDCP. At that time, in the words of one US security agent, 'a torrent of drugs was passing through the Caribbean.' The impact was already dislocating the structures of governance in the countries most intricately involved.

At the northern end of the region lie the Bahamas, a 100,000 square mile archipelago of some 700 islands, cays and large rocks. Being within striking range of the US coastline, the people of the Bahamas have a history of clandestine trading relationships with the US. During the Civil War Bahamian vessels were running guns into Confederate ports, and in the 1920s many a fortune was made by Nassau merchants, known as the Bay Street Boys, smuggling rum into any port along the 'dry' Eastern seaboard of the US. Half a century later their descendants were in government to curb the next trafficking enterprise – cocaine. This was a challenging project, as central government control is tenuous on some of the outer islands, where traffickers were establishing themselves. Carlos Lehder set up base on Norman's Cay in the Southern

Bahamas, where he was soon controlling economic and administrative structures and replacing the national currency with the US dollar.

The way that corruption worked at the local policing level is well illustrated by examples from the Bahamian police. Officers in the outer islands were advised not to patrol particular stretches of coastline on a given date or times. Financial rewards for compliance were matched by physical punishments against family members of officers with the impudence to perform their duty more conscientiously.

If drug trafficking groups were wresting control over the outer islands from out of the hands of the Bahamian government, it was a canker at the heart of the Jamaican political system. Since independence in 1962, Jamaican politics has been marred by high levels of violence. To secure electoral majorities in their constituencies, National Assembly members rely on local party activists, many of whom use force and intimidation to keep rivals out. Large parts of Kingston, the capital city, are now a mosaic of party-defined districts in a system known as garrison politics. In return for their loyalty, activists are rewarded with contracts for services. But during the 1980s the Jamaican economy suffered a severe downturn and the bitter ministrations of a structural adjustment programme, which restricted the opportunities for pork barrel policies. No longer benefiting from government handouts, the party machine in some constituencies set out to diversify their income-raising activities.

The island is conveniently located between the Colombian supply routes and northern markets, all the more accessible via large Jamaican diasporas in many US and British cities. Drug trafficking therefore provided a welcome opportunity, leading in the 1980s to the emergence of local crime figures, known as 'dons'. These local big men soon became independent from, though they were often in alliance with, the national assembly member for the constituency, and became the principal political authority and system of government. The hard currency income, the contacts and direct access to weaponry allowed them to loosen the ties with the political establishment and set out on their own. In many of the urban neighbourhoods of Kingston or Spanish Town it is the local don who today upholds basic security and stability and provides at least some level of welfare services. This rise to authority by non-state actors could only emerge in the vacuum left by state withdrawal during the sharp decline of the 1980s. The process is now generating its own momentum, fuelled by income from the international cocaine trade and other criminal operations, and their firepower relative to that of the law enforcement agencies. On occasion dons have challenged the authority of the state by blocking entry to their neighbourhoods to the police and even the Jamaica Defence Force.

Against the backdrop of these external and internal developments, Caribbean states throughout the 1990s began to engage with their major development cooperation partners and multilateral drug control efforts. Given the disparity of resources and power, the small island states have always preferred to negotiate collectively under the auspices of the regional organization, the Caribbean Community and Market (CARICOM), and via intermediaries such as the UN or Organization of American States. This created an opportunity for the UNDCP, which obtained funding from the EU in the 1990s to broker a loose working programme that became known as the Barbados Plan of Action (BPA). It brought the countries of the Caribbean region together with the main donors, the US and the members states of the EU, to sign up to a comprehensive regional programme. Without a closer definition and analysis, 'drugs' were identified as the source of political challenges and a major obstacle to the regions' development goals. The regional office of the UNDCP was strengthened to provide regional partners with the technical assistance without which they were sure to succumb to the designs of the traffickers. Most of the actions itemized in the BPA therefore referred to strengthening those parts of the state that deals with suppressing the drug trade and punishing the perpetrators. In subsequent years, most Caribbean countries began to introduce legislation that criminalized a range of drug-related activities, and to step up efforts by the requisite law enforcement agencies to enforce such legislation.

The document also recognizes the medical and social problems of drug use, and lists a number of recommendations for coordinating therapeutic and preventative measures. With generous EU funding, channelled through the UNDCP, this led to the inception of national drug councils modelled on the National

Council on Drug Abuse pioneered by Jamaica in 1991, and were usually staffed by personnel from national health or education ministries. Linking up with these bodies, the UNDCP began a systematic campaign of raising awareness. Caribbean governments had initially been alarmed by the security implications of the traffick in drugs, but had been sanguine about domestic use. The prevailing attitude of policy-makers and public alike could be paraphrased as, 'not our problem, let the Americans and Europeans kill themselves if that is what they want.' With technical assistance, the UNDCP introduced school surveys and so-called 'rapid assessments' to gather data on patterns of illicit substance use right across the region. The research established levels of drug use prevalence far higher than policy-makers had admitted to. Many older policy-makers and civil society leaders responded with a sense of outrage. Trade union leaders and church councils called for stiffer punishments and even the death penalty for traffickers, and external observers lamented that 'the Caribbean had lost its innocence'.[7]

With a sense of gathering doom spreading in the late 1990s, Caribbean governments began looking for international support to shore up their fragile state structures. In return they relinquished aspects of their hard-won sovereignty by granting access to their territorial waters to the US armed forces in 'hot pursuit' of suspected trafficking vessels via a series of shiprider agreements. These provide for an officer from the Caribbean nation to ride on board US vessels patrolling the area and authorize on-the-spot entry into Caribbean territorial waters. Caribbean governments also signed up to Mutual Legal Assistance Treaties to facilitate the extradition of arrested suspects to the US. Assistance came in the form of hardware, training and rafts of legal instruments wrapped in international conventions on drug control that countries signed up to. These contained clauses to criminalize the possession of small quantities of drugs in countries where marijuana use, in particular, was widely spread. The inevitable consequence has been that large numbers of young Caribbean men have been coming into conflict with the law as drug control moved up the agenda for law enforcement agencies patrolling the high seas and urban neighbourhoods. Prison populations, already comparatively high by international standards, have been on a sharp incline.

By 2005 the Caribbean as a region was competing with the former Soviet Union for the distinction of having the highest per capita incarceration rate in the world. (It is worth emphasizing that this excludes the US, which is by far the world champion in imprisoning its population.) Pressure on the existing capacity of the prison estate led to dramatic overcrowding, and the virtual dismantling of any effort at rehabilitation had the perverse consequence of driving up criminality.

By the early 2000s it was also becoming clear that, while the threat of external aggression against the state had dissipated, the measures taken against domestic drug use were a comprehensive failure. Across the islands, drug use was becoming endemic, yet somehow, the volcano around which society had been dancing – in the words of one commentator – was failing to erupt.[8] What were emerging as serious threats to the social fabric were in fact the product of the defensive measures taken under the influence of international donors. The most immediate of these was a growing volume of petty crime, which threatened the economic mainstay of many countries in the region, tourism.

A cruel logic is at work in small, highly stratified island communities where people who have spent time in prison are practically excluded from the already tight job market. Unable to reintegrate, these ex-convicts enter into the cycle of reoffending, arrest, incarceration and reoffending. The recidivist dilemma is familiar from other contexts, but accentuated by the scale of Caribbean states, where even small numbers suffice to create a critical mass of disillusioned ex-cons to form a criminal milieu. A political initiative that raises the number of people moving through the criminal justice system will push up the spiral of offending before the deterrent effect has had a chance to kick in. First, as one senior prison officer in Guyana explained, the ex-con is an embittered individual and more likely to extend his solidarity to other offenders than the mainstream. This leaves him at best unwilling to cooperate with the authorities, and at worst a willing accomplice for future offences. Secondly, as the numbers of released offenders increase, so offending behaviour becomes normalized. The most alarming feature, however, is the upscaling of offending behaviour.

Erstwhile drug offenders arrested on drug possession charges may not have been criminally active in the conventional sense.

They came into conflict with the law because of their drug-using behaviour, an offence that had no victims other than the perpetrators themselves. After their release, however, the stigma that attaches to the prison experience, and the acculturation to the offending culture within the prison, 'trains' ex-cons in the committal of other offences. Those known in Jamaican patois as 'rude' boys, with low expectations and a drug habit, are now pushed into extra narcotic offending behaviour that soon turns into a criminal lifestyle.

What has rendered this process particularly volatile in the Caribbean context has been the perceived imbalance in the application of the law. While debate rages across the region as to whether smoking marijuana has become 'normalized' or not, there is no denying that levels of use are fairly high. The intervention of the law, therefore, is widely felt to be out of step with cultural mores, and highly randomized. Failure of the judicial system to bring arrestees to trial swiftly exacerbates the problem further. In Guyana during the late 1990s, for instance, some unlucky offenders would have to wait up to two years in pre-trial detention for their possession cases to come before a magistrate. Once in court, the offender may receive anything from a dismissal with a warning to a custodial punishment. Sentencing across the region is inconsistent and erratic, illustrated by observation in a court in St Lucia in 2004, where in the course of a day's work the presiding magistrate sentenced one defendant to six months in jail for smoking a spliff in public, before determining the bail bond for a foreign national caught in possession of several kilograms of cocaine. There is method in such sentencing madness, however, as was revealed in an informal discussion with a senior police officer from one of the UK Overseas Territories. A Colombian go-fast (speedboat) had been intercepted in territorial waters and the crew was arrested, charged and brought to court. They posted a bail bond of several million dollars, were free to leave the court and promptly disappeared from the island. This, according to the officer, was a win-win situation where everybody was happy: the US Drug Enforcement Administration agents had the cocaine, which they could claim as their prize, the Caribbean police kept the impounded boat, and the government enjoyed the cash injection of unbudgeted bail money.

Raising the penalties against drug traffickers has created new opportunities for corruption of the courts, threatening a key pillar of Caribbean governance. Justice is perverted leading to the loss of public confidence in the law. This ever present danger has been actualized by stepping up the war on drugs through the glaring inequity of punishment meted out to different categories of offender and the downright corruption of magistrates. Less dramatically, possibly, is the impact on the capacity of the criminal justice system. International partners, it is to be recalled, have been supporting front-line services for over a decade. The US has led the way by equipping Caribbean law enforcement agencies with weaponry, communications equipment and vehicles. The EU, meanwhile, has been training police and customs officers and funded the formation of specialized anti-trafficking units. The UNODC, for its part, has assisted Caribbean states with the drafting of drug control legislation. As a consequence of these combined efforts at enhancing the capacity of Caribbean states to arrest, prosecute and penalize their drug-offending citizens, there has been a steep increase in activity across the criminal justice system. By the end of the 1990s the courts across the English-speaking Caribbean were struggling to keep up with the sheer case load. The resultant dilemma is illustrated by the civil case of Trinidad, where in the early 2000s the backlog had created waiting times of several years. With the court system blocked up by drug-related cases, it was becoming difficult for citizens and businesses to have their civil cases dealt with in a speedy manner. In effect the law, by working with several years' delay, was ceasing to function as a means of dispute settlement. Prison capacity, right down to police cells, was taken up by drug offenders, many in pre-trial detention. Ironically, even the police forces that had benefited directly from material assistance were being stretched. As one drug squad officer explained in 2003,

> Every time a trafficking case comes up, our officers have to appear in court, first, to give evidence, secondly to produce the exhibit. This means getting a vehicle to take the defendant to court, a separate vehicle for the drugs, both with an escort, of course. Now in Trinidad we only have a small number of senior defence counsels, all of whom have several cases at the same time. All too often we send our men with the defendant

and the drugs to the courthouse only to find that the defence lawyer has not turned up because he is appearing elsewhere in a different matter and the case has to be postponed.

The legal system inherited by Trinidad and other Commonwealth Caribbean countries draws on British tradition and maintains many features based on assumptions from the first part of the previous century. Once again smaller states struggle with keeping systems and structures updated to meet actual needs. Besides, key players often have no incentive to initiate reform. According to the police officer quoted above, legal counsel have no objection, for example, to the formal requirement of defendant and prosecutor having to be in attendance when the judge sets trial dates. Nor do the judges censor defence counsel for failure to appear in court for a hearing. It is difficult to assess in detail the dislocations wrought by the war on drugs onto the criminal justice system. It can be concluded, though, that in response to the perceived threat police, courts and prisons have all been stretched to and possibly beyond the limit.

Over the past twenty years traffickers and law enforcement have been playing cat and mouse over Caribbean waters and airspace. Reports of record seizures punctuate the game with the same regularity as the cries of alarm over proposed agency budget cuts. Fluctuations in flows and seizures may, in the case of the US, result from the revitalization of the Mexican transit route, while the British agencies discovered new West African networks after achieving a fall in Jamaican imports around 2005. In neither market has the sustained enforcement activity in the Caribbean achieved sustained results in the terms of availability. Cocaine remains plentiful and is becoming cheaper. Overall, in other words, it has made little difference with regard to ultimate policy objectives. Local Caribbean markets would seem to be easier to control, as the islands have relatively short stretches of coastline. Yet the combined efforts of Caribbean, US, Dutch and the Royal navies have at best produced temporary cocaine shortages, which are quickly corrected as markets set to work towards an equilibrium.

If cocaine is available and cheap enough for St Lucian jombees (the local insult for crack addicts, derived from 'zombies') to feed their habit from washing cars and other odd jobs, it has not reached epidemic proportions as feared. In all Caribbean countries crack cocaine use has stabilized, perhaps because of effective drug prevention programmes launched by national drug councils and various charities with support from the UNODC. On the other hand, these campaigns have been remarkably unsuccessful in containing marijuana use, which is high and rising, albeit with regional variation. More effective protective factors may be the cultural circumspection towards crack cocaine as a foreign, synthetic drug, and simple social learning processes. Growing up in Kingston, Port of Spain and Castries, young people have the opportunity to learn about the effects of regular crack use at first hand. Watching members of the community losing jobs, families, homes and dignity may be a far more effective deterrent than the legal instruments available to magistrates and judges, particularly in view of the low likelihood of arrest. During a training session at the police training centre in Kingstown, St Vincent, a group of officers made clear why, under normal circumstances, they would simply not bother arresting anyone for smoking drugs, just as they would not arrest anyone for using obscene language, an offence that remains in force on many Caribbean statute books. But if either offence were committed provocatively, showing disrespect to the officer and their uniform, they would take action. In other words, when and how the law was applied was decided not in parliament or court, but by the officer on the beat.

At the heart of the Caribbean dilemma lies the legal equivalence between the two different prohibited substances in use, cocaine and marijuana. Cocaine is a high-value commodity in the developed country markets and has, via spill-over, tourism and cultural emulation, become popular in the region. The sums of money involved in the trafficking business have created dislocations and destabilizing incentives in a developing country economy, while the enforcement efforts have pushed all involved outside of the protection of the law. As courts in the region and in the US penalize offenders harshly, violence has crept into the system and is now fuelled by arms imports from the US as well as from the conflict regions in Colombia. But cannabis, or marijuana, has a very different status to cocaine. It is arguably socially integrated, has become a cultural symbol, and is to all intents and purposes associated with neither crime nor violence. Conflating these two sets of illicit substances in the general war on drugs has not gone unchallenged.

There have been protests by Rastafarians across the region, the formation of an association of ganja farmers in St Vincent and a political démarche in Jamaica to align legal status with public opinion. In 2000 a team of public dignitaries without political affiliation was formed into the Ganja Commission under the leadership of a Professor of Anthropology from the University of the West Indies, and tasked with examining the evidence on marijuana and drawing up recommendations. In an exemplary democratic exercise they consulted with a wide range of stakeholders from across the social spectrum. As so many investigative commissions before them, they concluded that the risk posed by cannabis was widely misunderstood and needed to be addressed via effective public education. At a minimum, trust between the public and the authorities had to be repaired by depenalizing the possession of cannabis. This meant that it would still be considered a crime in keeping with Jamaica's obligations under the three UN treaties, as well as several hemispheric anti-drug conventions, but that these criminal offences would not lead to prosecution. Consumers, it was found, were no threat to anyone but themselves, and were finding the law at best irrelevant and at worst unjust. Punishing these people with fines and imprisonment for repeat offences or non-payment of fines was ineffective in preventing people from using marijuana, an odious abuse of state power, placed a heavy strain on state resources and, finally, was creating a gulf between the law and the people. Placed before cabinet the report was a short-lived cause for celebration among the region's drug policy reformers. On the eve of its publication, however, the US ambassador gave a public warning of the dire consequences facing Jamaica should the recommendations be implemented. In a country as dependent on US economic and political support as Jamaica, this was sufficient to pull the plug on the initiative. The report has been languishing in parliament since and is unlikely to come up again.

What the Ganja Commission and other critics had found was that the adverse consequences with regard to security, crime, public health and so on were not inherent to the drugs themselves. It was this unspoken and untested assumption of the regional programme encompassed by the BPA and propagated by the UNDCP that informed the sets of policies that have pitted governments and legislation against the cultural norm and social reality of their countries. Yet, because control policies are anchored in conventions drafted over half a century ago, and which were poorly informed about culturally integrated cannabis use, they are not open to change or amendment. New insights cannot be used to adjust policies in a developing country, even where the democratic process demands it, owing to the conventions policed by an appointed quango of international experts and enforced by the unilateral action of the US. Hence Caribbean states have continued to adhere to their repressive laws, with the support of the international agencies. The advice has been to tough it out or, in the words of a Bahamian civil servant, 'to imprison our way out of the problem', following the US model.

Hardest hit by this penal approach are the poor, with no money for legal representation, for posting bail or paying fines. They are also most frequently involved in the drugs economy, which across the Caribbean provides an illicit alternative to the formal economy, plagued by structural unemployment. The drug control bodies do recognize the economic needs of the poor, and have strategies to assist farmers in substituting other cash crops for the drugs they have been growing. 'Crop substitution', complemented by 'alternative livelihoods' programmes, has been much vaunted in the key cocaine and opium poppy production areas in South America, Afghanistan and Burma. In the Caribbean a different system was in place in the form of banana cultivation.

Rural communities in the small island states in the Eastern Caribbean, including Dominica, St Vincent, and Grenada, were producing bananas for export to the European Union. These bananas, cultivated by smallholders on mountainous farms, were not price-competitive with plantation-grown fruit from Latin America, and could only be brought to market sheltered by protective tariffs. Under pressure from the World Trade Organization and the US, the EU eroded these trade preferences in the early 2000s, dealing a deathblow to thousands of banana farms and the rural communities across the region. In St Vincent, the number of registered banana farmers declined from 7,800 in the late 1990s to 2,300 in 2003,[9] with knock-on effects as an estimated one-third of the entire labour force was dependent on this sector.[10] This has impoverished certain communities, and has closed employment opportunities for the young, with unemployment rates reaching 22 per cent in St Vincent in 2001. With an underdeveloped tourist sector and tightening restrictions on emigration, the only option left open to many Vincennian men has been marijuana cultivation. The island has now emerged as the largest marijuana producer in the Eastern Caribbean, supplying much of the region as well as markets farther afield. Interviews with marijuana growers in some of the jungle farms in the deep recesses of the island established, unsurprisingly, that many had been dislocated by the changes in the banana regime.[11] Some of the older men are still hankering for a crop that was easy to grow, good to eat and socially acceptable. It allowed farmers to live in dignity with their families in the heart of the village instead of roughing it in makeshift camps in the forest.

The European banana import regime was being dismantled at a time when concerns over Caribbean trafficking were reaching a high point. Yet, in spite of warnings from the State Department and the US military,[12] neither the UN nor the US drug control agencies took any precautionary measures, or even raised the issue of negative crop substitution. The only support that farmers did receive came from programmes funded and implemented by the European Commission. Today St Vincent is producing an estimated 10 to 20 tons of marijuana. Several thousand families are now depending on this illicit crop, particularly in the rural parts of the island. It is remarkable, in terms of policy analysis, how easily drug control could be subordinated to other interests. The opportunity to retain a drug-free island chain was squandered without a murmur in the face of pressure from a particular lobby, in this case agri-business. It seems senseless, furthermore, that large investments are made to induce farmers in one region to switch away from drug crops, while elsewhere nothing is done to defend an integrated licit rural economy, when the threat of drug production has arrived on the doorstep. Finally, it throws into question the claim of control agencies as advocates of the poor in developing countries.

Reviewing drug control in the Caribbean[13]

Within the course of a decade the problems and challenges have once again changed dramatically. The drug control measures brought into place during the 1990s to combat drugs in the Caribbean did succeed in averting the potential threat of takeover by drug cartels. In the light of us military interventions in Panama and Grenada the chances of this being tolerated, in any case, look very slim indeed. Such criticism notwithstanding, the political elites were caught by a sense of abandonment during the 1990s, when the end of the Cold War inaugurated a period of falling us investment coupled with the continuing withdrawal of benefits by former European colonial powers. No longer valued as partners, the small, democratic, free-market countries of the English-speaking Caribbean felt exposed to the harsher winds of a globalizing economy dealing in all commodities, licit and illicit. The message coming from the drug control agencies clearly confirmed national prejudices that the problem facing the region was drugs, and that a bundle of measures at supply and demand reduction level was needed. Well into the next decade all the indices suggest that drugs remain available and popular, but neither regional governments nor international development partners share any longer a sense of imminent social conflict or collapse. The us has redeployed some of its naval units away from trafficking patrols for anti-terror activities closer to home, while the EU has downgraded drug control to a 'cross-cutting' issue and no longer makes a dedicated budget available. Instead, a number of new trends have emerged that, when taken together, pose equally serious threats to the long-term attainment of development goals. Ironically, some of these problems have not been produced by the 'drugs' but by the very measures formulated by national governments with the assistance of the specialized international agencies to combat them. It is the very policy of penalization of drug use, and the criminalization of the users, that is overburdening the criminal justice system and straining social relations. Mass incarceration, in relative terms, has also backfired with respect to crime control and has failed to stem the flow of drugs. The prison experience has in all Caribbean countries enlarged the pool of lawbreakers, and is fuelling a crime wave that is already undermining the tourist industry on which much of the region's economy is hinged.

The conclusion from the Caribbean, then, is that the measures taken against a threat defined as stemming from drugs have eroded the institutions of the state, put stress on social relations and undermined the legitimacy of government. They have done little, to all intents and purposes, to curtail the use and availability of drugs with their adverse public health consequences. Indeed, the Caribbean is the only region in the western hemisphere where HIV is continuing to spread at alarming rates. Not only is crack cocaine a factor, but the attention of public health officials may have been diverted into drug control efforts. Cocaine and cannabis remain within the reach of the poorest street addict in Port of Spain, Roseau and Georgetown, crime is rife, and politics and drug crime are as entangled as ever. Yet the pressure of the 1990s and the attendant alarm over the crises of state have subsided. The UNODC has closed its offices in Barbados, the funding having run out before the mission could be accomplished. Partners, including HM Revenue & Customs and Dutch police, continue to work with counterparts in the region, and have even claimed tactical successes. The strategic coordination of drug control across the board to avert development challenges, however, has been forgotten. Funds for integrated drug control programmes have been withdrawn even though significant quantities of cocaine continue to be funnelled through the Caribbean towards Europe and North America. The one agency that has promoted the 'balanced approach' and vamped drugs as a development challenge, the UNODC, has directed its attention towards other regions. In some of these, including parts of the former Soviet Union, the agency is working against a very different institutional backdrop from the Caribbean. Yet it maintains that its methods, focused on controlling the menace of drugs, can assist the development and transition here as well as anywhere.

8 Drugs and Development Along the Silk Route

Since the fall of the Berlin Wall and the collapse of communism as a ruling ideology in Eastern Europe and Central Asia, the notion of 'development' has been extended to countries moving ostensibly from command economies and authoritarian government towards democratic market economies. While many of these had extensive industrial sectors, excellent health services and education systems, and scientific expertise to match the best of what had hitherto been called the First World, their public institutions and civil society were often much weaker than those found even in many developing countries. Public support by western countries, usually channelled via international agencies, foremost the European Commission, the UN and the Organization for Security and Cooperation in Europe (OSCE), have therefore concentrated on building up the instruments of governance, supporting the development of a modern state and invigorating non-governmental organizations.

This was easier in central Europe, where accession to the European Union provided incentives for recipient governments and a range of instruments. The so-called PHARE programme provided an umbrella for channelling billions of euros into eastern European institutions designed and implemented by the European Commission. The preferred method was to 'twin' institutions in the accession countries with a matching partner from among member states of the EU. The Bulgarian Ministry of Interior, for instance, partnered up with the UK Home Office to draft a drug strategy, introduce drug control legislation, and set up a number of institutions and mechanisms within government. The process was coordinated by a Pre-Accession Adviser seconded from the Home Office to Sofia, supported by more than a dozen short-term experts drawn from different UK government agencies. These experts would visit Bulgaria for a few days at a time to run assessments, draft recommendations and conduct training with their Bulgarian counterparts. The delegation of the European Commission would ensure that technical procedures were adhered to and coordinated with the activities of the European Union's technical agency concerned with drugs, the European Monitoring Centre on Drugs and Drug Addiction (EMCDDA).

Part of a wider strategy for integrating and harmonizing the institutions in accession countries with those in the existing EU member states, focal points were established to collate information on drugs. In the old member states these focal points were primarily located in health ministries, and even non-governmental organizations, and drew on data sets from across the board to provide an accurate picture on trends in consumption and availability, as well as the government responses in the form of a structured annual report. This information is open to the public and organized around a few key indicators: drug-related deaths, drug-related morbidity, drug use prevalence against the major types of drugs, the price, and the purity of the main drugs. Accompanied by technical protocols on how to define and measure controversial questions such as 'drug-related death', the entire system is intended as a set of technical instruments to support policy responses. It has been informed by the successive EU resolutions and strategy papers, in which the threat of drugs is defined as a public health issue requiring a rational, political response based on evidence and a sound understanding of what works.

Countries in the Balkans, Eastern Europe and Central Asia that are not accession candidates, that is are not partners for EU membership, have benefited from technical assistance modalities similar to PHARE. Experts from across the EU have been providing technical and managerial assistance, as well as financial support. Once again, the objectives are manifold: to raise technical, task-specific competence within the wider framework of nurturing good governance, the rule of law, democracy and the fledgling market economy. Without EU membership as a long-term goal, institutional compatibility and the 'twinning' process with existing EU organizations could be dispensed with. For implementation and project management, the EC therefore looked for partners with a mandate, technical competence and a regional presence, which meant, concretely, the UN and the OSCE.

In the drugs field the EC had already established a working relationship with the UNODC with regional programmes in the Caribbean and Southern Africa. These were components of a wider development cooperation programme, funded and managed by the Directorate for Development (DG8). In the late 1990s the competence for drug control was transferred to the Directorate for External Relations (Relex). Upon taking over the drugs portfolio, Relex staff re-evaluated programme priorities according to its own set of criteria. Containing the threats posed by drugs to Europe now took precedence over the consideration of benefits for the recipient. In a quick assessment of the respective risk to European health and security, the officials determined that heroin posed a far graver threat than the cocaine transiting the Caribbean.

For the past thirty years heroin from the 'Golden Crescent', comprising Afghanistan, Pakistan and Iran, had been passing though Turkey and the Balkans into Western Europe. Drug control assistance to Bulgaria, Romania and Hungary was already delivered under the PHARE programme and the administrative responsibility of the EC enlargement directorate. New routes were opening up after the fragmentation of the Soviet Union had facilitated the flow of heroin across Central Asia. It was already known that heroin was leaving Afghanistan across the northern border with Tajikistan, before moving across Central Asia, Ukraine and Russia into Europe. In the poetic jargon of border control, this became known as the 'silk route'.

A quick look at the map, however, suggested a more direct alternative route running via Iran into the southern Caucasus. To counter these eventualities, a number of programmes were developed with the objective of shoring up border defences and strengthening interception capacities in the newly independent countries. They were integrated with other technical assistance programmes for the different regions and known respectively as Border Management Central Asia Programme (BOMCA), Belarus, Ukraine, Moldova Anti-Drug Programme (BUMAD), Central Asia Drug Action Programme (CADAP) and Southern Caucasus Anti-Drug Programme (SCAD). In 2000, just as drug control funds were drying up for the Barbados Plan of Action, EU-funded drug control activities were taking off in the southern Caucasus.

Drug control in the southern Caucasus

The three countries of Armenia, Azerbaijan and Georgia were an integral part of the Soviet Union until 1990. Important aspects of culture, language and religion had survived long periods of Russian occupation and cultural assimilation, and could be revitalized at independence. The political structures, on the other hand, had been thoroughly Sovietized. After two centuries of colonization, there was no cultural memory of an alternative political system to develop into a post-independence political system, Indeed, Joseph Stalin, born and bred in Georgia, is still celebrated as one of the greatest sons of the region. Now part of the EU neighbourhood programme, the countries of the southern Caucasus can savour the prospect of EU membership as a long-term goal, while working through the legacy of authoritarianism. In the meantime they are hemmed in between a resentful Russia, still not reconciled to the independence and statehood of these former provinces, the Islamic Republic of Iran and an increasingly assertive Turkey.

Building up a democratic state in these adverse circumstances is a stark challenge even for countries like Georgia, driven by the popular energy of the 2003 Rose Revolution. The principles of EU engagement in the region have been very clear, defending regional stability, embedding democracy, and promoting the rule of law and good governance in the region. To achieve these objectives, programmes have sought to dismantle the inherited totalitarian state structures, and to assist in the creation of new forms of government. In the drugs field, the SCAD programme had to do both. Drug treatment centres in psychiatric institutions that had doubled up as political prisons had to be turned into centres for the treatment and rehabilitation of addicts, while border services had to be built out of nothing. For the EC this has always been an awkward task, as the creation of the common market with the free movement of goods and people presents the most celebrated achievement of the Union. Seeking to build on the experience of European cooperation and integration, many EC development packages are targeted at regions rather than individual countries. Assistance with drug control was therefore devised for the southern Caucasus, rather than each of the three countries individually. Regional cooperation in this, as in any field, is compromised by the unresolved territorial dispute between Armenia and Azerbaijan. In 1990 the predominantly Armenian population of Nagorno-Karabakh rose against the newly declared independent government of Azerbaijan. Supported by regular troops from the equally new Republic of Armenia, they swept out the Azeri forces to take control of the mountainous region. They have held on to this to the present day, when the area is under the control of an autonomous administration affiliated with Yerevan.

Azerbaijan refuses to recognize the autonomous republic and retains its claim to the territory. It has retaliated by closing the border, suspending diplomatic relations and breaking off all trading and transport links with Armenia. The government refuses to work on any joint regional project, with the exception of SCAD. The only EU, UN or OSCE programme to include all three regional players, SCAD, is run out of Tbilisi, the capital of Georgia, the one country that representatives from the other two can still travel to. Georgia meanwhile has its own share of problems in the two provinces of South Ossetia and Abkhazia, where local militias have seized the offices of states, evicted Georgian troops and declared independence. Though unrecognized by the international community, both statelets enjoy sufficient Russian protection and support to allow them a pretence of government.

It is against this background that SCAD has attempted to create an adequate legal and organizational framework, to support effective border controls, assist with the collection of accurate information on drug use and intelligence on drug trafficking, and to set up drug demand reduction and harm reduction measures. The United Nations Development Programme (UNDP) has been coordinating the programme out of its regional office in Tbilisi, while managing the national programmes from its national offices in Tbilisi, Baku and Yerevan.

Much of the work has focused on border controls. Across the former Soviet Union, the newly created border services are under-resourced and poorly trained. In Soviet times the military carried out this task along the external border, which in most cases was closed. Now border services have to manage a much greater volume of traffic over checkpoints that divide communities spread out over Georgia, Armenia, Azerbaijan and the Russian Federation. Often men with local knowledge have been recruited, sometimes former shepherds and hunters. In the words of one Finnish trainer attached to the Georgian border services, 'these men can shoot to kill, but they don't know how to arrest anyone.' Training of border guards is therefore an important aspect of building an independent, democratic state, though the question remains, what it is that these border guards should be controlling?

No security risks had been identified before the early 1990s when the traffic passed unimpeded. The UNODC helpfully suggested that borders should be secured against drug flows and decided in 2003 to provide drug testing kits to the uniformed guards at Larsi, where Georgia borders on the Russian Federation. At the point of evaluation in 2006 the kit appeared never to have been used. The station commander was perfectly content with visual inspections of travellers and cargo, because, he said categorically, 'no drugs pass along here'.

The same certainty has been shared by his colleagues at Sadakhlo on the Georgian–Armenian border. In the apparent absence of drug trafficking, the UNODC-supplied (and EU-funded) drug testing kit has been stored away in one of two dishevelled huts used by the Georgian border service. The searches of private passenger cars, though unsystematic, can be time-consuming and involve up to fifteen officers. These exercises are not so much about finding drugs, arms or fugitives from the law, than about raising revenue for the border service. The longer the queues of Armenian families returning from holiday on the Black Sea, the higher the informal charges that custom officers can extract for fast-tracking travellers. Evidently many officials, wealthy businessmen and impatient commercial vehicles avail themselves of this service. At this point at least, an unexamined crossing can be easily contrived for unscrupulous travellers with the means to resort to bribes.

The operation is far more organized on the Armenian side, at Bagratashen, where with US assistance a two-storey border post has been set up. The entire procedure appears much more orderly and systematic, even though privileged travellers are still being fast-tracked. Custom officers enter the details of all travellers into a computerized system provided as part of SCAD. For security reasons they cannot recall the information once it has been entered, although if a member of staff from the private company that developed the software happens to be on hand he can help detect and correct erroneous information. The traffic moves much faster than on the Georgian side, as it is the declared intention of the station commander to reduce the number and to improve the targeting and quality of each search, so that customs can protect the border without holding up trade. Drug trafficking is not a high priority: there is another UNODC kit gathering dust in a storeroom.

In 2004 law enforcement agencies across the region seized a total of just under 350 kg of drugs of all kinds, the majority of which was cannabis. This suggests that, in part, the risk assessment of the trans-Caucasian trafficking route as a major corridor for Europe-bound heroin shipments was at best premature. Were it not for the underwhelming performance of the border control services, the low seizure statistics could be construed as evidence of programme success. In reality, though, the multi-million euro investment in SCAD has contributed little to enhance the interception of drugs at the official points of entry in the region. Control efforts, it seems, were always going to founder on the politics of the region.

It is rarely admitted among policy-makers in each country that large tracts of territory in the region lie beyond the writ of national governments and are under the de facto control of armed groups. It is possible to plot a route from the Iranian border with Azerbaijan, through Nagorno-Karabakh, into Georgia, and the breakaway province of Abkhazia on the Black Sea, although there are no indications that any trafficking organizations are availing themselves of these opportunities at present. Most regional efforts seem to be going into marijuana cultivation and export in Nagorno-Karabakh. The UNDP in charge of the SCAD programme does not allow its officers to inspect alleged cultivation sites within the region for fear of offending the Azerbaijani authorities, who may interpret the visit by officers of an intergovernmental organization as recognition of Armenian suzerainty. On the Armenian side all allegations of marijuana cultivation are vigorously denied as Azerbaijani propaganda in spite of rich anecdotal evidence. The officers of the one international programme dedicated to drug control are therefore prevented by protocol from investigating the largest drug-producing area in the entire southern Caucasus.

It would be erroneous to project a Western European accommodation with cannabis onto the Caucasian authorities. There is no distinction in Armenian law between different substances, as found, for instance, in the US classification systems and derived from the schedules of the World Health Organization. The EU has funded legal experts from the UNODC to assist national governments with the drafting of anti-drug legislation under SCAD, yet a system of classification differentiating between the risks to users, families and communities of each substance was not on the agenda. In reality, neither government officials nor law enforcement agents have more than a scanty understanding of the pharmacology, the pattern of use or medical harm of the different drugs that they have been tasked, trained and funded to control. The level of debate is so poorly informed that Hollywood provides an official source of information. In Azerbaijan a department head in the Ministry of Education has published a book on the dangers of drugs for distribution in secondary schools. Without having ever seen any substances himself or interviewing any users, the author based his warnings on pamphlets and American films – not documentaries but feature films.

Many of the government officers whose work has a bearing on drugs in all three countries do have a visceral disgust for drugs and drug users. According to a senior police officer in Yerevan, 'most Armenian parents would rather see their children dead then have them use drugs.' One of his colleagues in the Ministry of Interior swept aside all the evidence about the rising popularity of cannabis produced in Nagorno-Karabakh among army recruits and students to pronounce: 'We can now say with confidence that there are no adolescent drug users in Armenia.'

There is indeed no data on prevalence levels available from Armenia. In Georgia, by contrast, some 24,000 drug users have been registered officially. Of these, around 14,400 are intravenous drug users (IDUs), with a further 16,900 IDUs registered in Azerbaijan. The true figures are widely believed to be far higher. In Armenia, recent changes in the legislation have made data gathering extremely difficult, leaving anecdotal information on cannabis use across different youth cultures and a small injecting drug scene as the only sources of alternative information. What has made this difficult to verify is drug control legislation introduced with the support of international legal experts paid by SCAD to travel to Armenia and present model legislation.

The first laws were passed in 2003, amended in 2005 and driven through cabinet by the head of the police, who has ministerial status, despite the opposition of the Prosecutor General, the Ministry of Justice and the Ministry of Health. The 2005 amendments deleted a clause allowing drug use or possession of small quantities to be punished by a fine under the administrative law. Since 2005 police officers have enjoyed the power to arrest people on the mere suspicion of having used a drug, to hold them for up to 72 hours and subject them to urine tests. Any arrestee who tests positive is transferred to a prison until the date of the trial, and then sentenced to custodial punishment. Within six months of the new law coming into force, more than twice as many people had been arrested for drug offences as in the previous six months. According to drug outreach workers, an even greater number of cases are settled outside the station, with bribes. As a result drug users are now wary about carrying needles with them. This has increased the incidence of needle sharing and thereby the risk of spreading infections. Some drug squad officers have extended their activities by conducting house searches of suspected users and their friends without warrants. The law, then, has hugely enhanced the powers of a police force already riddled with corruption, with the active support of an EU-funded and UN-implemented regional assistance programme.

An even crasser abuse of power was reported from neighbouring Georgia, where police officers were stopping young people to check their arms for injection marks. Anyone caught incurred an on-the-spot fine or, alternatively, imprisonment. In both countries police officers are said to be repeatedly extorting money from the drug users they have arrested for months or even years. Again this process has been aided by SCAD funding for computer programs, allowing police forces to store the personal data of all arrestees. There is little data protection and the idea of expunging data after certain time limits is met with incomprehension. According to one drug squad officer, 'If I arrest someone who was convicted of drug use ten years ago I need to know.' A drug offender, it seems, remains stigmatized and vulnerable to police predations for life.

Focus on Georgia

A number of features render Georgia's drug control profile particularly interesting. First, the political transition, with power being taken from the government of former Soviet foreign minister Shevardnadze during what is known as the Rose Revolution, has engendered a degree of openness and self-critical analysis with few parallels in the former Soviet Union. Part of the reform process has been a remodelling of law enforcement and an admission of widespread graft across the ranks. According to Giga Bokeria, deputy head of the parliamentary Commission for Constitutional and Legal Issues, 'the government and police had a deal – we do not pay your salary, but you can be bandits.' This included arbitrary arrests of citizens, the planting of arms or drugs, and other means for extorting bribes. In 2004 the government began to overhaul the law enforcement system in an effort to stamp out corruption and increase efficiency. Until then Georgia had been one of the most densely policed countries in the world, with one police officer for every 89 citizens, against a range of between 1:250 and 1:400 in democratic countries. Since then the ratio has increased to one officer for every 214 citizens, though many former police officers have been retained as uniformed security guards.[1] In these efforts the government has found itself in a bind. On the one hand, effective and functioning state services are recognized as a precondition for rapid development. On the other, state employment has for decades been the mechanism for social security in a country where macroeconomic changes have yet to deliver alternative job opportunities. With so many people on the payroll, it has been difficult to raise salary levels effectively to stave off temptation and eliminate the culture of corruption so entrenched across the force as well as other agencies.

Development partners from the EU, the US and the intergovernmental agencies have been assisting with a range of programmes to curb the power and the remit of the state, to foster accountability, transparency and the rule of law. Amid this overall engagement the SCAD programme is an anomaly. In Georgia, just as in Armenia, UN experts have assisted with the drafting of drug control legislation that has introduced harsh penalties for forms of behaviour that in the majority of EU member states are dealt with leniently.

It has facilitated the establishment of dedicated law enforcement departments and provided the drug squad with equipment and training. This level of international support has helped to insulate these departments from internal oversight processes and allowed for extraordinary practices to take root. Officers, for example, do not always record the amount of drugs that they have seized, which lends some credence to allegations that drug squad officers have participated in the drug market themselves. Critical voices from civil society organizations even suggest that the very importation and supply of heroin has traditionally been organized by law enforcement agents, who were cut out of the market by the eruption of injecting drug use as a youth phenomenon in the early 2000s.

SCAD, it has to be remembered, was called into being as a pre-emptive measure to protect EU countries from the inflow of Afghani heroin via a new and open route. In the event, the most serious drug trend to materialize unfolded in the opposite direction. It was Georgia where a new drug use pattern exploded overnight, and where the supply was sourced from the heart of the EU itself – France. In the late 1990s, with borders opening and trade in consumer goods thriving, Georgian traders were buying up secondhand cars in Western Europe. Some would stash in their vehicles small quantities of subutex, the commercial term for buprenorphine, an opiate antagonist used in the treatment of heroin addicts and available on prescription in France. Taken orally as a medicine, subutex has psychoactive properties when crushed, diluted and injected. In Georgia, as in other countries in the former Soviet Union, there is no needle phobia since injections were the chosen route for administering vaccinations and other medicine during Soviet times. Public health services would distribute the medication to be injected at home, often by the mother or grandmother. Buprenorphine has the added advantage of leaving a light chemical imprint and therefore escapes detection in most drug tests, which is one reason for its popularity in many Western European prisons. None of the three Caucasian countries had testing equipment capable of tracing the presence of buprenorphine, an important consideration for drug users in these heavily policed countries. Trading at 100 lari for a pill that could be shared by seven people, it was far cheaper than heroin costing 300–400 lari per gram (2006 prices) and gained great popularity.

The spread of subutex across Georgia convinced the authorities that they had a drug problem on their hands and needed to launch a 'drug education' campaign. The Ministry of Interior brought out posters bearing the message 'anything but Subutex' for distribution in schools and universities. The nascent NGO network protested that this suggested to students that they would be better off with heroin. Cynics argued that this was indeed the intended outcome, as the police were controlling the supply of heroin and resented being cut out of the market. Regardless, the high heroin prices in local markets lend some credence to the claim of the border services that only small quantities of heroin pass through the region. It also became clear that active drug users club together to organize their own supplies. Contrary to the calculations of EU strategists, they do not fly to Tehran or Kabul to source their drugs, but north to Moscow.

Russia is also the country from which Georgians have imported the habit of vodka drinking, now widely advertised on billboards and TV screens as the elixir of sophistication. In mountain villages it is making inroads into the traditional pattern of wine consumption. Georgia has a history of wine cultivation going back thousands of years, and there is strong evidence that it was from here that the domesticated Eurasian grapevine was transplanted to other parts of the world.[2] Today it produces a rich variety of wines, often from grape varieties unique to the country. Wine is integrated into social life and usually drunk with food. When groups of family or friends meet to socialize the drinking is punctuated by an appointed toastmaster, the *tamada*, who will regularly interrupt proceedings to make a toast.[3] The sequence of toasts is formalized but then open to the skill and dexterity of the individual *tamada*. In one setting, for instance, the first toast is drunk to welcome the guests, the second to thank the hosts, the next to bless the children, then one's country is toasted, women, our leaders, and so on. In newly independent Georgia British visitors could enjoy the unique experience of drinking to Margaret Thatcher and Joseph Stalin in a single session. These sessions can go on for a very long time, with considerable quantities of wine washing down the Mtkvari river. Yet the alcoholic impact is contained by the lower alcoholic content (Georgian wine often has 8–10 per cent alcohol, much less than what is presently found in Western European or New World wine), the accompaniment of food and, critically, the custom that restricts drinking to the toasts. Between toasts people do not touch their glasses, which puts a break on the overall consumption of the group and establishes limits on the overall length of the session. It also establishes drinking strictly as a social activity. As a result, addiction problems were largely unknown until relatively recently. Indeed, Tamara Sirbiladze of the Bemoni clinic in Tbilisi tells a story from her own university days studying narcology during Soviet times. According to her professor, there were no drink-related problems in Georgia and there was only one alcoholic in Tbilisi. And he, in any case, was a Russian.

Drug treatment in the southern Caucasus

Drug users who want to tackle their problems meanwhile have difficulty in finding help. The only facilities formally offering residential treatment in Azerbaijan and Armenia are the narcological institutes organized along the lines of mental health 'clinics', which were used in former times for incarcerating dissidents. SCAD funds were used in both countries to upgrade and refurbish the facilities. In Baku, the Republican Narcological Institute is an hour's drive away from the city centre, past the oil refineries in what is known as Gara Shahar ('black city'). Secured by a perimeter wall and uniformed guards, it is run along disciplinarian lines with strict controls on the movement of patients. Most of the facilities are used by the staff, numbering more than two hundred, to administer their own activities, while the reported fifteen clients are confined to a single residential unit. The director's office is decked out in Azerbaijani flags and photographs of the former president Haidar Aliyev and his son, Ilham Aliyefi the current president, so the Institute has at least a symbolic function as an outpost of government. All there is to show for the EU support are eight empty beds in an unused building, with the mattresses still in their plastic sheeting.

In Armenia the SCAD funds have gone much further – an entire floor of the Narcological Clinic of the Psychiatric Medical Centre in Yerevan has been refurbished. Treatment is phased from detoxification, stabilization, somatic recovery, to rehabilitation, over a minimum of twenty-one days and maximum of six months. The atmosphere in the upper floor, with its tiled floors, freshly painted walls and clean rooms, is conducive to client recovery. Yet at the point of visit the facility is empty, the sole client having been discharged earlier that day. On the floor below, however, a dozen or so residential patients share a few run-down and dirty rooms, the most noticeable feature of which is the barred windows. It emerges that only certain clients are eligible for treatment in the SCAD-funded facilities, and the director, although aware that keeping his existing capacity under-utilized was unlikely to unlock future funding, was not going to change his system to please donors. Indeed, most of the institute's activities revolved not around the treatment of addicts, but the analysis of urine samples for the police. This was again made possible by SCAD, which had provided the chromatographic spectrometer. The police call up the clinic to collect urine samples and return with the results. During 2005 some 1,200 such samples were analysed by the clinic.

In Georgia, at least, there are alternative facilities run by non-governmental organizations and based on talking therapies. Interestingly, these facilities also find it difficult to access clients, in part because the efficacy of these modes of treatment has yet to be recognized. There is a heavy medical bias in post-Soviet medicine, with little faith in interventions that do not employ powerful pharmaceuticals. While such treatment is available from the Georgian Research Institute on Addiction, it is also not widely utilized. To explain this shortfall, staff have suggested that potential clients may be deterred by the cost of treatment or the fear of the attendant stigma once their addiction is revealed. Alternatively, the incidence of problematic drug use may simply be very low. In the meantime, the institute keeps itself afloat financially by providing drug tests – not for the police, who have their own testing facilities, but for job applicants for government posts. One of the pieces of legislation brought in as part of the UN-sponsored crackdown on drugs is a requirement for all applicants for government positions to provide a negative drug test from the Research Institute on Addiction. The applicants have to pay out of their own pockets, although in most cases little is done by way of testing.

To all intents and purposes, treatment for addiction remains inadequate across the region. The combination of a poor and even punitive legislative system, the criminalization of drug use itself and the stigma attached to it have raised the barriers too high for most problem users in need. In the meantime, the designated narcological institutes have become, or continue to function, as extensions of the criminal justice system in the chemical surveillance of the population, rather than as agencies for public health.

Reinforcing the security apparatus

In all three countries the SCAD programme has helped to upgrade treatment facilities, with the setting up of outreach services that work with active users, and to support behavioural epidemiology activities. Only a fraction of the overall budget, however, was allocated to these public health interventions, with the bulk used to enhance the capacity of the state to apprehend and penalize drug offenders. The identification of drugs as a major social problem and a challenge to the development aspirations of these newly independent countries has played into the hands of the most conservative elements, who seek to preserve both the authority of the state and the privilege it affords its officials, many of whom are members of the old *nomenklatura*, the Communist Party elite. That these outcomes are diametrically opposed to the wider objectives of all development partners escapes notice in the fight against a common enemy – drugs. Prominent in the drug control networks emerging across the region are former members of the national security services, formerly known in the West as the KGB. Many carry their credentials with the pride of any elite, and have visibly mixed feelings about their new employers at the UN. Using western taxpayers' funds to recruit former KGB agents into drug control projects could be rationalized as a form of demobilization. It is equally rational to subject their activities to the closest scrutiny, as there are clear indications that networks of security agents are involved in a range of clandestine activities.

In Armenia one ex-agent has founded the company that is developing the software products used by the border services. This is partially funded by SCAD under a contract awarded by the national SCAD project manager, who happens to be another former national security officer. Yet neither the border services nor the police have full access to the system that has been developed for them. The eight members of the interagency drug profiling unit at Yerevan Zvarnots airport, set up under SCAD, have problems operating the equipment and are working to all intents and purposes without computer support. Half a mile up the road, however, in the head offices of the software company, the system is working perfectly and the names of passengers entering a flight can be called down in seconds. It seems puzzling that a private company has better access to such sensitive data than the law enforcement agencies who are ostensibly owners of system and data sets. More disturbing still is the role taken by private contractors in analysing the data. One of the activities in which they have become involved, it emerges, is tracking the movement of prostitutes to countries like Turkey or Dubai, which falls into their remit under the rubric of 'people trafficking'. As it is known that sex workers travel in groups, they now look for other single women travellers within the age group on the same flight and put them under surveillance. This information is passed on to the law enforcement officers, who pull female passengers aside for questioning before departure or after arrival. What happens next is subject to speculation, but the use of this information to extract financial or sexual favours is a distinct possibility.

A critical appraisal of the EU-funded drug control programme in the southern Caucasus cannot help but question why a multi-million euro programme has been initiated to to strengthen the authority of states that have at best shaky democratic systems and poor records in respecting human rights. Far from assisting their transition towards the rule of law, the SCAD programme in particular and the wider issue of drug control in general have been

shoring up corrupt agencies and provided an alibi for rogue
officers. It has provided a screen for the abuse of state power
over its citizens at the expense of public health and transparency.
While drugs clearly present a challenge to these societies, the
responses fashioned in the name of drug control only compound
the problems without addressing the real risks. The countries of
the southern Caucasus are trying to move towards the ideal of the
modern, democratic state but are pulled into a different direction
by internal forces. The role of security, including the secret police,
the military and the various law enforcement agencies,
is only beginning to be recognized.

Nowhere is this more evident that in the Russian Federation,
where the Federal Security Service (FSB), the successor to the KGB,
has aggregated immense political power and economic privilege
and is now controlling the Kremlin. Contemporary recruitment
patterns are showing the first signs of solidification, as today's intake are often the children and grandchildren of security agents.
Could this be the making of a ruling class based on shared values,
an *esprit de corps* and intense sense of loyalty? To retain and
legitimize its position within the wider society, this new elite will
always be in need of an enemy, which, next to Islamic terrorists,
ethnic minorities and western sympathizers, is readily provided
by the domestic drugs scene. Not surprisingly, then, the head of
the drug control agency, Victor Cherkesov, is a former KGB agent
'who was still hunting dissidents in the late 1980s'.[4]

9 Positives and Negatives of the Drugs Economy

The difficulties arising from increases in crime, corruption and medical problems, ranging from the spread of infectious diseases to psychological dependency, are plain to see for developed and developing countries alike. Indeed, the character of these challenges is the same for governments anywhere, regardless of development status. It is mainly the quality of the threat that divides rich post-industrial nations, worried about obesity and successful ageing, from Third World countries struggling to stave off hunger, improve infant survival and extend school enrolment. Only an internal engine of self-perpetuating economic growth, argues standard development theory, can generate the wealth needed to provide these benefits. According to the school of thought that character-izes 'drugs as a development obstacle', this economic development process is impaired by the illicit drugs trade.

The argument is multi-layered and needs to be analysed at each level. First of all, it holds that productive energies are diverted from more constructive activities into the drugs trade. One of the examples provided is the dominant economic role of the drug trade in urban areas such as the inner-city neighbour-hoods of Kingston, Jamaica, or the *favelas* of Rio de Janeiro. The second argument claims that drug economies will suffer from 'Dutch Disease': drug money circulating through the economy will drive up production costs, rendering alternative economic activities unprofitable.[1] Thirdly, the use of drugs by workers and non-workers alike will adversely affect their productivity. Fourthly, the illicit drug earnings laundered through bogus businesses will distort the economy and impede the growth of genuine enterprises.

On the other hand it is possible to claim positive contributions made by the drugs economy, including informal sector employment, foreign exchange earnings for entire economies and a rare competitive advantage for marginal regions and poorly governed states. The argument made by the UNODC that such income is not invested in productive enterprise is poorly supported by evidence; it is also audacious, given that such investment has been made difficult by the money-laundering legislation pressed for by the agency itself. First, the drugs economy is so vast and comprises so many different operations that it is difficult to arrive at any generalization. Ethnographic accounts of drug dealers in New York, for instance, demonstrate how income is often used quite conventionally to maintain families.[2] As the war on drugs has hit the ethnic minorities particularly hard, some women are using the opportunities arising in the drugs economy, not for diversifying into other criminal areas, but simply to maintain households, including male partners:

> When women breadwinners support men's alcohol and drug use and sustenance need they secure and retain a companion in an era when men, especially minority men, are becoming a scarce commodity due to increased social control policies. This helps keep them anchored in conventional roles and identities and aids preservation of the family.[3]

The proceeds of the drug trade are also used to secure the survival of families in drug-producing countries, such as Afghanistan. The only other alternative for pauperized Afghani families is to give away daughters into marriage.[4] Some aspects of the dynamics of cash-cropping drug products in a developing economy are illustrated by the case of the banana farmers who have turned to cannabis cultivation on the Caribbean island of St Vincent.

Working on patches of land high up on the mountain slopes, farmers can hope to raise three crops in the course of a year. A small farm worked by three or four men may yield between 200 and 1,000 pounds of cannabis, which in 2002 was selling for up to 300 East Caribbean dollars (US$110.00) per pound. In most cases the farmer has been close to subsistence levels in the run-up to the harvest and suddenly finds himself in possession of a large amount of cash. The first test is to bring this money home, past the dangers of a forest road and the temptations of the city lights. These challenges are faced by farmers taking produce to market all over the world and are the stuff of folklore in many traditions. Yet in St Vincent the farmer faces danger not only from thieves and robbers, but also from police and soldiers. Moreover, even when he reaches home he won't be able to bank his money since he cannot account for how he has come by it, as is required under anti-money laundering legislation introduced under the BPA. Storing wads of cash under the mattress carries the risk of attracting the attention of criminal elements in the neighbourhood and raises the temptation to spend it quickly on consumer items, such as motorbikes or 'boom boxes'.

It is ironic that legislation brought in as a package of drug control measures, and advertised as a way of reducing crime, has effectively contributed to destabilizing vulnerable communities since these are no longer able to use the banking system for their savings and investment. By injecting large amounts of cash into areas with poor levels of security, the policy has created opportunity for violent crime and has lowered the safety of families overall. We find, in summary, that the initiatives launched at international level to impede the cashflow of organized crime groups and to protect the financial system only accentuate the deprivations of disadvantaged rural populations in poor countries, who have no voice or representation at the negotiating table. It does little to dissuade farmers from planting cannabis, because they have so little choice.

This is, of course, the overriding reason why farmers in developing countries turn to drug crops in the first place. In Afghanistan, poppy cultivators will happily switch to other crops if this makes economic sense. They do not produce opium because of some criminal disposition, but because poppy provides maximum stability in a low-security environment. Farmers will turn to food crops such as wheat, onions and potatoes, provided that they can obtain the necessary farming inputs, fetch good prices and sell the crops on functioning markets.[5] Equally in the opium-producing hill country of Laos, 'farmers readily surrendered the poppy culture if alternative cashcrops became available.'[6]

In both countries the vast expansion of opium production was a function of market signals and the devastation of war. Laos was ravaged first by the fight for independence and subsequently the ideological rivalries between communist factions. In Afghanistan the destruction of the general fabric of rural society by the Soviet occupation created a necessary precondition for the opium economy. It has since driven the country into a vicious cycle, where opium provides the best insurance to farmers in an unstable political situation, while attracting the interventions of external forces and the criminal elements that prevent the country from gaining the very stability necessary for economic growth. Blunt measures for controlling the problem can be counterproductive. Eradication, for example, has worsened the problem of opium-related indebtedness, as farmers whose fields have been eradicated fall deeper into debt, which they can manage only by planting a fresh crop of poppy. The notoriously successful Taliban opium ban – as well as more recent campaigns – has therefore created a class of desperately poor farmers forced into mortgaging land, giving their daughters away into marriage, selling household goods to pay off debt, in addition to producing more opium. Even where local reductions can be achieved, this has only had the effect of shifting production to other established cultivating areas or to new areas. Eradication at a time of rising demand, sets perverse incentives by boosting farm gate prices, which helps to spread poppy cultivation across the country.[7] Moreover, in these eradication exercises poorer farmers seem to be disproportionally affected while the better off can often escape by means of political connection or bribes.[8]

Poverty alone, it seems, does not explain why certain countries emerge as drug producers. If it did, the largest coca producer in the western hemisphere, it has been suggested, would not be the middle-income country of Colombia, but Haiti.[9] Other factors are required, such as a cultural history of use of the psychoactive substance in question and a sufficient level of organization for integrating drug production into the wider economy. It is this combination of variables that explains the predominance of Bolivia, Colombia and Peru as by far the most significant coca producers for most of the twentieth century.

There is yet another twist to the issue of drug production, highlighted in a study of Afghanistan, Burma and Laos. By remarkable coincidence these three largest opium producers were all Cold War flash points and arenas for CIA activity. In each of these the secret services cultivated hill tribes, who, far from government reach, became centres of anti-communist activity. For the external CIA agents the expansion of poppy cultivation proved serendipitous, in that it provided an endogenous form of income for their clients that reduced dependency on US support. Production shot up exponentially in all three countries. In Burma it rose from 18 tons in 1958 to 400–600 tons in 1970, and in Afghanistan production increased from 100 tons in 1971 to 2,000 tons by 1991.[10]

The clandestine promotion of drug production by US secret services appears contradictory, given that the US has always been the most vociferous activist for drug control. Yet it is not unusual for secret services to collude with criminal elements if this provides a perceived advantage in the defence of national interest. Indeed, the Drug Enforcement Administration has repeatedly complained about its efforts being thwarted by other agencies.[11] The war on drugs has on successive occasions been subordinated to what the secret services have considered as their more central tasks, such as the war against communism in Asia and Latin America, although the long-term consequences of such activities are increasingly being criticized for contributing to 'blow back'[12] and for leaving a legacy of ashes at home as well as abroad.[13]

Coca cultivation

A different pattern of production and consumption still obtains in the coca complex of Latin America. During the 1990s coca cultivation in the two traditional producing countries, Peru and Bolivia, was driven back with considerable US involvement and at great economic and social cost. In Peru, large sections of the security services, the Servicio de Inteligencia Nacional, under the leadership of Vladimiro Montesinos were simultaneously involved in both coca crop eradication and cocaine trafficking, while the disaffection of farmers fed into the rural insurrection organized by the Maoist movement of the *senero luminoso* (the 'Shining Path') across large parts of the country. In Bolivia entire coca-growing districts came under quasi-occupation by the armed forces, sparking off confrontations with farmers. The coca growers (*coqualeros*) organized themselves politically and started campaigning. Ultimately the agitators succeeded in overthrowing the government and electing one of their number: in 2004 the former coca farmer Evo Morales became the first national leader of native American origin to lead the country. In the meantime farmers in Colombia, who had never cultivated coca on any scale before, began making up for the shortfall. By the late 1990s Colombia was the largest coca producer in the world.

To better understand these unintended political outcomes, which were deeply damaging to the long-term interests and standing of the US in the region, as well as to the social and economic development of the two countries concerned, we should consider the threefold fallacy of crop eradication-centred drug control policy.

Firstly, it is culturally insensitive, as coca production has been established in Bolivia and Peru for centuries and has deep cultural roots. The bulk of coca production has traditionally been and remains for local consumption, not for cocaine production. Banning unlicensed coca production caused tens of thousands of coca-producing peasants to lose their livelihood, simply because some of that production was diverted for refinement into cocaine that was being produced and consumed overseas.

Secondly, it is economically anachronistic, since the crop substitution projects advocated so vigorously by the UNODC, and funded by agencies such as the United States Agency for International Development, are based on an already discredited model of economic planning. At a time when experts from the World Bank and the International Monetary Fund were exhorting Latin American policy-makers to cut government assistance to the agricultural sector and to align their economies with the demand and rigors of the market, drug control experts were telling Bolivian farmers that they should be growing fruit and flowers instead of coca.

Thirdly, ignoring the fundamental laws of demand and supply, the drug control technocrats were overwhelmed by the subsequent displacement effect. With eradication adding to the cost of production in Bolivia and Peru, coca cultivation relocated to Colombia in another instance of the 'sausage' effect.

In view of the hefty financial commitment to the ongoing coca eradication programme under the auspices of Plan Colombia, this deserves some reflection. For more than a decade planes have been dropping their toxic loads on the fields of poor farmers in one of the ecologically most diverse environments, all to prevent 'addicts' in the us from snorting or smoking the chemical derivatives of the coca leaf. Yet the farmers in Colombia's Putomayo province are often new to coca. There is no history of either coca cultivation or coca use in Colombia, but today it is by far the world's largest producer and exporter. This is not testimony to the criminal tendencies of the Colombian peasantry or to the calculations of the guerrilla or terrorist movements that draw rents from coca farmers. It is simply the workings of market mechanisms, with Colombian production rising to fill the gap created by coca eradication in Bolivia and Peru.

Already the consequence of the Colombian eradication campaign is being felt in neighbouring Ecuador and Venezuela, where coca production has been reported from regions bordering Colombia. In the meantime, with focus and investment shifting away from Bolivia and Peru, coca producers there are once again re-entering the export trade. Supply side-centred drug control, then, has this counterintuitive consequence of spreading the very phenomenon that it ostensibly seeks to suppress. Short-term results can be achieved in a particular area, but only at the cost of displacing production to other regions. The interdiction programme only adds to the spectacular value increases that coca undergoes across the various stages of the commodity chain. This may have increased the attractiveness of the industry to the newcomer, meaning that 'interdiction may in practice turn into a coca price support programme'.[14] The problem is that drug production, like trafficking, leaves a footprint in terms of criminality, corruption and the loss of government control.

The reason that this well-evidenced and theoretically predictable result does not loop back into policy formulation is rooted in agency politics and one of the most notable features of Plan Colombia – outsourcing. Many aspects of this particular part of the war on drugs have, in fact, been privatized. The planes spraying glyphosate over the coca fields, the radar control systems scanning Andean skies for trafficking planes and the training of

Colombian troops are all operated by private-sector companies, whose main loyalty is to shareholders. Their ultimate interest, then, lies not in eradicating coca but in continuing the contract.

For Third World countries with any level of drug crop production, the most serious development impediment is in effect to become implicated in the war on drugs. The measures introduced to suppress production or trafficking will in all likelihood exacerbate existing social tensions and have a devastating effect on security agencies and the criminal justice system. Drugs themselves, providing an economic and political opportunity from which farmers can at best hope to eke out a living, are just one element in a chain. Whether the key beneficiaries of the drugs economy are criminals or the state, depends on the determination of legal status, as the example of khat goes to show.

10 The Khat Economy

Khat, *Catha edulis*, is the latest, though probably not the last, psychoactive substance to transform from a regional trading item into a global commodity. The process is currently masked because mainstream western consumers have not taken up the habit. Within many of the communities affected in developed and developing countries alike, however, the sudden appearance or unprecedented availability of this drug has been the cause of considerable alarm.

Until the end of the twentieth century khat use was confined to the production areas of Yemen, southern Arabia, the Hararghe highlands of Ethiopia, the Nyambene hills in Kenya and their immediate environs. The plant flourishes in an equatorial climate at an altitude of about 1,500–2,500 m, where it can grow in excess of 24 m. In contrast to most psychoactive substances, khat is taken by chewing the unprocessed leaves and twigs in their raw form. Cathine and cathinone, two of the naturally occurring psychoactive alkaloids found in the leaves, are highly unstable and degrade within less then 72 hours. Only the construction of roads and the development of commercial air cargo made possible the export of khat from the 1980s. New markets have typically been opened up by migrants from the khat zone. In East Africa this process has been driven by Yemenis, while in Europe and North America the main consumers are Somalis, who are themselves recent converts to the khat habit.[1] In countries like Uganda, farmers have responded to market signals and embarked on small-scale khat cultivation.

Khat is classified as a stimulant. Within ten to fifteen minutes of onset it provides a high-energy rush that lasts for twenty minutes and is followed by a longer period of dreamy introspection known in Arabic as *mirkana*. Experienced users distinguish several stages of differing quality in the 'high', and wrap up the session within three hours. The intensity of the 'buzz' and the length of the experience is determined by the quality of the leaves, their cathine and cathinone content, and the number of 'bundles' that the chewers consume in each sitting. In the heartlands, however, khat sessions were traditionally integrated into the daily cycle of chores to provide entertainment and relaxation, and were punctuated by the obligations to work and family.

Khat, by heightening the senses and stimulating the mind, has both inspired spiritual fervour and drawn moral condemnation, particularly from the followers of Wahabist Islam, who are in ascendancy across the Arabian peninsula. Policy-makers have often taken the view that khat adversely affects productivity and diverts resources. Most of all they have been concerned that the khat chew provides a rare opportunity for socialization. Repressive regimes, including successive colonial administrations, the theocracy of Saudi Arabia and the military Somali dictator Siad Barre, have all tried to ban khat, with varying degrees of success. In this endeavour they have enjoyed the full support of the international drug control establishment. In 1933 the Advisory Committee on the Traffic in Opium and Other Dangerous Drugs of the League of Nations discussed khat for the first time, but was unable to agree on a course of action. In 1962 the Commission on Narcotic Drugs determined that clarification on the chemical and pharmacological identification of the active principles of khat was needed.[2] Funds became available via the UN Fund for Drug Abuse Control for the formation of an experts group on khat meeting in 1983 at an international conference in Madagascar.[3] The WHO expert committee concluded that there was sufficient evidence to justify a technical review in 2002[4] and the INCB, in its Annual Report for 2006, made a strong recommendation that khat should be brought under international control.[5]

While many countries, including the US, Canada and Sweden, have anticipated tighter international restrictions in their respective national legislation, many others, including the main producers in Ethiopia, Kenya and Yemen, but also the UK and the Netherlands, have not. The contrast among the importing countries has been remarkable. Against a general backdrop of high levels of poverty and social exclusion among the Somali communities in all points of immigration in Europe and North America, the countries in which khat is banned score yet another disadvantage – the breakdown of trust between the community and the police. In Toronto zealous policing has led to the physical abuse of Somali suspects and has sparked off riots over arrests of alleged khat dealers.[6] Perhaps the worst aspect is the regular descent of police officers onto Somali cafes and restaurants, where men are made to open their mouths so police officers can satisfy themselves that no khat is being chewed.

North American and Scandinavian markets are now being supplied by well-organized trafficking networks, who have taken to recruiting British and Canadian nationals as couriers for delivering their cargo. The prohibition of a cultural pastime against the backdrop of persistent demand has created a criminal economy with predictable consequences. In Scandinavia the trafficking groups have already diversified their activities and are now carrying cocaine and cannabis as well as khat. As the penalties against khat have been raised, the tariff differential between offences relating to khat and other drugs has narrowed, making it more economical to deal in substances of higher value.

One of the reasons for the ban, and an argument advanced for the reclassification of khat in the UK, is the alleged adverse effect of khat on the integrity of Somali families. It is claimed that men abandon their loved ones to spend time and money in the khat cafes (*mafrishes*). Instead of caring for their dependents, finding work or learning English, they are getting high, and becoming addicted and mentally unstable. These are powerful and entirely plausible arguments, reminiscent of the calls of nineteenth-century temperance campaigners, who saw the demon drink as the downfall of the labouring classes. This also provides an easy response to deeply entrenched and complex problems; it furthermore shifts the burden of guilt onto the victims of deprivation and exclusion. The evidence from studies among UK Somalis, however, suggests a far more complex situation, with many families fractured long before the arrival of husbands and fathers. In many cases women and children found asylum long before the men, who followed years later. By then their families had adjusted to a new life and were reluctant to return to a traditional patriarchal structure, especially when the role of breadwinner had been compromised. Most Somali refugees are largely dependent on social security payments, and middle-aged or older men with few appropriate qualifications, poor language skills, no support networks or political contacts are firmly shut out of the job market. In addition, many had been brutalized during the long years of civil war and were suffering post-traumatic stress disorders.

For many Somali men in the UK and the Netherlands there is solace in the pharmacological uplift of khat and the company of fellow nationals. While a regular habit does prove both a drain on resources and a block to integration, removal of this one factor is no guarantee of rapid social inclusion. The social profile of Somalis as one of the poorest immigrant communities, with high levels of unemployment, poor educational attainments and high welfare dependence, is similar for countries with prohibitionist and permissive khat control regimes. While a ban may succeed in preventing men from gathering in *mafrishes* for a communal chew, they do not convert this into more time spent at home with their families. In Canada much of this time seems to be invested in running across town to find somewhere to score an illicit bundle, chasing leads and swapping rumours of imports. Once the khat is bought, the men do not chew it stretched out companionably along their divans, but while walking the streets or cruising in their cars. Each bundle trading at CAN$50–70 is a far greater burden on the fragile family budget than the £3–5 it costs in London.

Across the UK there are several hundred cafes or *mafrishes* selling khat, providing one of the few economic opportunities where Somalis have a clear advantage. In many cities Somali immigrants congregate in neighbourhoods where *mafrishes*, cafes, shops, and telephone and banking services provide some form of community. It is also the dynamo for economic development, which promises a better future and attracts Somalis from other parts of the diaspora, including Sweden. Starting a business is far less cumbersome in the UK and accumulating capital is much easier; this includes, of course, by trading in khat.

Like all psychoactive substances, khat is implicated in a number of mental health conditions. A number of case reports have recorded instances in Europe and North America where khat is identified as an aggravating factor. Moreover, in Somaliland, the as yet unrecognized breakaway northern part of the collapsed state of Somalia, endemic levels of khat use parallel high prevalence of serious mental disorders.[7] Yet the authors are clear that a direct causal relation cannot be established. Indeed, the literature so far cannot state positively that khat has any adverse effects on its users.[8] While it may complicate some conditions, it may arguably be a form of self-medication for others. It is certainly used as a performance enhancer by agricultural labourers, students studying for examinations, long-distance drivers and nightwatchmen.[9] Temporary increases in performance may of course be compensated by subsequent lapses, but these rhythms may also be managed perfectly well within established cycles of work and rest.

There is more concrete evidence for the economic benefits of khat in the key production areas of Haraghe, Ethiopia. Farmers supply a network of markets where khat is bought up, graded, packaged and sold on to the large urban market within Ethiopia and export. Over recent years cultivation has become established in many other parts of the country, as improvements in the road system have facilitated the marketing of the crop. Most producers are smallholders, who intercrop khat with food crops and cultivate it for sale in local markets. In contrast to coffee, the other mainstay of Ethiopian export agriculture, khat has the advantage of price stability based on strong domestic demand. It is also a hardy crop, with few demands in terms of input and labour, and therefore favours the rural poor. Rising khat production over the past decade is positively reflected in the contribution that it has made to the revenue collected by local government. It is one area of the economy where there has been dynamic development, at a time of stagnation and arrested development.

Between 1990/91 and 2003/04 Ethiopia earned over us$413 million from exporting 86,625 metric tonnes of khat. Over 10.7 billion birr was collected in revenue between 1980–2002 from taxing domestic and export trade. Khat tax revenue as a share of GDP in Ethiopia averaged 1.7 per cent for the 1990s, while public health expenditure as a share of GDP averaged 1.2 per cent, which means that khat revenues more than finance national expenditure on health.[10]

Ironically perhaps, the khat economy has emerged without any support from agricultural extension services or development inputs. The importance of khat as a foreign exchange earner for the Ethiopian economy is all the more significant in that it is the product entirely of endogenous entrepreneurship. The positive benefits for the national economy, for rural producers and a wide range of ancillary service industries may well accrue precisely because the entire process, from the farm to marketing, export and overseas distribution, is in the control of small-scale African enterprises.

The positive knock-on effects are ready for all to see in the Eastleigh district of Nairobi, where literally thousands of people are employed in preparing khat for export. Every day the produce arrives by truck from the production areas to be sorted according to quality, is then wrapped into banana leaves, packed into wooden crates weighing 40 kg each, and then taken to the airport. It can also be seen all over Kenya, where the sale of khat provides tens of thousands of women traders with a precarious livelihood.

Less dramatic than the airborne export is the more gradual extension of the khat frontier in East Africa. Farmers in Uganda have begun producing khat in sufficient quantities to supply a lively khat-chewing scene that has sprung up in the centre of Kampala. To the residents of East Africa's rapidly expanding urban conglomerations, khat provides an alternative form of recreation. In the Kisenyi district of Kampala a number of simple establishments offer fresh bundles of khat and rough benches where customers can sit and chew. It attracts aficionados from different social and ethnic groups, and provides a low-cost source of entertainment. Overlooked in the discussion of mental health, diversion of income and impact on productivity is the principal reason why people all over Africa are increasingly inclined to chew khat – the pursuit of pleasure.

11 Drugs and the Management of Pleasure

The absence of pleasure as a category for consideration is an unwholesome elision in the discourse on drugs that needs to be rectified if an appropriate policy is ever to be formulated. We have defined the drug control system as part of the Enlightenment project, with an emancipatory ideal and a progressive teleology. It was formulated by an ascending class, the bourgeoisie, during the early modern period and furnished with their evolving moral and aesthetic values, which owed much to the Protestant experience of religion. One of the central thematic areas of the Protestant ethos was and is the management of pleasure, particularly in relation to consumption and intoxication. It is important to remember that much of the Protestant critique, and particularly that formulated by its so-called Puritan denominations, was not a denial of pleasure per se. There were strictures on dancing and certain forms of music, on libertine sexual conduct, bans on blood and other types of sport, and on consumption of both food and drink. But the exhortations of the Puritans do not amount to a Yogic denial of the world itself, or the embrace of pain as advocated by some of the more extreme Catholic sects, to share in the sufferings of Christ on the cross. Puritan morality censured those forms of entertainment that were deemed degrading or exploitative, and indulged in what was known as 'beastliness' in the eighteenth century. The purpose of the project was to replace these with other more uplifting pastimes, allowing for self-improvement. Hence the wine was to be poured out, but the cup was kept and filled instead with a drink that cheered – stimulating tea, which kept the mind clear and the body coordinated.

Consumption was readily embraced as the earned reward for work, a predisposition that paved the way for production increases and cumulative innovation. In the employment of psychoactive substances the contrast between Catholic and Protestant uses of cocoa is notable. For the first century after contact with the Americas, the Catholic clergy kept cocoa as a closely guarded secret. Unsweetened, this nourishing and bitter drink allowed monks to concentrate on their devotional duties without interrupting their fast. In the nineteenth century Protestant entrepreneurs in Switzerland and Holland combined it with sugar and pasteurized milk into an energy-rich snack for the rising number of urban workers.

While this emphasis on work continues an old Christian tradition of disciplining the flesh, the Protestant ethic refines the mortification into a fulfilment of duty that feeds into an ethos of liberation. It is through work that people can free themselves from the chains of poverty, ignorance and servitude. The self-determining, autonomous subject of history was realizing the dignity of man. In the perfection of skills and the realization of gifts, people would be able to actualize themselves. To that end pharmacological aids are readily assimilated, be these tea, sugar, cocoa or – by the emerging Yuppie in the 1970s – a dabbling with cocaine.

The object of consumption becomes abhorrent, however, as soon as the pattern ceases to be utilitarian and becomes an end in itself. And once the consumer is compelled by the object to direct activities towards its consumption, the very autonomy of the human subject is in jeopardy. He is no longer master of his own destiny, but an object driven by the desire for consumption. Moreover, this is no longer the free-willed pursuit of pleasure, but the effect of bio-social determination.[1] Not only does this frustrate the efforts of the individuals to fulfil their potential, but it is a menace to the social order, especially when these patterns of consumption are endemic among groups of people who actively seek, or would passively benefit from, the categorical reform of the system. It can at worst fan the flames of revolution, and at best lead to drops in productivity.

There have been successive attempts at channelling the use of mind-altering substances under what are now known as public health initiatives. The most common one found in all western countries is the exhortation to enjoy alcohol sensibly. This is a rare concession in official, that is to say government, formulated discourses that pleasure is indeed a factor in the use of substances. Alcohol advertising, of course, has always been based on hedonistic appeal, suggesting that alcohol was not simply a factor in, but a precondition for adult pleasure.

There are strong indications as to what is meant by sensible alcohol use, including refraining from driving, staying within limits and care of personal safety. Yet there is also an inherent contradiction because alcohol is used precisely to leave sensibility and all the other constraints behind. Indeed, for most people in the UK alcohol is the quick, cheap ticket to deactivate our social inhibitions and take leave of our senses. Fortunately, for most this is a temporary departure: even at a time of rising concern over alcohol misuse, it is accepted that the vast majority of drinkers return to a state of steady sobriety.

Interestingly, the same is the case for most consumers of illicit substances. The vast majority of cannabis smokers, including several members of the Cabinet, return to sober, work-governed normality.[2] For a growing number of people the regular but controlled use of a range of substances is a part of their recreational repertoire.[3] Indulging in illicit pleasures at the weekend or over a holiday is a voluntary decision, not a craving. In the UK, as in most European countries, government messages on drugs are mixed. Policy documents are full of tough talk about fighting drug trafficking, disrupting markets and going after the dealers. Yet there is also a strand of harm reduction (HR), based on an acceptance of drug use and aiming at reducing the risks it entails. Messages about the dangers of needle sharing are not that different, in principle, from the call for sensible drinking. As are the leaflets, websites and packs targeted at minorities, such as clubbers and other groups of young people. This includes information about the effects of drugs, both desired and unwanted, the inherent risks and how to contain them. Leaflets on MDMA, for instance, will warn against dehydration. In some European countries clubs may even provide pill testing by a laboratory, where pills are analysed for adulteration and impurities. Though these activities are normally contracted out to non-governmental organizations, they are government-funded and in support of general harm reduction principles. Yet the important concession of the HR discourse is that drug use is a voluntary choice, not the product of cravings and addiction.

Another revealing trend has been the alcohol industry's reaction to the promise and popularity of illicit substances. Many alcohol products have been repackaged with the introduction of high-strength bottled beers, iced lagers and white ciders, alcopops and bottled spirit mixers, and the promotion of high-strength spirits consumed as 'shots' or 'chasers' alongside beer.[4] Accompanied by a redesign of bars and drinking venues, with an emphasis on experience and style, they have targeted a clientele who had already been socialized into illicit drugs as part of their early consumer experience, and were prepared to experiment. Key to the success of these ventures in the new 'night-time economy' is the realization that risk-taking is an inextricable part of the pleasure complex, including the pharmacologically induced altered mental states.

In a political and social sense, these pleasures, whether gained from licit or illicit drugs, are quite innocent. They are not part of a 'dropping out' or a turning away from society. Much of the policy on drugs is still modelled on the image of the drug user as rebel, featured for instance in Harold Finestone's work with African-American heroin users in Chicago during the 1950s. They identified themselves as 'cats', puzzling creatures of contrasts, defined in opposition to their antitheses, the 'squares'. While the square worked the cat would hustle; while the square would live a humdrum routine, the cat was spontaneous; while the square pursued respectability the cat went for kicks. Kicks were invariably pleasures that were tabooed and illegal; heroin was the ultimate kick because 'No other substance was more profoundly tabooed by conventional middle-class society.'[5]

Today's clubbers, ravers and bingers, by contrast, do return to the office on Monday morning to pursue their careers. Many regard these weekend excesses as well-deserved rewards for their professional success. Drug use no longer forms part of an alternative reward system for social dropouts, but is an aspect of a calculating hedonism,[6] where pleasure is integrated into the rhythm of work and life. It may, in the sense of providing a vent to the pressures of work and life, prove to be a facilitator for social contact, not too different from the coffee machine.

It would therefore be useful to revisit the purpose of the Puritan objection against the background of seventeenth-century Europe, still suffering periodic visitations by the horsemen of the Apocalypse – famine, epidemics, warfare and pillage. The economy was governed by scarcity, with a constant need to raise productivity and output. In this positive assessment of work as the key to resolving humanity's afflictions lies the root of a very contemporary optimism in progress as an ineluctable historic determination, which will deliver ever rising material wealth and corresponding human happiness.

The process is strictly 'this worldly' about increasing, not negating, consumption, albeit only of such products and produce that do not overly distract from the central task of self-propelling, cumulative growth. Alcohol and opiates were problematic, in the same way as the more indulgent forms of sexuality, in that they distracted and debilitated from the worldly mission of work, and presented alternative goals for human ambition. Had the objection been simply to the altered state per se, the phenomenal enthusiasm in the early nineteenth century surrounding the scientific exploration of novel substances, such as nitrous oxide, would be hard to explain.[7] The substances that subsequently became known as drugs were such anathema to the bourgeois sensibility because they induced the utter dissolution of the work ethic, first during the state of intoxication, then by directing human endeavour to the gratification of the habit, and thirdly, when taken by the lower classes, through their potential threat to the social order.

The techniques developed throughout the eighteenth and nineteenth centuries to control the human body, as documented by Foucault, were designed to improve productivity by coordinating inputs and reducing waste. Reactions to this rationalization of human functions included the discovery of the unconscious in the late nineteenth century and its diverse neurotic manifestations. With the increasing technological complexity and the commodification of an ever growing register of goods and services, the world became, as Max Weber put it, disenchanted. Urbanization triggered the growing isolation of people, who were fragmented into smaller families and lost their sense of community as the village and the tribe were being replaced by the imagined community of the nation. The human need for social bonding, for society to get together and celebrate itself, as stipulated by Emile Durkheim, had to be met by different mechanisms. Sports, popular music events, festivals and, of course, attendance of religious services all provided new outlets. But the relatively short period of time available, within a calendar dominated by work in the competitive world market, required chemical stimuli to enable people to reach the stage of abandon that provided relief from routine and the hegemony of reason. It needed that brief moment of insanity where oppressive social norms and the confines of propriety could be suspended, and new forms of being flirtingly explored. Mind-altering substances therefore provide an ecological adaptation to the living conditions of post-modernity, and have slotted easily into the commodity markets of modern consumerism.

The harm reduction ethos recognizes the reality of the recreational use of illicit mind-altering substances and, implicitly perhaps, its social function. In the practice of outreach it works in the venues of communality and otherness – in dance clubs, bars and holiday resorts – alerting people to risk and educating in ways of minimizing harm.

Why this has been resisted so vehemently in the us is part of a historical process that relates to what is perhaps the strongest contrast between the New World and the Old, namely the religiosity of the former and the secularism of the latter. In the us regular church attendance is far higher: God and prayer form part of everyday life. There are straightforward functionalist explanations in that the religions provide a sphere for experience beyond rationale and calculus. In the most thoroughly capitalist country in the world, religion provides an important escape from the pressures of the market and the dictates of work. It is not for nothing that, in contrast to Europe, the us has never had a strong, organized labour movement. The churches, then, compete with the experience of drug use as a setting for the non-rational, and many provide a mantle of legitimacy to the persecution of drug users. The rigorous stance of the churches on a 'drug-free America' is a continuation of what is known as the 'social gospel'. Part of the strategy is to enlarge the power of government to strike down social conditions that inhibit human freedom and deny fulfilment of human potential.[8]

The obverse of this process has been the intrusion of moral notions into the formulation of policy. In the US the concession that drug use may be the outcome of informed choice is never made in the government policy discourse. What is provided in so-called drug education remains 'fear-based', by concentrating on the often exaggerated negative consequences of drug use. The possibility of voluntary and educated drug-taking is never entertained, and no advice provided on how to avoid drug-related harms once the substance has entered the system. Needle exchanges are rare and funded by charities, not public health bodies. It also marks a refusal to engage compassionately with the addict, who is not considered a patient in need of medical assistance, but an abuser who is morally culpable and deserving of punishment.[9] This is why the country that champions both markets and individual freedom in most other spheres has also developed the most extraordinary apparatus of oppression for drug users.

Drug control as a perversion of state functions

In the historic struggle between the classes, the triumph of the bourgeoisie was completed by winning absolute control of the state in the course of the American and French revolutions. This was not merely a political victory, but the fulfilment of the Enlightenment project. According to Hegel, the state was the realization of reason and a necessary condition for the apprehension of reality.[10] The instrument for translating puissance into orderly administration was a rational bureaucracy, which became a defining feature of the modern state.[11] At the cusp of the exponential state expansion that characterized the twentieth century, it was difficult to foresee what the inflation of tasks and the appropriation of powers would entail – the proliferation of vested interests, the construction of administrative empires, and a domain for power struggles with ever more tenacious relations to an external reality.

In the communist bloc and many developing countries the state was shaped into an instrument of exploitation and used to run national economies into the ground. While the worst excesses of bureaucratic growth have been held in check in the capitalist democracies, the sheer proliferation of state functions has diluted its rational function. Strangely, at the very point where the state impinges on ever more areas of life, national governments have ceded part of their authority, their sovereignty even, to multilateral organizations. These have often vaulted ambitions dressed in the language of rights. Yet when formulated by international bureaucrats these are a parody of the original declarations of human rights as universal, that is non-culturally specific, and inalienable. They smack instead of sanctimony and professional interest, as in Article 33 of the UN Convention on the Rights of the Child, which obliges treaty countries to 'take all appropriate measures, including legislative, administrative, social and educational measures, to protect children from the illicit use of narcotic drugs and psychotropic substances as defined in the relevant international treaties, and to prevent the use of children in the illicit production and trafficking of such substances'.[12]

It is at national level, however, that drug control is implemented in earnest, and where objective rationality in the exercise of state power has been abandoned. We have already discussed how the repressive approach has a counterproductive effect on the ostensible goals of improving public health and reducing crime. Yet government after government has rejected the suggestions of expert commissions and discarded scientific evidence as to the effectiveness of policy, because relenting on the strict proscriptions on drugs and drug use 'would send the wrong message'. The policy, then, is determined not by proven efficacy but by a persistent faith in the righteousness of those policies.

When the US president first declared the war on drugs in 1971, to be followed in moderated form by the UK government, there was an underlying rationale beyond the cynical manipulation of symbols to attack a vociferous political opposition. At the time there was a genuine alarm that mass drug use would have serious health consequences. Secondly, there was hope, vain as it turned out, that a strong repressive stance could succeed in, and justify the costs of, keeping drugs out. One generation later, it is plain that mass drug use has not had the devastating fallout that was feared in the late 1960s, and that many of the associated problems are produced by the control measures, not by the consequence of drug use. After a massive investment in the criminal justice system and high social costs borne by the tens of thousands of people and their families dragged through courts and prisons, it has become equally plain that the repressive approach has failed in keeping drugs out of societies once use has become established. The market proves once again that it cannot be bucked.

Variants on the third argument that drug control was serving the purpose of controlling socially disruptive elements,[13] or the assertions of a restless working class,[14] or keeping recalcitrant minorities in check, also had a rationale. Cracking down on problematic minorities to maintain the social order is a plausible justification that seems to have a lot of traction in the US. African-Americans are ten times more likely to be arrested and imprisoned for drug offences than their white compatriots, even though patterns of use are no higher. And crack, the drug preferred by African-Americans, attracts one hundred times the penal sanctions stipulated for the powder cocaine used predominantly by white Americans: mandatory sentences established in the 1986 Anti Drug Abuse Act created a penal equivalence between offences involving 50 grams of crack cocaine and 5 kilograms of cocaine powder.

Building on historic evidence on how opium legislation was used to restrict Chinese immigrants in the western states, and allegations that drug laws in the early twentieth century were used to control African-Americans and Mexicans, the argument is one of crass utility for racist domination. A more subtle argument has been advanced by Thomas Szasz, with his notion of 'ceremonial chemistry'.[15] Attributing a primordial need to societies to exact some form of sacrifice, he argues that drug users have become the ceremonial victims of modern society, with psychiatrists standing by in the role of an officiating priesthood.

Psychiatrists and many other therapists can be seen as the natural beneficiaries of the growing need for drug treatment, increasingly ordered through the courts. Known as drug courts in the US, Scotland and many other countries, and implemented either within prisons or as an alternative to custodial punishment, this system of coerced drug treatment has been introduced to re-duce drug-related offending. With a large proportion of property crime, so goes the paradigm, motivated by drug addiction, weaning heavy users off their habit will pay in terms of crime reduction. The massive investment in treatment systems, including maintenance on substitution medication, has dramatically increased the treatment budget and the numbers of staff.

The biggest winner in the war on drugs, however, is the law enforcement sector. For police forces across the world, drug control continues to be used as a fund-raiser and as a bargaining chip for greater powers. Nowhere has this been demonstrated as clearly as in the US, where the Federal Bureau of Narcotics set policy on drug control from the 1930s onwards and where the need for controlling national cocaine flows was a key argument used in the creation of federal police forces. It was under the leadership of Harry Anslinger that drug addiction was defined as a crime and the policy response one of repression. When, in 1961, the American Medical Association and the American Bar Association published a joint report arguing against this position and in favour of treating addiction as a disease, the FBN responded with a dirty tricks campaign, accusing the organizations of spreading lies.[16] The successor organization, the Drug Enforcement Administration, has since benefited from the most spectacular budget increases during the second escalation in the war on drugs, initiated by President Reagan and reinvigorated by George Bush Sr.

Drug control has arguably changed not only the scale but also the nature of policing. Police departments have received military training and ageing ordnance phased out by the military. Indeed, 'the drug war exceptions have encouraged a dangerous culture of paramilitarism in police departments.'[17] The upgrading of law enforcement agencies with increasingly lethal and intrusive hardware was accompanied by a sweeping expansion of their powers beyond random searches to entry into homes, wiretaps and entrapment. This is where police officers pose as drug dealers to tempt suspected drug seekers into attempting to make a purchase, and then arresting them. While judicial approval was less forthcoming during the period of alcohol prohibition, often owing to sympathy for alcohol use among the judiciary, the situation is very different when it comes to cannabis, cocaine or heroin: even Thurgood Marshall, perhaps the best-known liberal on the Supreme Court, remarked, 'If it's a dope case, I won't even read the petition. I ain't giving no break to no dope dealer.'[18]

Suspects in a drug case get neither the benefit of the doubt nor the protection of the law, a fact that has been used to good advantage by materially minded police officers all over the world. Within the law, officers in many jurisdictions are now 'policing for profit', using asset forfeiture legislation introduced against law offenders to finance new buildings, cars and training. There is a risk that some officers are motivated by the prospect of confiscating private assets. One analysis of the DEA database, for instance, found that, out of 25,297 items seized in a twelve-month period, only seventeen were valued at more than $50,000.[19] In most cases the owners of these items decided not to contest the case, as the costs of litigation outweighed the value of the goods in question. Many of these items, such as cars and powerboats, were then sold off at closed auctions to end up in the possession of the officer who made the seizure.

The means at the disposal of the state have been enhanced significantly by advances in the technologies of control. Closed circuit TV cameras are covering many public spaces and are found increasingly in areas used for drug consumption, such as toilets in bars and clubs. They are complemented by chemical surveillance via urine and blood tests, which are now routinely performed in police stations and increasingly in places of work. Many employers ostensibly conduct these to see if staff are 'fit for work', but, interestingly, many multinational companies use them to police the behaviour of employees. The suggestion is that positive test results can be manipulated so as to strengthen the hand of employers in dismissal procedures or to absolve the company of liability in cases of personal injury.

The widespread US practice of testing schoolchildren for drugs, and periodic visits by drug sniffer dog teams, has been copied in parts of the UK. It serves to habituate young people to the practice of drug testing, and to accept as normal the requirement of proving innocence, a clear inversion of an established legal principle. Not surprisingly, the number of people caught in the ever widening net is running into hundreds of thousands. In the US an estimated 500,000 people are serving prison sentences at present for drug-related offences, the majority of which involve marijuana. As convicted felons they lose their right to vote in elections in many states, get evicted from public housing projects, and become ineligible for higher education grants. They suffer what has been termed a 'social death' and become a high-risk group for further crime.

Taking leave of our senses

In the face of such costs it is worth revisiting the starting position – the introduction of drug control in order to protect core values, such as the dignity of man and, most importantly, freedom. Drugs were placed under control to help people avoid falling into the thrall of addiction and stay in control of their lives. Yet in the process many far more concrete liberties have been sacrificed, and the powers of the state have been strengthened exponentially. The policy of incarcerating people to protect their freedom, tenuous to start with, has become a grotesque perversion of public policy.

What has accentuated the problem with drug control is that as part of an international control system it has been exported to countries with very different systems of governance, such as Saudi Arabia, Nigeria or Uzbekistan. In these countries with a tradition of authoritarianism and chronic institutional corruption, drug laws are employed to silence dissidents or to collect bribes. At best there appears a randomized draconianism, where individuals caught in possession, or who show up positive drug tests, are subjected to severe punishments, but the majority escapes detection. It is particularly unfortunate that countries like the US and agencies like the UN, which normally champion civil liberties and the cause of freedom, simply turn a blind eye to these abuses. They actually encourage countries in taking a hard line and will often provide technical assistance and hardware.

While it is increasingly clear that the costs of prohibition are outweighing the benefits, there is no shift in policy in view, with policy-makers shrugging off critical voices. They can draw on advice and data from the drug control establishment instead, a dynamic, well-endowed internal lobby with a strong institutional basis in the UN and at national level. Professionals working for the drug control industry have no interest in dismantling the machinery that provides benefits and prestige. This means that the very experts closest to the problem have most to lose if the system's failure is exposed.

Drug prohibition is likely to continue lumbering on, destroying the lives and livelihoods of millions in its wake. The collateral damage is borne mainly by marginal communities in developed and developing countries, and is therefore considered sustainable by technocrats and their political paymasters in the developed world. The victims' cries will be muffled by the reports and solemn declarations on the advances in the war produced by the drug war technocracy. Change in all likelihood will come when the original pretext of the drugs war, to police and control certain populations and to strengthen the arm of the state, is no longer required. In the wake of 9/11 the system may already be in decline.

References

1 **Taking Leave of Our Senses: Drug Use and Drug-taking in the 21st Century**

1 Kettil Bruun, Lynn Pan and Ingemar Rexed, *The Gentlemen's Club: International Control of Drugs and Alcohol* (Chicago, IL, 1975).
2 James Chin, *The AIDS Pandemic: The Collision of Epidemiology with Political Correctness* (Oxford, 2007).
3 J. L. Himmelstein, 'Drug Politics Theory: Analysis and Critique', *Journal of Drug Issues*, v (1978), pp. 37–52.
4 Drug War Facts, http://www.drugwarfacts.org/corrupt.htm, accessed 22 January 2008.
5 In fairness, the Government of Singapore attaches the highest importance to the rights of every individual to life, liberty and security of person. Article 9 (1) of the Constitution of the Republic of Singapore states that 'no person shall be deprived of his life or personal liberty *save in accordance with law*'. This important exception has propelled Singapore to the highest per capita execution rate in the world. International Harm Reduction Association, *Death Penalties for Drug Offences: A Violation of International Human Rights Law* (London, 2007).
6 Ronald J. Ostrow, *Los Angeles Times*, 6 September 1990.
7 Peter Reuter and Alex Stevens, 'An Analysis of UK Drug Policy: A Monograph Prepared for the UK Drug Policy Commission', UK Drug Policy Commission (London, 2007).
8 Herbert Asbury, *The Great Illusion: An Informal History of Prohibition* (New York, 1950).
9 Peter H. Odegard, *Pressure Politics: The Story of the Anti-Saloon League* (New York, 1928).
10 S. Holloway, 'The Regulation of Drugs in Britain before 1868', in *Drugs and Narcotics in History*, ed. Roy Porter and Mikuláš Teich (Cambridge, 1996), pp. 77–96.
11 The DEA is a law enforcement agency in the US Department of Justice responsible for fighting the war on drugs both within the US and

abroad. In 2006 the agency employed 10,800 people, who between them made some 29,800 arrests and commanded a budget of US$ 2,415 billion.

12 'Current Supply of Legal Opium Adequate to Meet World Demand, Says INCB President', 12 November 2007, http://www.incb.org/incb/en/press_release_2007-11-12_01.html.

13 Shane Blackman, *Chilling Out* (London, 2006).

14 Partnership for a Drug-Free America, 'Polls Find American Teens and Parents Perceive New Link Between Drugs and Terrorism, Suggesting a Possible New Anti Drugs Approach', 12 April 2001, http://www.drugfree.org/Portal/About/NewsReleases/Polls_Find_A merican_Teens_and_Parents_Perceive_L, accessed 22 February 2008.

15 Chris Allen, *Crime, Drugs and Social Theory: A Phenomenological Approach* (Aldershot, 2007).

16 Geoffrey Hunt and Judith C. Barker, 'Drug Treatment in Contemporary Anthropology and Sociology', *European Addiction Research*, v (1999), pp. 126–32.

17 Julia Buxton, *The Political Economy of Narcotics: Production, Consumption and Global Markets* (London, 2006), p. 69.

18 Mary Douglas, ed., *Constructive Drinking: Perspectives on Drink from Anthropology* (Cambridge, 1987).

19 Claude Lévi-Strauss, *The Raw and the Cooked* (Paris, 1964).

20 Pierre Bourdieu, *Distinction: A Social Critique of the Judgement of Taste* (London, 1984), p. 14.

2 The Pathology of Drug Use

1 Oscar Wilde, *The Picture of Dorian Gray* (London, 1891)

2 Antonio Escohotado, *A Brief History of Drugs: From the Stone Age to the Stoned Age* (Rochester, VT, 1999).

3 'My Honourable Friend referred to the Prime Minister's use of the phrase "tough on crime, tough on the causes of crime". The greatest cause of crime, as all law-abiding people know, is drugs. The Government have not been tough on drugs as a cause of crime, they have been soft. There can be no argument about that; everybody in the country knows it. The Government have given misleading signals, especially to the young. I feel strongly that the Government have created a situation in which the drug barons, who use guns so ruthlessly, can take advantage of the greater market for drugs and the lower street price for drugs. They have moved into our inner cities in increasing numbers and that has led to the rise in organised crime over which the Government have presided. I put the finger of blame firmly on the Government, because all those matters are linked.' Hansard, 18 October 2004.

4 *Strategy Unit Drugs Report* (12 May 2003).

5 'The Results of the First Two Years of the NEW-ADAM programme', *Home Office Online Report 19/04* (London, 2004).

6 Michael Gossop, John Marsden and Duncan Stewart, NTORS *after Five Years (National Treatment Outcome Research Study): Changes in Substance Use, Health and Criminal Behaviour in the Five Years after Intake* (London, National Addiction Centre, 2001).

7 Christine Godfrey, Gail Eaton, Cynthia McDougall and Anthony Culyer, *The Economic and Social Costs of Class A Drug Use in England and Wales 2000*, Home Office Research Study 249 (London, 2002).

8 Mike Jay, *Emperors of Dreams: Drugs in the Nineteenth Century* (London, 2001).

9 David Courtwright, 'The Rise and Fall and Rise of Cocaine in the United States', in Jordan Goodman, Paul E. Lovejoy and Andrew Sherratt, eds, *Consuming Habits: Global and Historical Perspectives on How Cultures Define Drugs*, 2nd edn (London, 2007), pp. 215–37.

10 *New York Times*, 17 February 1914.

11 Courtwright, 'The Rise and Fall and Rise of Cocaine', p. 227.

12 Prime Minister's Strategy Unit, *Alcohol Misuse: How Much Does It Cost?* (London, Cabinet Office, 2003); available at www.cabinet office.gov.uk/upload/assets/www.cabinetoffice.gov.uk/strategy/eco n.pd, accessed 6 April 2007.

13 Edward Preble and John Casey, 'Taking Care of Business – The Heroin User's Life on the Street', *International Journal of Addiction*, IV/1(1969), pp. 1–24.

14 Ric Curtis, Travis Wendel and Barry Spunt, *We Deliver: The Gentrification of Drug Markets on Manhattan's Lower East Side* (New York, 2002); Paul Goldstein, 'The Drugs-Violence Nexus: A Tripartite Framework', *Journal of Drug Issues* (1985), pp. 493–506.

15 Nicholas Dorn, Karim Murji and Nigel South, *Traffickers: Drug Markets and Law Enforcement* (London, 1992).

16 Kirby R. Cundiff, 'Homicide Rates and Substance Control Policy', *Independent Institute Working Paper Number 34* (Washington, DC, 2001); J. A. Miron, 'Violence and the U.S. Prohibitions of Drugs and Alcohol', *American Law and Economics Review*, 1–2 (1999), pp. 78–114.

17 David Garland, *The Culture of Control: Crime and Social Order in Contemporary Society* (Oxford, 2001).

18 Matrix, 'The Illicit Drug Trade in the United Kingdom', *Home Office Online Report 20/07* (London, 2007), v.

19 Nicholas Dorn and Lesley King, 'Literature Review on Upper Level Drug Trafficking', *Home Office Online Report 22/05* (London, 2005).

20 National Crime Intelligence Service, *The 2002 United Kingdom Threat Assessment* (London, 2002), p. 13.

21 Toby Muse, 'US Troops "Tried to Smuggle Cocaine"', *Guardian*, 9 May 2005.

22 Penny Green, *Drugs, Trafficking and Criminal Policy: The Scapegoat Strategy* (Winchester, 1998).

23 J. Fagan, 'Women and Drugs Revisited: Female Participation in the Cocaine Economy', *Journal of Drug Issues*, XXIV/1 (1994), pp. 179–225.

24 Philippe Bourgeois, *In Search of Respect: Selling Crack in El Barrio* (Cambridge, 1995).

25 Sudhir Alladi Venkatsh, *American Project: The Rise and Fall of a Modern Ghetto* (Cambridge, MA, 2000).

26 G. Bammer, W. van den Brink, P. Gschwend, V. Hendriks and J. Rehm, 'What Can the Swiss and Dutch Trials Tell Us about the Potential Risks Associated with Heroin Prescribing?', *Drug and Alcohol Review*, XXII (2003), pp. 363–71.

27 Ryan S. King and Marc Mauer, 'The War on Marijuana: The Transformation of the War on Drugs in the 1990s', *Harm Reduction Journal*, III/6 (2006).

28 Information from Daniel Macallair of the Centre on Juvenile and Criminal Justice, San Francisco.

29 Marc Mauer and Meda Chesney-Lind, eds, *Invisible Punishment: The Collateral Consequences of Mass Imprisonment* (New York, 2002).

30 Tiggey May, Martin Duffy and Mike Hough, *Policing Cannabis as a Class C Drug: An Arresting Change?* (York, 2007).

31 Peter Cohen, 'The Culture of the Ban on Cannabis: Is it Political Laziness and Lack of Interest that Keep this Farcical Blunder Afloat?', *Drugs and Alcohol Today*, XIII/2 (2008).

32 Harry G. Levine and Deborah P. Small, *The Great Marijuana Arrest Crusade: Racial Bias and the Policing of Marijuana in New York City, 1997–2006* (New York, 2008).

33 Robert West, *Theory of Addiction* (Oxford, 2006).

34 Harry Levine, 'The Discovery of Addiction: Changing Conceptions of Habitual Drunkenness in America', *Journal of Studies on Alcohol*, XV (1979), pp. 493–506.

35 Michel Foucault, *The Birth of the Clinic: An Archaeology of Medical Perception* (New York, 1975).

36 Gavin Dingwall, *Alcohol and Crime* (Cullompton, 2005).

37 Nick Heather and Ian Robertson, *Problem Drinking* (London, 1985), p. 45.

38 World Health Organization, *Neuroscience of Psychoactive Substance Use and Dependence* (Geneva, 2004).

39 Michael Gossop, *Living with Drugs*, 6th edn (London, 2007).

40 Gossop, Marsden and Stewart, NTORS *after Five Years* (2001).

41 Nick Heather, 'Motivational Interviewing: Is It All Our Clients Need?', *Addiction Research & Theory*, XXIII/1 (2005), pp. 1–18.

42 Tim Leighton, 'How can we (and why should we) develop better models of recovery?', *Addiction Research & Theory*, XXV/5 (2007), pp. 435–8.

43 Irvin Yalom, *The Theory and Practice of Psychotherapy* (New York, 1985).

44 G. A. Marlatt and K. Fromme, 'Metaphors for Addiction', in

Stanton Peele, ed., *Visions of Addiction: Major Contemporary Perspectives on Addiction and Alcoholism* (Lexington, MA, 1988), pp. 1–23.

45 Louis Berger, *Substance Abuse as Symptom: A Psychoanalytic Critique of Treatment Approaches and the Cultural Beliefs that Sustain Them* (Hillsdale, NJ, 1991).

3 Possible Benefits of Drug Use

1 Neil McKeganey, from the University of Glasgow, is a lone voice in the British drug research community in advocating a morality-based approach to public health.

2 Barbara Ehrenreich, *Blood Rites: Origins and History of the Passions of War* (London, 1997).

3 Terence McKenna, *The Food of the Gods: A Radical History of Plants, Food and Human Evolution* (London, 1992), p. 52.

4 Brent Berlin, 'The First Congress of Ethnozoological Nomenclature', *Journal of the Royal Anthropological Institute*, Special Issue, Ethnobiology and the Science of Humankind (2006).

5 Gordon Wassoon, *The Wondrous Mushroom: Mycolatry in Mesoamerica* (New York, 1980).

6 C. Ruck, J. Bigwood, D. Staples, J. Ott and R. G. Wassoon, 'Entheogens', *Journal of Psychedelic Drugs*, XI/1–2 (1979), pp. 145–6.

7 Carlos Castaneda, *The Teachings of Don Juan: A Yaqui Way of Knowledge* (New York, 1969).

8 Richard Rudgley, *The Alchemy of Culture: Intoxicants in Society* (London, 1992).

9 J. D. Lewis-Williams and T. A. Dowson, 'Signs of All Times: Entoptic Phenomena in Upper Palaeolithic Art', *Current Anthropology*, XXXIX (1993), pp. 201–45.

10 Riane Eisler, *The Chalice and the Blade: Our History, Our Future* (San Francisco, CA, 1987).

11 Marshall Sahlins, *Stone Age Economics* (New York, 1972).

4 How Drugs Have Shaped History in the Modern Era

1 Massimo Montanari, *Food Is Culture* (New York, 2006).

2 Andrew Sherratt, 'Peculiar Substances. Drugs: Attitudes and Approaches', in *Consuming Habits: Global and Historical Perspectives on How Cultures Define Drugs*, ed. Jordan Goodman, Paul E. Lovejoy and Andrew Sherratt, 2nd edn (London, 2007), pp. 1–10.

3 Norbert Elias, *The Civilizing Process* (Cambridge, 1994).

4 W. Schivelbusch, *Tastes of Paradise: A Social History of Spices, Stimulants and Intoxicants* (New York, 1992).

5 Eric Wolfe, *Europe and the People Without History* (Berkeley, CA, 1982).
6 Karl Polanyi, *Dahomey and the Slave Trade* (Seattle, WA, 1966).
7 Fernand Braudel, *Civilization and Capitalism, 15th–18th Century*, I: *The Structures of Everyday Life* (Berkeley, CA, 1975), p. 256.
8 Ibid. p. 258.
9 Montanari, *Food Is Culture* (2006).
10 Quoted in Schivelbusch, *Tastes of Paradise* (1992), p. 39.
11 Ibid.
12 David Courtwright, *Forces of Habit: Drugs and the Making of the Modern World* (Cambridge, MA, 2001).
13 Braudel, *Civilization and Capitalism*, I: *The Structures of Everyday Life* (1975), p. 251.
14 Arjun Appadurai, ed., *The Social Life of Things: Commodities in Cultural Perspective* (New York, 1986), p. 24.
15 Zheng Yangwen, *The Social Life of Opium in China* (Cambridge, 2006), p. 46.
16 Mike Jay, *Emperor of Dreams* (London, 2000), p. 72.
17 Frank Dikotter, Lars Laamann and Zhou Xun, *Narcotic Culture: A History of Drugs in China* (London, 2004), p. 100.
18 Ibid., p. 203.
19 Ibid., p. 141.
20 Ibid., p. 191.
21 Mimi Sheller, *Consuming the Caribbean* (London, 2004).
22 Axel Klein, '"Have a piss, drink *ogogoro*, smoke *igbo*, but don't take *gbana*": Hard and Soft Drugs in Nigeria. A Critical Comparison of Official Policies and the View on the Street', *Journal of Psychoactive Drugs*, XXXIII/2 (2001), pp. 111–19.
23 Brian du Toit, *Cannabis in Africa* (Rotterdam, 1980).
24 James Fernandez, *Bwiti: An Ethnography of the Religious Imagination in Africa* (Princeton, NJ, 1982).
25 Barry Chevannes, 'Criminalizing Cultural Practice: The Case of Ganja in Jamaica', in *Caribbean Drugs: From Criminalization to Harm Reduction*, ed. Axel Klein, Anthony Harriott and Marcus Day (London, 2004).

5 **Redefining the Issue: Symptom of Decadence or Development Problem?**

1 William Butler, *HIV/AIDS and Drug Misuse in Russia: Harm Reduction Programmes and the Russian Legal System* (London, 2003).
2 James Chin, *The AIDS Pandemic: The Collision of Epidemiology with Political Correctness* (Oxford, 2007).
3 Kettil Bruun, Lynn Pan and Ingemar Rexed, *The Gentlemen's Club: International Control of Drugs and Alcohol* (Chicago, IL, 1975).

4 Jay Sinha, *The History and Development of the Leading International Drug Control Conventions*, Report prepared for the Canadian Senate Special Committee on Illegal Drugs (Ottawa, 2001).
5 Rick Lines, 'Death Penalties for Drug Offences: A Violation of International Human Rights Law', International Harm Reduction Association (London, 2007).
6 David Bewley-Taylor, 'Emerging Policy Contradictions between the United Nations Drug Control System and the Core Values of the United Nations', *International Journal of Drug Policy*, xxvi/6 (2005), pp. 423–31.
7 UN Charter, Article 1 paragraph 3, and Article 62 paragraphs 1–2.

6 International Drug Control: System and Structure

1 W. Willoughby, *Opium as an International Problem: The Geneva Conferences* (Baltimore, MD, 1925).
2 Report of the meeting of the ad hoc intergovernmental advisory group held pursuant to Commission on Narcotic Drugs resolution 3 (xxxvii), 18 November 1994. UNDCP/1994/AG.7:par.5.
3 Special Session of the General Assembly Devoted to Countering the World Drug Problem Together, 8–10 June 1998, 'Political Declaration; Guiding Principles of Drug Demand Reduction; and Measures to Enhance International Cooperation to Counter the World Drug Problem', New York, USA.
4 UNDCP, 1998. UNGASS 1998, Factsheet 6.
5 The internal management problems are detailed in the 24-page letter of resignation by the former Director of Operations and Analysis, Michael v.d. Schulenberg. While two subsequent OIOS investigations resulted in a slap on the wrist for the former director Pino Arlacchi, they also exonerated the organization in 2003. This was seen by the independent UN watchdog Iowatch as 'double-soft' and particularly worrying as the allegations were levelled at the very UN office leading the global battle against crime and corruption, and because the way the two whistle-blowers were dealt with: 'they have no future in this organisation.' www.iowatch.org/archive/recentdevelopments/topcorruptioncos supted.shtml, accessed 12 March 2008.
6 Emmanuel Akyeampong, *Drink, Power and Cultural Change: A Social History of Alcohol in Ghana, c. 1800 to Recent Times* (Portsmouth, NH, 1996); Lawrence Armand French, *Addictions and Native Americans* (Westport, CT, 2000).
7 Helen Codere, 'The Social and Cultural Context of Cannabis Use in Rwanda', in *Cannabis and Culture*, ed. Vera Rubin (The Hague, 1975), p. 225.

7 How Drugs Became a Development Issue

1 Susan Beckerleg, 'Brown Sugar or Friday Prayers: Youth Choices and Community Building in Coastal Kenya', *African Affairs*, XCIV (1995), pp. 23–38.
2 Axel Klein, Anthony Harriott and Marcus Day, eds, *Caribbean Drugs: From Criminalization to Harm Reduction* (London, 2004).
3 Peter Andreas and Ethan Nadelmann, *Policing the Globe: Criminalization and Crime Control in International Relations* (Oxford, 2006).
4 Europena monitoring Centre on Drugs and Drug Addiction, Annual Report, 2006. Lisbon, 2006.
5 United Nations Drug Control Programme, *The Drugs Nexus in Africa* (Vienna, 1999), accessible online at www.undoc.org/pdf/report_1999-03-01_1.pdf.
6 West India Commission, *Time for Action: A Report by the West India Commission* (Bridgetown, Barbados, 1992).
7 I. L. Griffith, 'Drugs and the Political Economy in a Global Village', in *The Political Economy of Drugs in the Caribbean*, ed. I. L. Griffith (Basingstoke, 2000), pp. 11–28.
8 Scott MacDonald, *Dancing on a Volcano: The Latin American Drug Trade* (New York, 1988).
9 European Commission, 'Working Briefs on the SFA Programme in Dominica, St Lucia and St Vincent and the Grenadines' (Bridgetown, Barbados, 2004).
10 International Labour Office, 'Restructuring and the Loss of Preferences: Labour Challenges for the Caribbean Banana Industry' (ILO, 1999).
11 Axel Klein, Anthony Harriott and Marcus Day, eds, *Caribbean Drugs: From Criminalization to Harm Reduction* (London, 2004).
12 Gordon Myers, *Banana Wars: The Price of Free Trade* (London, 2004).
13 The point was made in the annual report of the International Narcotic Control Board published in early 2004: 'Article 14 of the 1988 Convention requires parties to adopt appropriate measures aimed at eliminating or reducing illicit demand for narcotic drugs and psychotropic substances, with a view to reducing human suffering. The ultimate aim of the conventions is to reduce harm' (INCB para 218).

8 Drugs and Development Along the Silk Route

1 Zoran Krunic and George Siradze, *Reports on the Current Situation with Recommendations for Reform*, Ministry of Internal Affairs of Georgia (Tbilisi, 2005).
2 Patrick McGovern, *Ancient Wine: The Search for the Origins of Viniculture* (Princeton, NJ, 2003).

3 Tamara Dragadze, 'Gender, Ethnicity and Alcohol in the Former Soviet Union', in *Gender, Drink and Drugs*, ed. Maryon MacDonald (Oxford, 1994); Gerald Mars and Yochanan Altman, 'Alternative Mechanism of Distribution in the Soviet Economy', in *Constructive Drinking: Perspectives on Drink from Anthropology*, ed. Mary Douglas (Cambridge, 1987).

4 *Economist*, 25–31 August 2007.

9 Positives and Negatives of the Drugs Economy

1 William Byrd and Christopher Ward, 'Drugs and Development in Afghanistan', *World Bank, Social Development Papers, Conflict Prevention and Reconstruction, Paper 18* (Washington, DC, 2004).

2 Philippe Bourgeois, *In Search of Respect: Selling Crack in El Barrio* (Cambridge, 1995).

3 Tammy Anderson, 'Dimensions of Women's Power in the Illicit Drug Economy', *Theoretical Criminology*, IX/4 (2005), pp. 371–400.

4 David Mansfield, 'What is Driving Opium Poppy Cultivation? Decision Making Amongst Opium Poppy Cultivators in Afghanistan in the 2003/4 Growing Season', UNODC/ONDCP *Second Technical Conference on Drug Control Research* (Kabul, 2004).

5 David Mansfield, *Governance, Security and Economic Growth: The Determinants of Opium Poppy Cultivation in the Districts of Jurm and Baharak in Badakhshan* (Kabul, 2007).

6 Joseph Westermeyer, 'Opium and the People of Laos', in *Dangerous Harvest: Drug Plants and the Transformation of Indigenous Landscapes*, ed. Michael Steinberg, Joseph Hobbs and Kent Mathewson (Oxford, 2004), p. 130.

7 Byrd and Ward, 'Drugs and Development in Afghanistan' (2004).

8 Mansfield, 'What is Driving Opium Poppy Cultivation?' (2004).

9 Francisco E. Thoumi, *Political Economy and Illegal Drugs in Colombia* (Boulder, CO, 1995).

10 A.W. McCoy, 'The Stimulus of Prohibition: A Critical History of the Global Drug Trade', in *Dangerous Harvest*, ed. Steinberg, Hobbs and Mathewson (Oxford: 2004).

11 A. W. McCoy, *The Politics of Heroin: CIA Complicity in the Global Drug Trade* (New York, 1991); David MacDonald, *Drugs in Afghanistan: Opium, Outlaws and Scorpion Tales* (London, 2007).

12 Robert Baer, *See No Evil: The True Story of a Ground Soldier in the CIA's War on Terrorism* (New Jersey, 2002).

13 Tim Weiner, *A Legacy of Ashes: A History of the CIA* (London, 2007).

14 Menno Vellinga, The Political Economy of the Drug Industry: Latin America and the International System (Gainesville, FL, 2004).

1 Axel Klein and Susan Beckerleg, 'Building Castles of Spit: The Role of Khat Chewing in Worship, Work and Leisure', in Jordan Goodman, Paul E. Lovejoy and Andrew Sherratt, eds, *Consuming Habits: Global and Historical Perspectives on How Cultures Define Drugs*, 2nd edn (London, 2007), pp. 238–54.
2 World Health Organization Expert Report on Addiction-Producing Drugs, 'Khat (*Catha edulis*)', *Bulletin on Narcotics*, XVI/2 (1964).
3 World Health Organization Advisory Group, 'Review of the Pharmacology of Khat', *Bulletin on Narcotics*, special issue devoted to *Catha edulis* (khat), XII/3 (1980).
4 World Health Organization Expert Committee on Drug Dependence, *World Health Organization Technical Report Series, 915* (2003), i–v, 1–26.
5 International Narcotics Control Board, 2006, Annual Report.
6 K. Grayson, 'A New Drug Khatastrophe: Khat and Somali-Canadians', in *Governance and Global (Dis)Orders: Trends, Transformations and Impasses*, ed. A. Howell (Toronto, 2005).
7 M. Odenwald, F. Nener, M. Schauer, T. Elbert, C. Catani, B. Lingefelder, H. Hinkel, H. Hafner and B. Rockstroh, 'Khat Use as Risk Factor for Psychotic Disorder: A Cross-sectional and Case Control Study in Somalia', *BMC Medicine*, III/5 (2005).
8 Nasir Warfa, Axel Klein, Kam Bhui, Gerard Leavey, Tom Craig, Stephen Stansfeld and Aboker Ajab, 'Associations between Khat Use and Mental Disorders: An Emerging Paradigm', *Social Science & Medicine*, LXV/2 (2007), pp. 309–18.
9 Neil Carrier, 'The Need for Speed: Contrasting Timeframes in the Social Life of Kenyan Miraa', *Africa*, LXXV/4 (2005), pp. 539–58.
10 David Anderson, Susan Beckerleg, Degol Hailu and Axel Klein, *The Khat Controversy: Stimulating the Debate on Drugs* (Oxford, 2007).

11 Drugs and the Management of Pleasure

1 P. O'Malley and M. Valverde, 'Pleasure, Freedom and Drugs: The Uses of "Pleasure" in Liberal Governance of Drug and Alcohol Consumption', *Sociology*, XXXVIII (2004), pp. 25–42.
2 Alex Stevens, 'My Cannabis – Your Skunk: Reader's Response to the Cannabis Potency Question', *Drugs and Alcohol Today*, VII/3 (2007), pp. 13–17.
3 Fiona Measham, John Aldridge and Howard Parker, *Dancing on Drugs: Risk, Health and Hedonism in the British Club Scene* (London, 2002).
4 Fiona Measham, 'The Decline of Ecstasy, the Rise of "Binge" Drinking and the Persistence of Pleasure', *Journal of Community*

and Criminal Justice, LI/4 (2004), pp. 309–26.

5 Harold Finestone, 'Cats, Kicks and Colour', in *Perspectives on Deviance*, ed. S. Becker (New York, 1964).

6 M. Featherstone, 'The Body in Consumer Culture', in *The Body, Social Processes and Cultural Theory*, ed. B. Turner (London, 1991).

7 Mike Jay, *Emperors of Dreams: Drugs in the Nineteenth Century* (London, 2001).

8 Austin Kerr, *Organized for Prohibition: A New History of the Anti-Saloon League* (New Haven, CT, 1985).

9 D. Matza and P. Morgan, 'Controlling Drug Use: The Great Prohibition', in *Punishment and Social Control*, ed. T. Blomberg and S. Cohen (Chicago, IL, 1995).

10 Herbert Marcuse, *Reason and Revolution: Hegel and the Rise of Social Theory* (Oxford, 1941).

11 Max Weber, 'Bureaucracy', in *From Max Weber: Essays in Sociology*, ed. H. H. Gerth and C. Wright Mills (London, 1946).

12 United Nations, 'The UN Declaration on the Rights of the Child', UN General Assembly Resolution 1386, 1959.

13 Jock Young, *The Exclusive Society* (London, 2006).

14 Rowdy Yates, 'A Brief History of British Drug Policy, 1950–2001', *Drugs: Education, Prevention and Policy*, IX/2 (2002).

15 Thomas Szasz, *Ceremonial Chemistry: The Ritual Persecution of Drugs, Addicts and Pushers* (Garden City, NY, 1975).

16 Richard Davenport-Hines, *The Pursuit of Oblivion: A Social History of Drugs* (London, 2001), p. 290.

17 Gene Healy, 'Deployed in the USA: The Creeping Militarization of the Home Front', *Cato Institute Policy Analysis*, 503 (Washington, DC, 2003), p. 16.

18 Douglas Husak, *Legalise This! The Case for Decriminalizing Drugs* (New York, 2002), p. 147.

19 A. Schneider and M. P. Flaherty, 'Government Seizures Victimize Innocent', *Pittsburgh Press*, 27 February 1991.

Select Bibliography

Akyeampong, Emmanuel, *Drink, Power and Cultural Change: A Social History of Alcohol in Ghana, c. 1800 to Recent Times* (Portsmouth, NH, 1996)

Allen, Chris, *Crime, Drugs and Social Theory: A Phenomenological Approach* (Aldershot, 2007)

Anderson, David, Susan Beckerleg, Degol Hailu and Axel Klein, *The Khat Controversy: Stimulating the Debate on Drugs* (Oxford, 2007)

Anderson, Tammy, 'Dimensions of Women's Power in the Illicit Drug Economy', *Theoretical Criminology*, IX/4 (2005), pp. 371–400

Andreas, Peter, and Ethan Nadelmann, *Policing the Globe: Criminalization and Crime Control in International Relations* (Oxford, 2006)

Appadurai, Arjun, ed., *The Social Life of Things: Commodities in Cultural Perspective* (New York, 1986)

Asbury, Herbert, *The Great Illusion: An Informal History of Prohibition* (New York, 1950)

Baer, Robert, *See No Evil: The True Story of a Ground Soldier in the CIA's War on Terrorism* (New Jersey, 2002)

Bammer, G., W. van den Brink, P. Gschwend, V. Hendriks and J. Rehm, 'What Can the Swiss and Dutch Trials Tell Us about the Potential Risks Associated with Heroin Prescribing?', *Drug and Alcohol Review*, XXII (2003), pp. 363–71

Beckerleg, Susan, 'Brown Sugar or Friday Prayers: Youth Choices and Community Building in Coastal Kenya', *African Affairs*, XCIV (1995), pp. 23–38

Berger, Louis, *Substance Abuse as Symptom: A Psychoanalytic Critique of Treatment Approaches and the Cultural Beliefs that Sustain Them* (Hillsdale, NJ, 1991)

Berlin, Brent, 'The First Congress of Ethnozoological Nomenclature', *Journal of the Royal Anthropological Institute*, Special Issue, Ethnobiology and the Science of Humankind (2006)

Bewley-Taylor, David, 'Emerging Policy Contradictions between the United Nations Drug Control System and the Core Values of the United Nations', *International Journal of Drug Policy*, XXVI/6 (2005), pp. 423–31

Blackman, Shane, *Chilling Out* (London, 2006)

Bourdieu, Pierre, *Distinction: A Social Critique of the Judgement of Taste* (London, 1984)

Bourgeois, Philippe, *In Search of Respect: Selling Crack in El Barrio* (Cambridge, 1995)

Braudel, Fernand, *Civilization and Capitalism, 15th–18th Century*, I: *The Structures of Everyday Life* (Berkeley, CA, 1975)

Bruun, Kettil, Lynn Pan and Ingemar Rexed, *The Gentlemen's Club: International Control of Drugs and Alcohol* (Chicago, IL, 1975)

Butler, William, *HIV/AIDS and Drug Misuse in Russia: Harm Reduction Programmes and the Russian Legal System* (London, 2003)

Buxton, Julia, *The Political Economy of Narcotics: Production, Consumption and Global Markets* (London, 2006)

Byrd, William, and Christopher Ward, 'Drugs and Development in Afghanistan', *World Bank, Social Development Papers, Conflict Prevention and Reconstruction, Paper 18* (Washington, DC, 2004)

Carrier, Neil, 'The Need for Speed: Contrasting Timeframes in the Social Life of Kenyan Miraa', *Africa*, LXXV/4 (2005), pp. 539–58

Chevannes, Barry, 'Criminalizing Cultural Practice: The Case of Ganja in Jamaica', in *Caribbean Drugs: From Criminalization to Harm Reduction*, ed. Axel Klein, Anthony Harriott and Marcus Day (London, 2004)

Chin, James, *The AIDS Pandemic: The Collision of Epidemiology with Political Correctness* (Oxford, 2007)

Codere, Helen, 'The Social and Cultural Context of Cannabis Use in Rwanda', in *Cannabis and Culture*, ed. Vera Rubin (The Hague, 1975), pp. 219–30

Cohen, Peter, 'The Culture of the Ban on Cannabis: Is it Political Laziness and Lack of Interest that Keep this Farcical Blunder Afloat?', *Drugs and Alcohol Today*, XIII/2 (2008)

Courtwright, David, *Forces of Habit: Drugs and the Making of the Modern World* (Cambridge, MA, 2001)

——, 'The Rise and Fall and Rise of Cocaine in the United States', in *Consuming Habits: Global and Historical Perspectives on How Cultures Define Drugs*, ed. Jordan Goodman, Paul E. Lovejoy and Andrew Sherratt, 2nd edn (London, 2007), pp. 215–37

Cundiff, Kirby R., 'Homicide Rates and Substance Control Policy', *Independent Institute Working Paper Number 34* (Washington, DC, 2001)

Curtis, Ric, Travis Wendel and Barry Spunt, *We Deliver: The Gentrification of Drug Markets on Manhattan's Lower East Side* (New York, 2002)

Davenport-Hines, Richard, *The Pursuit of Oblivion: A Social History of Drugs* (London, 2001)

Dikotter, Frank, Lars Laamann and Zhou Xun, *Narcotic Culture: A History of Drugs in China* (London, 2004)

Dingwall, Gavin, *Alcohol and Crime* (Cullompton, 2005)

Dorn, Nicholas, Karim Murji and Nigel South, *Traffickers: Drug Markets and Law Enforcement* (London, 1992)

Dorn, Nicholas, and Lesley King, 'Literature Review on Upper Level Drug Trafficking', *Online Report Home Office* OLR 22/05 (London, 2005)

Douglas, Mary, ed., *Constructive Drinking: Perspectives on Drink from Anthropology* (Cambridge, 1987)

Dragadze, Tamara, 'Gender, Ethnicity and Alcohol in the Former Soviet Union', in *Gender, Drink and Drugs*, ed. Maryon MacDonald (Oxford, 1994)

Drug War Facts, http://www.drugwarfacts.org/corrupt.htm, accessed 22 January 2008.

Du Toit, Brian, *Cannabis in Africa* (Rotterdam, 1980)

The Economist, 25–31 August 2007

Ehrenreich, Barbara, *Blood Rites: Origins and History of the Passions of War* (London, 1997)

Elias, Norbert, *The Civilizing Process* (Cambridge, 1994)

Eisler, Riane, *The Chalice and the Blade: Our History, Our Future* (San Francisco, CA, 1987)

European Commission, 'Working Briefs on the SFA Programme in Dominica, St Lucia and St Vincent and the Grenadines' (Bridgetown, Barbados, 2004)

Fagan, J., 'Women and Drugs Revisited: Female Participation in the Cocaine Economy', *Journal of Drug Issues*, XXIV/1 (1994), pp. 179–225

Featherstone, M., 'The Body in Consumer Culture', in *The Body, Social Processes and Cultural Theory*, ed. B. Turner (London, 1991)

Fernandez, James, *Bwiti: An Ethnography of the Religious Imagination in Africa* (Princeton, NJ, 1982)

Finestone, Harold, 'Cats, Kicks and Colour', in *Perspectives on Deviance*, ed. S. Becker (New York, 1964)

Foucault, Michel, *The Birth of the Clinic: An Archaeology of Medical Perception* (New York, 1975)

French, Lawrence Armand, *Addictions and Native Americans* (Westport, CT, 2000)

Garland, David, *The Culture of Control: Crime and Social Order in Contemporary Society* (Oxford, 2001)

General Accounting Office, Report to the Honorable Charles B. Rangel, House of Representatives, Law Enforcement: Information on Drug-Related Police Corruption (Washington, DC: USGPO, May 1998), p. 37

Godfrey, Christine, Gail Eaton, Cynthia McDougall and Anthony Culyer, 'The Economic and Social Costs of Class A Drug Use in England and Wales 2000', *Home Office Research Study 249* (London, 2002)

Goldstein, Paul, 'The Drugs-Violence Nexus: a Tripartite Framework', *Journal of Drug Issues* (1985), pp. 493–506

Goodman, Jordan, Paul Lovejoy and Andrew Sherratt, eds, *Consuming Habits: Drugs in History and Anthropology*, 2nd edn (London, 2007)

Gossop, Michael, *Living with Drugs*, 6th edn (Aldershot, 2007)

Gossop, Michael, John Marsden and Duncan Stewart, NTORS *after Five Years (National Treatment Outcome Research Study): Changes in Substance Use, Health and Criminal Behaviour in the Five Years after Intake* (London, National Addiction Centre, 2001)

Grayson, K., 'A New Drug Khatastrophe: Khat and Somali-Canadians', in *Governance and Global (Dis)Orders: Trends, Transformations and Impasses*, ed. A. Howell (Toronto, 2005)

Green, Penny, *Drugs, Trafficking and Criminal Policy: The Scapegoat Strategy* (Winchester, 1998)

Griffith, I. L., 'Drugs and the Political Economy in a Global Village', in *The Political Economy of Drugs in the Caribbean*, ed. I. L. Griffith (Basingstoke, 2000), pp. 11–28

Healy, Gene, 'Deployed in the USA: The Creeping Militarization of the Home Front', *Cato Institute Policy Analysis, 503* (Washington, DC, 2003)

Heather, Nick, 'Motivational Interviewing: Is It All Our Clients Need?', *Addiction Research & Theory*, XXIII/1 (2005), pp. 1–18

Himmelstein, J. L., 'Drug Politics Theory: Analysis and Critique', *Journal of Drug Issues*, V (1978), pp. 37–52

Holloway, S., 'The Regulation of Drugs in Britain before 1868', in *Drugs and Narcotics in History*, ed. Roy Porter and Mikuláš Teich (Cambridge, 1995), pp. 77–96

Home Office, 'The Results of the First Two Years of the NEW-ADAM Programme', *Home Office Online Report 19/04* (London, 2004)

Hunt, Geoffrey, and Judith C. Barker, 'Drug Treatment in Contemporary Anthropology and Sociology', *European Addiction Research*, V (1999), pp. 126–32

Husak, Douglas, *Legalise This! The Case for Decriminalising Drugs* (New York, 2002)

International Labour Office, 'Restructuring and the Loss of Preferences: Labour Challenges for the Caribbean Banana Industry' (ILO, 1999)

International Narcotics Control Board, Annual Report, 2006

——, 'Current Supply of Legal Opium Adequate to Meet World Demand, Says INCB President', http://www.incb.org/incb/en/press_release_2007-11-12_01.html

Jay, Mike, *Emperors of Dreams: Drugs in the Nineteenth Century* (London, 2001)

Kerr, Austin, *Organized for Prohibition: A New History of the Anti-Saloon League* (New Haven, CT, 1985)

Lines, Rick, *Death Penalties for Drug Offences: A Violation of International Human Rights Law*, International Harm Reduction Association (London, 2007)

King, Ryan S., and Marc Mauer, 'The War on Marijuana: The Transformation of the War on Drugs in the 1990s', *Harm Reduction Journal*, III/6 (2006)

Klein, Axel, '"Have a piss, drink *ogogoro*, smoke *igbo*, but don't take *gbana*": Hard and Soft Drugs in Nigeria. A Critical Comparison of Official Policies and the View on the Street', *Journal of Psychoactive Drugs*, XXXIII/2 (2001), pp. 111–19

——, Anthony Harriott and Marcus Day, eds, *Caribbean Drugs: From Criminalization to Harm Reduction* (London, 2004)

——, and Susan Beckerleg, 'Building Castles of Spit: The Role of Khat Chewing in Worship, Work and Leisure', in *Consuming Habits*, ed. Jordan Goodman, Paul Lovejoy and Andrew Sherratt, 2nd edn (London, 2007), pp. 238–54

Krunic, Zoran, and George Siradze, *Reports on the Current Situation with Recommendations for Reform*, Ministry of Internal Affairs of Georgia (Tbilisi, 2005)

Leighton, Tim, 'How can we (and why should we) develop better models of recovery?', *Addiction Research & Theory*, XXV/5 (2007), pp. 435–8

Lévi-Strauss, Claude, *The Raw and the Cooked* (Paris, 1964)

Levine, Harry G., and Deborah P. Small, *The Great Marijuana Arrest Crusade: Racial Bias and the Policing of Marijuana in New York City, 1997–2006* (New York, 2008)

Levine, Harry, 'The Discovery of Addiction: Changing Conceptions of Habitual Drunkenness in America', *Journal of Studies on Alcohol*, XV (1979), pp. 493–506

Levitt, Stephen, and Steven Dubner, *Freakonomics: A Rogue Economist Explores the Hidden Side to Everything* (London, 2005)

Lewis-Williams, J. D., and T. A. Dowson, 'Signs of All Times: Entoptic Phenomena in Upper Palaeolithic Art', *Current Anthropology*, XXXIX (1993), pp. 201–45

MacDonald, Scott, *Dancing on a Volcano: The Latin American Drug Trade* (New York, 1988)

MacDonald, David, *Drugs in Afghanistan: Opium, Outlaws and Scorpion Tales* (London, 2007)

Mansfield, David, 'What is Driving Opium Poppy Cultivation? Decision Making Amongst Opium Poppy Cultivators in Afghanistan in the 2003/4 Growing Season', UNODC/ONDCP *Second Technical Conference on Drug Control Research* (Kabul, 2004)

——, *Governance, Security and Economic Growth: The Determinants of Opium Poppy Cultivation in the Districts of Jurm and Baharak in Badakhshan* (Kabul, 2007)

Marcuse, Herbert, *Reason and Revolution: Hegel and the Rise of Social Theory* (Oxford, 1941)

Marlatt, G.A., and K. Fromme, 'Metaphors for Addiction', in *Visions of Addiction: Major Contemporary Perspectives on Addiction and Alcoholism*, ed. Stanton Peele (Lexington, MA, 1988), pp. 1–23

Mars, Gerald, and Yochanan Altman, 'Alternative Mechanism of Distribution in the Soviet Economy', in *Constructive Drinking: Perspectives on Drink from Anthropology*, ed. Mary Douglas (Cambridge, 1987)

Matrix, 'The Illicit Drug Trade in the United Kingdom', *Home Office Online Report 2007* (London, 2007)

Matza, D., and P. Morgan, 'Controlling Drug Use: The Great Prohibition', in *Punishment and Social Control*, ed. T. Blomberg and S. Cohen (Chicago, IL, 1995)

Mauer, Marc, and Meda Chesney-Lind, eds, *Invisible Punishment: The Collateral Consequences of Mass Imprisonment* (New York, 2002)

May, Tiggey, Martin Duffy and Mike Hough, *Policing Cannabis as a Class C Drug: An Arresting Change?* (York, 2007)

McCoy, A. W., 'The Stimulus of Prohibition: A Critical History of the Global Drug Trade', in *Dangerous Harvest: Drug Plants and the Transformation of Indigenous Landscapes*, ed. Michael Steinberg, Joseph Hobbs and Kent Mathewson (Oxford, 2004)

——, *The Politics of Heroin: CIA Complicity in the Global Drug Trade* (New York, 1991)

McGovern, Patrick, *Ancient Wine: The Search for the Origins of Viniculture* (Princeton, NJ, 2003)

McKenna, Terence, *The Food of the Gods: A Radical History of Plants, Food and Human Evolution* (London, 1992)

Measham, Fiona, 'The Decline of Ecstasy, the Rise of "Binge" Drinking and the Persistence of Pleasure', *Journal of Community and Criminal Justice*, LI/4 (2004), pp. 309–26

——, John Aldridge and Howard Parker, *Dancing on Drugs: Risk, Health and Hedonism in the British Club Scene* (London, 2002)

Miron, J. A., 'Violence and the U.S. Prohibitions of Drugs and Alcohol', *American Law and Economics Review*, 1–2 (1999), pp. 78–114

Montanari, Massimo, *Food Is Culture* (New York, 2006)

Muse, Toby, 'US Troops "Tried to Smuggle Cocaine"', *Guardian*, 9 May 2005

Myers, Gordon, *Banana Wars: The Price of Free Trade* (London, 2004)

National Crime Intelligence Service, *The 2002 United Kingdom Threat Assessment* (London, 2002)

New York Times, 17 February 1914

Odegard, Peter H., *Pressure Politics: The Story of the Anti-Saloon League* (New York, 1928)

Odenwald, M., F. Nener, M. Schauer, T. Elbert, C. Catani, B. Lingefelder, H. Hinkel, H. Hafner and B. Rockstroh, 'Khat Use as Risk Factor for Psychotic Disorder: A Cross-sectional and Case Control Study in Somalia', *BMC Medicine*, III/5 (2005)

O'Malley, P., and M. Valverde, 'Pleasure, Freedom and Drugs: The Uses of "Pleasure" in Liberal Governance of Drug and Alcohol Consumption', *Sociology*, XXXVIII (2004), pp. 25–42

Ostrow, Ronald, *Los Angeles Times*, 6 September 1990

Partnership for a Drug-Free America, 'Polls Find American Teens and Parents Perceive New Link Between Drugs and Terrorism, Suggesting a Possible New Anti Drugs Approach', 12 April 2001; available on http://www.drugfree.org/Portal/About/NewsReleases/Polls_Find_Am

erican_Teens_and_Parents_Perceive_l, accessed 22 February 2008

Polanyi, Karl, *Dahomey and the Slave Trade* (Seattle, wa, 1966)

Porter, Roy, and Mikuláš Teich, eds, *Drugs and Narcotics in History* (Cambridge, 1996)

Preble, Edward, and John Casey, 'Taking Care of Business – The Heroin User's Life on the Street', *International Journal of Addiction,* iv/1 (1969), pp. 1–24

Prime Minister's Strategy Unit, *Alcohol Misuse: How Much Does It Cost?* (London, Cabinet Office, 2003), www.cabinetoffice.gov.uk/upload /assets/www.cabinetoffice.gov.uk/strategy/econ.pdf

——, *Drugs Report: Understanding the Issues* (London, Cabinet Office, 2003), www.cabinetoffice.gov.uk/upload/assets/www.cabinetoffice. gov.uk/strategy/drugs_report.pdf, accessed 10 March 2008

Reuter, Peter, and Alex Stevens, 'An Analysis of uk Drug Policy: A Monograph Prepared for the uk Drug Policy Commission', uk Drug Policy Commission (London, 2007)

Ruck, C., J. Bigwood, D. Staples, J. Ott and R. G. Wassoon, 'Entheogens', *Journal of Psychedelic Drugs,* xi/1–2 (1979), pp. 145–6

Rudgley, Richard, *The Alchemy of Culture: Intoxicants in Society* (London, 1992)

Sahlins, Marshall, *Stone Age Economics* (New York, 1972)

Schneider, A., and M. P. Flaherty, 'Government Seizures Victimize Innocent', Pittsburgh Press, 27 February 1991

Schivelbusch, W., *Tastes of Paradise: A Social History of Spices, Stimulants and Intoxicants* (New York, 1992)

Sheller, Mimi, *Consuming the Caribbean* (London, 2004)

Sherratt, Andrew, 'Peculiar Substances. Drugs: Attitudes and Approaches', in *Consuming Habits: Global and Historical Perspectives on How Cultures Define Drugs,* ed. Jordan Goodman, Paul E. Lovejoy and Andrew Sherratt, 2nd edn (London, 2007), pp. 1–10

Sinha, Jay, *The History and Development of the Leading International Drug Control Conventions,* Report prepared for the Canadian Senate Special Committee on Illegal Drugs (Ottawa, 2001)

Stevens, Alex, 'My Cannabis – Your Skunk; Reader's Response to the Cannabis Potency Question', *Drugs and Alcohol Today,* vii/3 (2007), pp. 13–17

Szasz, Thomas, *Ceremonial Chemistry: The Ritual Persecution of Drugs, Addicts and Pushers* (Garden City, ny, 1975)

Thoumi, Francisco E., *Political Economy and Illegal Drugs in Colombia* (Boulder, co, 1995)

United Nations, 'The un Declaration on the Rights of the Child', un General Assembly Resolution 1386, 1959

United Nations Drug Control Programme, *The Drugs Nexus in Africa* (Vienna, 1999), accessed online at www.undoc.org/pdf/report_1999-03-01_1.pdf

Vellinga, Menno, *The Political Economy of the Drug Industry: Latin America and the International System* (Gainesville, fl, 2004)

Venkatsh, Sudhir Alladi, *American Project: The Rise and Fall of a Modern Ghetto* (Cambridge, MA, 2000)

Warfa, Nasir, Axel Klein, Kam Bhui, Gerard Leavey, Tom Craig, Stephen Stansfeld and Aboker Ajab, 'Associations between Khat Use and Mental Disorders: An Emerging Paradigm', *Social Science & Medicine*, LXV/2 (2007), pp. 309–18

Wassoon, Gordon, *The Wondrous Mushroom: Mycolatry in Mesoamerica* (New York, 1980)

Weiner, Tim, *A Legacy of Ashes: A History of the CIA* (London, 2007)

West India Commission, *Time for Action: A Report by the West India Commission* (Bridgetown, Barbados, 1992)

West, Robert, *Theory of Addiction* (Oxford, 2006)

Westermeyer, Joseph, 'Opium and the People of Laos', in *Dangerous Harvest: Drug Plants and the Transformation of Indigenous Landscapes*, ed. M. Steinberg, Joseph Hobbs and Kent Mathewson (Oxford, 2004)

Wilde, Oscar, *The Picture of Dorian Gray* (London, 1891)

Willoughby, W., *Opium as an International Problem: The Geneva Conferences* (Baltimore, MD, 1925)

Wolfe, Eric, *Europe and the People Without History* (Berkeley, CA, 1982)

World Health Organization, *Neuroscience of Psychoactive Substance Use and Dependence* (Geneva: WHO, 2004)

World Health Organization Advisory Group, 'Review of the Pharmacology of Khat', *Bulletin on Narcotics*, special issue devoted to *Catha edulis* (khat), XII/3 (1980)

World Health Organization Expert Report on Addiction-Producing Drugs, 'Khat (*Catha edulis*)', *Bulletin on Narcotics*, XVI/2 (1964)

World Health Organization Expert Committee on Drug Dependence, *World Health Organization Technical Report Series, 915* (2003), i–v, 1–26

Yalom, Irvin, *The Theory and Practice of Psychotherapy* (New York, 1985)

Yangwen, Zheng, *The Social Life of Opium in China* (Cambridge, 2006)

Yates, Rowdy, 'A Brief History of British Drug Policy, 1950–2001', *Drugs: Education, Prevention and Policy*, IX/2 (2002)

Young, Jock, *The Exclusive Society* (London, 2006)

Index